The Monterey Bay Shoreline Guide

THE MONTEREY BAY

SHORELINE GUIDE

Jerry Emory

With photographs by
Frank Balthis

UNIVERSITY OF CALIFORNIA PRESS

BERKELEY
LOS ANGELES
LONDON

MONTEREY BAY AQUARIUM

University of California Press
Berkeley and Los Angeles, California

University of California Press, Ltd.
London, England

MONTEREY BAY AQUARIUM

© 1999 by The Regents of the University of California

Library of Congress Cataloging-in-Publication Data
Emory, Jerry.
    The Monterey Bay shoreline guide / Jerry Emory : illustrations by
Frank Balthis and others.
    p.   cm. — (University of California Press/Monterey Bay Aquarium
series in marine conservation)
    Includes bibliographical references (p.   ) and index.
    ISBN 0-520-21153-7 (alk. paper). — ISBN 0-520-21712-8 (alk. paper)
    1. Natural history—California—Monterey Bay Region—Guidebooks.
2. Monterey Bay Region (Calif.)—Guidebooks. I. Title. II. Series.
QH105.C2E56   1999
508.794'76—dc21   98-36120
                                                                        CIP

Printed and bound in Hong Kong
9 8 7 6 5 4 3 2 1

Printed on acid-free paper.

The frontispiece: Monterey Bay, from Wilder Ranch State Park in the
north to Point Lobos State Reserve in the south. Note the Monterey
Canyon meandering shoreward toward Moss Landing and Elkhorn
Slough. To obtain a copy of this image, contact Friends of Monterey Bay,
P.O. Box 1011, Felton, CA 95018.

All images are by Frank Balthis, except where indicated.

Maps by Seventeenth Street Studios

University of California Press / Monterey Bay Aquarium
Series in Marine Conservation, 1

"Healthy oceans are critical to the future of all life on Earth, yet by and large the underwater world remains hidden to us, unknown and mysterious. The mission of the Monterey Bay Aquarium is to inspire conservation of the oceans, and this series of books is intended to further that goal. By helping people discover their connection with the natural world, we hope to foster a lifelong commitment to learning about and caring for the oceans on which all life depends."

—*Julie Packard*
EXECUTIVE DIRECTOR
MONTEREY BAY AQUARIUM

To the memory of my father, Jerome Campbell Emory.
He explored the shores of Monterey Bay as a child,
then returned for the last 25 years of his life.
He talked with the dolphins along the bay's shoreline,
and retold their stories to my young daughters.

Contents

Acknowledgments

A book such as this one is truly a collective effort. It is a collective effort in the following sense: I did the fieldwork, countless hours of research, and months of writing, but without the ideas, insights, and enthusiasm of the people living and working along the shoreline of the greater Monterey Bay, this work would be less thorough, and less interesting. I talked with hundreds of people while conducting my fieldwork and subsequent research from my office. I can't name them all here. In fact, I don't even know the names of a few local residents I ran into along stretches of beach, or atop lonely bluffs. But these nameless residents are just as important, and just as appreciated, as the following list of people I leaned on for information.

Gary Strachan and Kim Hayes (Año Nuevo State Reserve); Diane West-Bourke (resident naturalist and teacher, Rancho Del Oso); Janet Web and Frank McCrary (Big Creek Lumber); Ken Kannegaard (RMC Lonestar, Davenport); Allen Blum (Wilder Ranch State Park); Lee Summers and Julie Sidel (Natural Bridges State Beach); Sally Real (Long Marine Lab); Bob Culbertson (California State Parks, Santa Cruz District); Lisa McGinnis (Santa Cruz Parks and Recreation); Carrie Maze and Katrina Paz (Santa Cruz County Conference and Visitors Council); Marla Novo, Rachel McKay, and Nikki Silva (Santa Cruz Museum of Art and History); Carol Champion (U.C. Santa Cruz, Special Collections); Jessica Kusz (Santa Cruz Mission State Historic Park); Bev Dyc (Santa Cruz Surfing Museum); Roberta Hunter and Kate Sandusky (Friends of Santa Cruz State Parks); John Akeman (County of Santa Cruz, Parks, Open Space, and Cultural Services); Julie Munnerlin (Santa Cruz County Regional Transportation Commission); Charles Prentiss (Santa Cruz City Museum of Natural History); Sean Van Sommeran (Pelagic Shark Research Foundation); Jan Bollwinkel-Smith (Santa Cruz Seaside Company, the "Boardwalk"); Carrie Arnone and Tony Castro (Capitola Chamber of Commerce); Carolyn Swift (Capitola Museum); the staff of New Brighton State Beach (for allowing me to recharge my portable computer batteries while working out of their campground); John Mandel (old friend and Watsonville resident); Ken Silviera

(Watsonville Wastewater Treatment Facility); Dave Dixon (Marina State Beach); Christopher Mychajluk (Marina Coast Water District); Steve Addington and Andy Hunter (Bureau of Land Management, Fort Ord); Greg Thornton (California Land Management); Bob Leos, Jeannine DeWald, and Bruce Elliot (California Department of Fish and Game, Monterey); Tim Jensen (Monterey Peninsula Regional Park District); Kelly Seely (Monterey Chamber of Commerce); Doug Stafford (City of Monterey Parks); Lisa Hulse Davies (Transportation Agency for Monterey County); Molly Laughlin (Pacific Grove Chamber of Commerce); Molly Joest (Pebble Beach Company); Joyce Stevenson (Carmel resident and conservation guru); Bob Pavlik, Teri Leaf, Laurel Clark, and Elizabeth McKee (CalTrans); Don Roberson (birds); Mark Stromberg (Hastings Natural History Reservation); Bill Rainey and Elizabeth Pierson (bats); Mill Valley Library's excellent staff; and all the other city, county, and state employees who answered my incessant questions. Any inaccuracies in this book are the author's.

I also want to thank Adam Fuchs at PowerFood for providing me with several months' worth of PowerBars to keep me fueled during my long days of bike riding, running, walking, and note taking. Start to Finish—a Bay Area–based bicycle company with nine stores—tuned up my mountain bike before I started my fieldwork, gave me some new equipment, and outfitted me.

Special thanks go to Nikki Nedeff and Kevin Dummer —good friends, fellow geographers, and residents of Carmel Valley—for their knowledge of the local landscape and natural history. Their animal-filled house next to the Carmel River became a second home, and a welcome sight after long days of exploration. Liz Love and Kip Evans of the Monterey Bay National Marine Sanctuary's office in Monterey were helpful and encouraging from the onset of this project.

Nora Deans, head of publications at the Monterey Bay Aquarium, was the first to read this book proposal (with extreme enthusiasm, I might add). Eventually Nora ran the idea past Doris Kretschmer, executive editor at the University of California Press. Their excitement for this project, and their guidance, made an amazing difference. Roxane Buck-Ezcurra, editor at the Aquarium, was there for me every step of the way. I sent e-mail messages to Roxane almost daily, and she answered them promptly— more often than not with a dose of much-appreciated humor—with the help of Aquarium scientist Steven Webster. If I had a problem, or a scientific question, Roxane was usually my salvation. The illustrations for this book could not have been organized without her. After I finished the manuscript it was delivered to Anne Canright, an editor who knows the Monterey Bay region well. Anne's eye for detail and her countless questions improved the text more than I would like to admit. Her guidance through the rewriting process is greatly appreciated. I consider myself a very lucky author to have worked with such a superb editor.

Photographer and naturalist Frank Balthis seems like an old friend, even though I only introduced myself to him halfway through preparing this book. Everywhere I looked during my fieldwork I saw Frank's wonderful photographs. I soon realized I needed to meet him and get him involved in this project. His interest, enthusiasm, flexibility, and years exploring the Monterey Bay shoreline have made a tremendous difference. Look for Frank at Año Nuevo State Reserve, where he works part time as a ranger. Additional photographs were generously donated by my friends Stacy Geiken, Nikki Nedeff, and Mark Palmer. William Rainey also kindly let me use one of his excellent bat photographs.

Authors gather inspiration from many sources. I'm no exception, and gardening, exercise, and good writing are high on my list. However, during the long days of producing the text for this book, music—typically turned up very loud—was often my salvation. I'd like to acknowledge in particular the tunes of Craig Chaquico, Sammy Hagar, Martin Hayes, B. B. King, Los Lobos, Bob Marley, Bonnie Raitt, Roy Rogers (the slide guitar player, not the cowboy), Carlos Santana, Joe Satriani, Ludwig Von Beethoven, and Neil Young.

And last, but by no measure least, heartfelt thanks go to my wife, Jeannie Lloyd (The Beans), and our two young daughters, Sarah and Samantha. This dynamic threesome is my salvation. Without their love, support, and tolerance I couldn't have undertaken, and then finished, this book. Without their close and constant presence, my life wouldn't be the same.

Introduction

Sunset State Beach

One Monday evening, about halfway through my fieldwork for this book, I was walking from my campsite at Sunset State Beach down to the Pajaro River. It was a beautiful warm evening, fog free and calm. The tide was out and the beach felt cool and firm under my bare feet. Terns cried above the waves, surfers migrated upslope to their cars and dry clothes, and peeping shorebirds began to assemble in huddled groups to wait out the evening. As I was walking and thinking about my day's adventures I came across a large chunk of whale blubber on an isolated section of the beach. I had never seen blubber before, but it was unmistakable.

Down the beach families were playing in the fading light, and the shoreline was surprisingly quiet save for the gentle crashing of the waves and the distant squeals of children.

As I stood over this yard-square piece of marine mammal flesh I looked out into the bay and wondered aloud, "Where did this come from? What happened out there?" I was at once awestruck, a bit horrified, and very excited. When I returned to my office several days later I called Kip Evans at the Monterey Bay National Marine Sanctuary office in Monterey and told him my blubber story. There was a brief pause, and then he said, "Amazing! Last Friday a pack of killer whales was seen attacking, then eating, an immature gray whale in the bay. What you saw were dinner scraps!"

Amazing is right. When I think of the greater Monterey Bay shoreline I think of many things, but above all I think of its wildness. I've been fortunate to have experienced this wildness for many years, first as a child camping at the area's numerous state beaches and most recently while working on this guide. The shoreline's wildness presented itself to me in many different ways during my fieldwork. One evening it was the blubber discovery—a bit gruesome, true, but incredible when you think about it. Another time, while I sat on a bluff watching the sunset near Rio Del Mar, wildness arrived in the form of birds. From the direction of Elkhorn Slough tens of thousands

Sooty shearwaters feeding
in the bay

of sooty shearwaters streamed over the water just beyond
the breakers. Suddenly they circled and began a collective
feeding frenzy on a large school of bait fish. You could
hear the roar and slicing of their wings through the
humid marine air. The nearshore waters foamed white
with their repeated plunging.

Everyone on the beach below me stopped what they
were doing and stared out at the water, transfixed. Out
of thin air a mob of gulls formed over the boiling water,
jagged lines of terns dropped from the sky, and determined brown pelicans shouldered in on the swirling
mass of shearwaters to share in the booty and pick up
leftovers. Just as quickly as it began, it stopped, and the
undulating gray cloud of shearwaters lined out north in
the fading light, heading toward Capitola.

Of course, the wildness is just as wild—and just as
awesome—when you see the fin of a smoothhound shark
parting the still waters of Elkhorn Slough or you hear a
raucous colony of cormorants at Pt. Lobos through a
curtain of fog. Wildness can also be small in scale and
relatively still, as in the numerous tidepools I inspected
around the bay. A keen eye and patience will help you to
see life-and-death struggles as tidepool species go about
their intricate dance of existence. And for sheer colorful
decoration, tidepools and their inhabitants are unsur-
passed.

It's all amazing, large and small alike. While you sun-
bathe, exercise, and laugh along the calming, safe shore-

line, drama and beauty are all around you. Even the sand beneath your feet is teeming with life.

Envisioning that attack on the gray whale, knowing that white sharks occasionally patrol just offshore, and realizing that innumerable krill, squid, and jellyfish—and countless other marine species—live in these deep, cold waters sends an exciting chill down the back of my neck. As we stand on this shoreline we are near to something wonderful—a largely unsuspected world. This combination of a welcoming and accessible shoreline, coupled with abundant wildlife and the mysteries of the deep, will quickly capture your attention and inspire you to return for years to come.

We will never know what the first human inhabitants of this magnificent shoreline thought about their home. We will never know because they had no written language and the vast majority of their stories can no longer be heard along these coastal plains. The few stories that remain, dutifully kept alive for us today, are mere threads of a once-intricate tapestry. But if social complexity and an intimate knowledge of the natural world can be considered measures of contentment, then these coastal people loved their land deeply. In fact, there is reason to believe they felt their home was a magical place.

After all, for over 10,000 years the Quiroste, Cotoni, Uypi, Aptos, Calendaruc, Ensen, Rumsien, and Sargentaruc people—to name just a few of the Ohlone tribes that once ringed the bay—chose these shores to hunt, collect nuts and seeds, raise their young, worship, and ease the pain of their elderly. They flourished with the help of abundant resources and were kept sharp and forever watchful by their neighbor the grizzly bear.

How could these coastal peoples have known what would transpire after the arrival of Europeans? And how could Cabrillo, Vizcaíno, or Portolá have foreseen, even in their wildest dreams, what would follow their explorations? There are many tragic aspects to this region's early history, and yet it is fascinating and important for us to remember and contemplate that history, for it has shaped the human landscape we know today. Numerous museums along the shoreline maintain excellent exhibits about these first inhabitants and the European settlers, helping you to imagine what life was like in this area before California became a state.

It seems to me that Monterey Bay's shoreline has always been a magical place. It is neither terra firma nor open ocean, but an inviting mix of the two. Creeks, rivers, redwoods, fields, chaparral, beach, and sea: the shoreline. This magnificent coast is a place of history, commerce, residence, and holiday relaxation, as well as a region for countless weekend explorations and adventures. Along some 110 miles—between Point Año Nuevo in the north and Point Sur in the south—you can experience everything from two-ton elephant seals to palm-sized monarch butterflies. You can hike unimpeded along miles and miles of public beaches, or spend an entire day contemplating the horizon or a tidepool. It's all here: incredible vistas, fascinating wildlife, recreation, entertainment, dining, and even world-class wines from local vineyards.

But the bay's varied shoreline is the real attraction. Along the shore you are walking on the fine blue edge of the Pacific Ocean. Even while you explore the shore's neighboring canyons, valleys, and waterways, the Pacific is your constant companion. You may not be able to see it all the time as you work your way down the coast, but you can almost always hear it. And if you can't see it or hear it, you will surely be able to smell the foggy, salty essence of the sea, and feel its moist presence as cool winds blow inland off an even cooler ocean.

As you gaze across the bay, it is all but impossible to imagine that one of the area's most important physical features—the Monterey Bay Submarine Canyon—hides below the surface. This canyon is so deep that the Grand Canyon would fit inside it, with room to spare. In fact, it's analogous to a classic V-shaped river valley in the adjacent coastal mountains. Narrow at its head, the canyon begins its descent just 100 yards offshore of Moss Landing. It plunges precipitously at first, to a depth of 4,300 feet, dissecting the continental shelf. It then broadens and levels out; where it exits the bay and opens up, the canyon is already 13 miles wide and approximately one mile deep.

MONTEREY BAY AQUARIUM

Sixty miles offshore, the Monterey Canyon has dived to a depth of 12,000 feet. This impressive marine trench has a powerful influence on local ecology, weather, and human commerce.

Yet another reason this region is so special is that this exquisite stretch of shoreline, as well as the Monterey Canyon, is part of the Monterey Bay National Marine Sanctuary. Established in 1992, the sanctuary presently takes in more than one-quarter of the California coast, from Marin County in the north to Cambria, 360 miles to the south in San Luis Obispo County, and extends an average of 35 miles offshore; in all it covers some 5,300 square miles. The nutrient-rich waters of the sanctuary support thousands of species, from minute zooplankton to blue whales, as well as the nation's most extensive kelp forests.

Because of this wealth of species and the accessibility of so many different marine ecosystems within close proximity, more than 20 marine-oriented institutions flourish along the edge of the bay. They range from Stanford University's Hopkins Marine Station, established in 1892, to the relatively new Monterey Bay Aquarium, which thrills 1.8 million visitors annually. Individually and collectively, these institutions are recognized as models for marine research and education both in the United States and abroad.

Geography and Other Notes

Monterey Bay, and therefore its shoreline, is typically defined as the section of coast from Point Santa Cruz in the north to Point Pinos on the Monterey Peninsula. I decided to broaden the view a bit and explore the shoreline from Point Año Nuevo down to Point Sur on the Big Sur Coast. Not only are all these lands and nearshore environments ecologically related, but also there are simply too many fantastic places to visit just north of Point Santa Cruz and immediately south of Point Pinos. After all, the idea behind a book like this is to encourage the reader to enjoy the information it contains, then get out there and experience these places in person. By expanding the scope of the book, I simply offer you more places to explore, including a few inland destinations.

Efforts are being made today to organize a trail system along the entire bay so future explorers can spend hours or even days biking or walking along it. Many sections of this trail are already in place, such as the 30 or so paved miles of the Monterey Bay Coastal Trail between the cities of Marina and Carmel. The Monterey Bay trail system complements the California Coastal Trail (CCT), which will one day follow the state's entire shoreline. For information about the status of the CCT in the Monterey region, and elsewhere along the coast, contact Coastwalk at 1-800-550-6854, or go to their website at http://www. sonic.net/coastwalk.

Also, the shoreline adjacent to the bay proper is within the Monterey Bay State Seashore. Although this designation is at the moment rather symbolic, eventually the state seashore will work with city and county agencies to complete projects such as the shoreline trail and to further improve public access.

It is my hope that you will find this book to be a comprehensive, thoughtful, and useful introduction to the shoreline's human history, natural history, public access points, parklands, and inviting coastal towns. Each chapter contains information about bicycling and public transportation within that specific stretch of shoreline. Overview maps are included, and "Getting Around" sections provide detailed directions, and mileage where appropriate. The "Information" sections are filled with telephone numbers, as well as the occasional website address. These were all accurate when I completed the guide, but don't be surprised if a few numbers or websites have changed. If you have a name or a subject, you'll be able to track down the new information. Before visiting a specific park, museum, or other facility, always call ahead to check on the hours and current events.

Throughout, you will find information about specific sites, including plant and animal species, both on the shore and in the bay. I've also incorporated material on weather, history, geology, ecology, and a variety of notes and trivia. General information about shoreline and pier fishing is provided as well, but there are so many jurisdictions along the shore, and such a mix of regulations, that it is best to call specific parks, piers, or marinas before you head out with your rod and tackle box.

To research this book and organize material, I rode my bicycle, walked, or ran almost all public portions of the shoreline between Point Año Nuevo and Point Sur. I drove all the coastal roads, logging some 2,500 miles with my aging truck. It is astonishing to me how much of the shoreline is open to everyone. However, some sections of land adjacent to the shore are private. If land is posted as private property, that means don't cross it. Sometimes a public easement allows access through private land, so you may come across a confusing situation where a trail or dirt road is bordered by threatening signs. Don't worry: it's safe to proceed, as long as you stick to the path. If this book says an accessway is public, it is. Proceed without worry.

That brings me to some thoughts on how to use this book. First, acquaint yourself with the layout of the guide. Use the index, study the maps, and read about a given section of shoreline before going there. Then when you venture to the shore, bring this book along for quick reference. If you have a specific interest in a species or a subject (bird-watching, botany, seashells, geology), scan the reference section for suggested books, most of which can be purchased in the numerous shoreline visitors' centers and museums.

Besides bringing this guide with you, come prepared in other respects. The weather along the coast can change rapidly at any time of the year. Dress in layers and keep a dry set of clothes in your car. You can hike for hours along public stretches of the shoreline, so be sure to carry some water, a snack, and maybe a few dollars just in case. If you are biking, also pack a repair kit and a pump. You'd be surprised how many unprepared bicyclists I helped out while I was traveling the highways and backroads.

Above all, enjoy this book as you get to know and love this extraordinary section of California's coast.

Año Nuevo State Reserve to Natural Bridges State Beach

The Año Nuevo region is the perfect location to either start or wrap up your exploration of the Monterey Bay shoreline and the Monterey Bay National Marine Sanctuary. The coastline is defined by miles of impressive cliffs, marine terraces, and a scattering of jewel-like coves and hidden beaches. And just inland you'll find spots renowned for their natural beauty and rich human history.

From Año Nuevo's shore you can look south across the entire bay to the Monterey Peninsula some 50 miles distant and the roughened silhouette of the Sierra de Salinas and Santa Lucia Range. Just beyond the visitor center at the Año Nuevo Reserve, the meeting of land and sea is marked by miles of abrupt cliffs stretching away toward Santa Cruz. The sweeping vista draws your eyes south. Follow the prevailing winds and currents along the shoreline here, moving slowly and confidently around the smooth curve of the bay as you explore this remarkable shoreline.

The Año Nuevo elephant seal colony. Año Nuevo Island can be seen in the distance.

Año Nuevo State Reserve

The reserve's landscape is so packed with human and natural history that first-time visitors could spend a long weekend here (based, say, out of nearby Butano State Park) without even crossing the county line to the immediate south.

Father Antonio de la Ascensión, a member of the Sebastián Vizcaíno sailing expedition, named this point of land Punta de Año Nuevo—New Year's Point—in early January 1603. Today, despite the fact that these reserve lands have been used as mission-era pasturelands, a private rancho, a long-lived dairy operation, a farm, and a sand-mining enterprise, they remain much as Vizcaíno and his crew saw them: wild and teeming with life.

One major change is that Año Nuevo now accommodates some 200,000 visitors annually. Nonetheless, elephant seals, sea lions, and other animals own the beach

◄ Wilder Ranch's coastal bluffs and marine terraces
JERRY EMORY

9

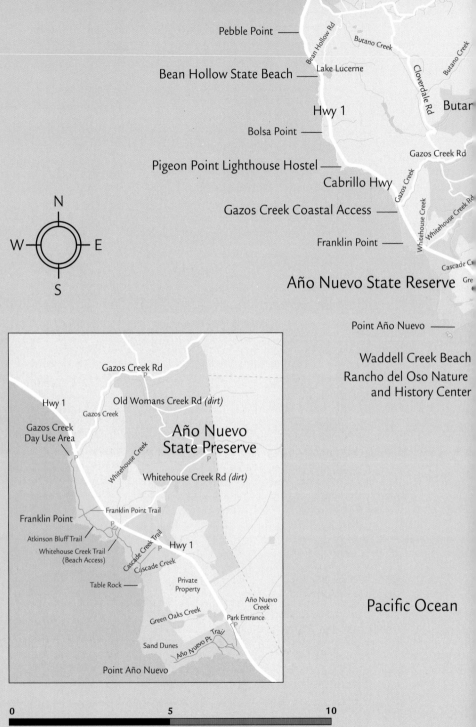

Pebble Point

Bean Hollow State Beach
Lake Lucerne

Bean Hollow Rd
Butano Creek
Cloverdale Rd
Butano Creek

Hwy 1

Butar

Bolsa Point

Gazos Creek Rd

Pigeon Point Lighthouse Hostel

Cabrillo Hwy

Gazos Creek Coastal Access

Gazos Creek
Whitehouse Creek Rd
Whitehouse Creek

Franklin Point

Cascade Cr

Año Nuevo State Reserve
Gre

Point Año Nuevo

Waddell Creek Beach
Rancho del Oso Nature
and History Center

N
W   E
S

Gazos Creek Rd
P

Hwy 1
Old Womans Creek Rd *(dirt)*
Gazos Creek

Año Nuevo
State Preserve

Gazos Creek
Day Use Area
P

Whitehouse Creek
P

Whitehouse Creek Rd *(dirt)*

Franklin Point Trail

Franklin Point
P

Atkinson Bluff Trail
Whitehouse Creek Trail
(Beach Access)

Cascade Creek Trail
P   Hwy 1
Cascade Creek

Table Rock

Private
Property

Año Nuevo
Creek
Park Entrance
P

Green Oaks Creek

Pacific Ocean

Sand Dunes
Año Nuevo Pt Trail

Point Año Nuevo

0   5   10

MILES

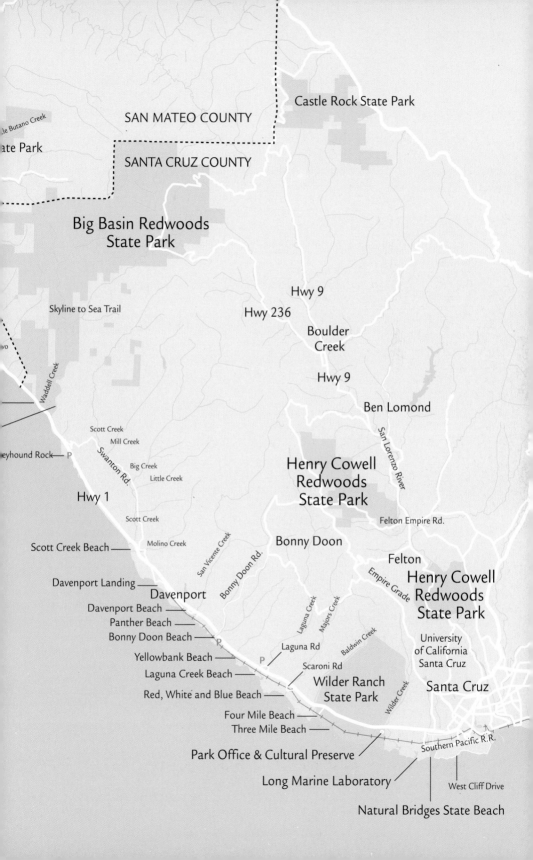

Castle Rock State Park

SAN MATEO COUNTY

SANTA CRUZ COUNTY

ttle Butane Creek

ate Park

Big Basin Redwoods
State Park

Hwy 9

Hwy 236

Skyline to Sea Trail

Boulder
Creek

Hwy 9

Ben Lomond

Waddell Creek

Scott Creek

Mill Creek

eyhound Rock— P

Swanton Rd.

Big Creek

Little Creek

San Lorenzo River

Henry Cowell
Redwoods
State Park

Hwy 1

Scott Creek

Felton Empire Rd.

Scott Creek Beach ———

Molino Creek

Bonny Doon

Felton

Davenport Landing ——

Empire Grade

Henry Cowell
Redwoods
State Park

Davenport

San Vicente Creek

Bonny Doon Rd.

Davenport Beach ——

Panther Beach ———

University
of California
Santa Cruz

Bonny Doon Beach ——

P

Laguna Creek

Majors Creek

Yellowbank Beach ——

P

Laguna Rd

Baldwin Creek

Santa Cruz

Laguna Creek Beach ——

Scaroni Rd

Red, White and Blue Beach ——

Wilder Ranch
State Park

Wilder Creek

Four Mile Beach ——

Three Mile Beach ——

Southern Pacific R.R.

Park Office & Cultural Preserve ———

Long Marine Laboratory

West Cliff Drive

Natural Bridges State Beach

During the 1800s it is estimated that hundreds of thousands of elephant seals were killed for the oil that could be rendered from their blubber. By the late 1800s, only 50 to 100 individuals survived off the coast of Baja California. The Mexican government passed laws in 1922 to help protect the seals, and the U.S. government passed similar measures when the seals returned to U.S. waters several years later. They've been reclaiming their range and increasing their numbers ever since. Today, about 2,000 pups are born at Año Nuevo every year.

and dunes here. Humans are simply visitors. The near-shore waters are rich with life, above and below the choppy surface. Dunes, grasslands, and chaparral offer protection and food for an array of birds and animals. As just one indication of this area's riches, over 320 bird species have been seen within the reserve. No matter what time of year you visit, you will come away amazed at the abundance and diversity of life both on land and near shore.

Future plans for this 4,000-acre reserve include protection of neighboring lands. One day, visitors will be able to explore a contiguous swath of public land between Año Nuevo, Butano State Park, and Big Basin Redwoods State Park.

Elephant Seals

The most popular attraction for visitors to Año Nuevo is the northern elephant seal colony that assembles here each winter. (Late spring and early summer are great for birds and plants.) Once you spot one of these pinnipeds—animals with finlike feet, or flippers—especially a mature male calling on the beach, you'll immediately realize why they are called elephant seals. Not only are they enormous (males can weigh up to 2.5 tons), but they also have long, pendulous noses that look like an elephant trunk.

Año Nuevo's beaches and dunes really start hopping in December. During this month the diminutive females (they weigh "only" 1,200–2,000 pounds) arrive onshore. Within a week they give birth to a single pup. Feeding on their mothers' rich milk, pups grow from about 75 pounds at birth to 250–350 pounds when they are weaned less than a month later. At this point, mothers abandon their offspring, now called weaners.

Females begin mating about a month after giving birth, but the fertilized egg does not start developing for several months. This phenomenon, called "delayed implantation," is believed to give mothers time to regain some strength, after giving birth and nursing, for the gestation of a new pup. This adaptation also helps time events so that pups are born soon after the females' arrival at Año Nuevo every winter.

During this hectic season of pupping and mating, the beaches are covered with harems ruled by a dominant male. It may look like mayhem to a human visitor, but all the birthing, nursing, mating, and disputes follow fairly rigid rules and timelines.

Bull elephant seal

Infant elephant seals, known as weaners

When this site was named in 1603, Año Nuevo Island was still part of the mainland. It was the *punta*—or point—in Punta de Año Nuevo. Since then wave action has slowly eaten away at the point, creating a 13-acre island. To warn modern-day mariners of this area's rocky shores a fog whistle was installed on Año Nuevo Island in 1872, and a five-story light tower in 1890. In 1904, a large house was constructed here for the lighthouse keeper and his assistant. An automatic buoy replaced the lighthouse in 1948.

Only sea lions and birds live on the island now. The ground around the old structure is peppered with the burrows of pigeon guillemots and rhinoceros auklets, and elephant seals congregate on the big beach just in front of the house.

The males lie there like so many soft-skinned minivans with their wheels buried in the sand, or patrol the surf-line, occasionally rising with great effort to bellow out their territorial calls. An impossibly deep, large-diameter-drain-pipe-sounding "glub-glub-glub" booms out of their blubber-lined chests and rolls across the assembled masses. After they have performed, they fall back down to the sand or crash into the water as if they couldn't hold their weight for another second. And yet these calls are often the precursor to bloody territorial battles between males.

By March adult elephant seals begin to leave the colony. Males are first to disperse, followed by females. Weaned pups linger along the shoreline here for two and a half months to practice swimming and feeding on their own. Then they venture north to feed, along with the adults, off the coast of northern Washington and Vancouver Island, eventually returning the following September.

During breeding season (December 15 through March 31) only guided visits are permitted within the reserve, and reservations are highly recommended. Call 1-800-444-4445 for information and reservations. From April through November, hiking permits must be obtained at the visitors center (650-879-2025) before entering the Wildlife Protection Area.

The Bluffs

The reserve's Whitehouse Creek Trail leads to several bluff-hugging pathways (the main one being the Atkinson Bluff Trail) and a nicely protected little beach. Both along this bluff and at Franklin Point you will find scores of small trails branching off here and there. Instead of following a rabbit or fox run, stay to the well-signed pathways. It will be easier on you, and on the land. For example, there is a small footpath along Atkinson Bluff that heads south, but the principal trail is about 50 feet inland—and for good reason. The bluffs here are very unstable, and the drop to the beach is steep.

The trail between Whitehouse Creek and Cascade Creek to the south is about two miles long. When you approach the line of cypress and decrepit eucalyptus, you are nearing the end of the trail. At Cascade Creek, a low-lying marshy area can be enjoyed from a distance but not crossed—this portion of the reserve is closed to the public in order to protect the elephant seals and other wildlife. Here you are standing on a very distinct marine terrace, now topped with a coastal prairie, overlooking the fertile mouth of Cascade Creek. To the south, in the reserve's Wildlife Protection Area, acres and acres of new

Of all the birds of prey found in and around Año Nuevo, the northern harrier *(Circus cyaneus)* is perhaps the most abundant. If it's not, it's at least the most visible as it slowly teeters across the grasslands and dune fields in search of prey. Harriers can also be seen standing on the ground not far from many trails. In fact, they nest on the ground in the middle of tall grass. Frequently a male and a female can be seen hunting the same area.

The sexes of these slim birds are easy to distinguish. The adult male is a uniform gray above and white below and sports a striking white facial disk of feathers. The female is slightly larger than the male, shares the facial pattern, but is covered with buff plumage. Both can be identified at a distance by their rocky flight close to the ground and by their white rump patches.

Look closely at the ground where harriers hunt. You'll probably see a maze of runways and tunnels in the grass: voles! The relationship between these birds and their small rodent prey is so interdependent that one researcher describes the northern harrier as "the hawk that is ruled by a mouse." When vole populations soar, harriers can

Northern harriers are common birds of the shoreline, where they hunt for voles and other prey across coastal prairies and scrub.

become polygamous (a male having more than one mate). When vole numbers plummet, harriers may forgo nesting altogether or disperse. The vole found along the central coast is the California vole *(Microtus californicus)*.

and stabilized dunes predominate—a striking transition. Dunes also exist at the northern end of the bluff, but they are less developed.

The entire terrace between Cascade and Whitehouse Creeks is spectacular for spring wildflowers and for studying northern harriers and white-tailed kites. This area has also been burned with controlled fires set by park personnel to control exotics (nonnative species), such as pampas grass and European gorse.

European Gorse: The Spiny Invasive

Out along the bluff trail you might find a specimen or two of a nasty-looking weed with impressive thorns. It might be trying to pretty itself up with brilliant yellow pealike flowers, but don't let it fool you. It's European gorse *(Ulex europaeus)*, one of the Pacific coast's toughest exotics. This dense grayish-green shrub can grow up to nine feet tall, and its small leaves are typically shorter than its hazardous spines.

Native to the Mediterranean region, gorse is well adapted to survive in a number of environments. A typical gorse shrub produces about 8,000 seeds every year, which may lie dormant in the soil for up to 40 years.

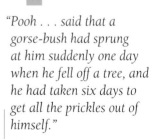

"Pooh . . . said that a gorse-bush had sprung at him suddenly one day when he fell off a tree, and he had taken six days to get all the prickles out of himself."

A. A. Milne,
Winnie the Pooh
(1926)

Harbor seals can be seen on protected beaches along the Monterey Bay shoreline.

Who's making all that racket anyway? What is that thing that looks like an overstuffed sausage resting on those rocks? Año Nuevo Island and the adjacent mainland beaches make up the most important pinniped rookery and resting areas within the marine sanctuary. Here are the various species of marine mammals present.

▪ Elephant seal
(Mirounga angustirostris)
These show-stoppers dominate the mainland's beaches and dunes. By far the largest of the pinnipeds gracing these shores, elephant seals are also the deepest diving of all marine mammals. They spend most of their life at sea, where they routinely dive 2,000 feet in search of their favorite foods, such as rays, squid, and small sharks. Scientific observers report their amazing feats: one male seal dove to a depth of just over 5,000 feet; a female seal stayed underwater for almost two hours. Scientists admit they still have a lot to learn about these pinnipeds.

▪ Harbor seal
(Phoca vitulina)
Harbor seals (and their relatives, fur seals) have a completely different personality from that of their gargantuan neighbors the elephant seals. These elusive, plump, speckled creatures live on Año Nuevo Island year round, but their growls can be heard from the mainland only on a day with onshore winds. When fully grown they tip the scales at about 250 pounds, and they can dive some 1,500 feet in search of food. Harbor seals can be spotted poking their heads out of the water just off the reserve's beaches—and around the entire bay—as if keeping their eyes on things without wanting to get involved. They also rest on offshore rocks, and being much more agile than elephant seals, they can perch atop precarious places. (With binoculars you can easily see their mottled coats.) Unlike sea lions, however, they can't walk any distance on land.

▪ Steller's sea lion
(Eumetopias jubatus)
The brown-to-yellowish Steller's sea lion is a raucous member of the island's pinniped neighborhood. In the past three decades the population of Steller's sea lions has declined by half, down to some 116,000 individuals in

Steller's sea lions come ashore on Año Nuevo Island.

the north Pacific. As a result they are now included as a threatened species on the federal Endangered Species List, compiled by the U.S. Fish and Wildlife Service. Año Nuevo Island is the southernmost breeding site for Stellers. They stick to the edges of the island and rocky outcrops. Males can reach a length of ten feet and weigh in at 2,200 pounds, much larger than the popular and well-known California sea lion.

California sea lion
(Zalophus californianus)

Hundreds of dark brown California sea lions arrive at Año Nuevo Island each September, where the principally male group rests for several months before venturing far-ther north to feed. Summer months find many returning south to breeding grounds in the Channel Islands. The penetrating bark of the male California sea lion can be heard for miles. These are the seals typically trained for shows and for scientific research because of their cognitive abilities. They also commandeer portions of Monterey Harbor and San Francisco's Pier 39 seasonally.

Northern fur seal
(Callorhinus ursinus)

The northern fur seal, a rare visitor to the island, was heavily hunted for its prized coat during the past century. When you scope the waves or nearshore waters, look for a seal with thick, dark fur and you'll have a positive identification. The fur seal's snout is also more pointed than that of the sea lion.

Southern sea otter
(Enhydra lutris nereis)

Otters are not pinnipeds, but they too can be seen offshore from the reserve. Typically, they are accompanied by a gull or two waiting for food scraps the otter might discard. Like the elephant seal and many other marine mammals, the otter is returning from near-extinction and recolonizing its former range. The first mother and pup were seen at Año Nuevo in 1980, after an absence of more than a century (see pp. 279–281). The reserve now constitutes the northern limit of their range.

The raucous bark of the California sea lion is a constant sound around the bay.

The plant is also able to fix nitrogen from the air, and so can grow in just about any soil type. Rendering fields inaccessible, it out-competes native species with ease—just one reason State Parks is actively removing it. And that is no easy task. Gorse is extremely adaptable: its seeds can spread by water, in animal fur and droppings, on the soles of shoes, and by hitching a ride with cars or other machinery. To help the cause, do not plant gorse and do not collect its seeds.

San Francisco Garter Snake

As you walk the shoreline around the Año Nuevo Reserve you might come across a snake with striking body stripes of greenish yellow, red, and black. Its head is red, its belly blue green, or sometimes turquoise. It is the San Francisco garter snake (*Thamnophis sirtalis tetrataenia*), a state- and federally-designated endangered species.

This slim snake, which can grow to about four feet long, once thrived around the edges of freshwater—where it chased down its favorite food, frogs—from San Francisco County to Año Nuevo. Over the years it fell victim to loss of habitat as the marshes and waterways it inhabited were altered or paved over. Today it is confined to a handful of small populations throughout San Mateo County and in northwestern Santa Cruz County. Recovery efforts are being made to safeguard this species' future through habitat preservation and restoration. If you do come across one of these brilliant snakes, observe, but please don't pick it up or bother it.

The endangered San Francisco garter snake at Año Nuevo

The California mussel (*Mytilus californianus*) is one of the most common creatures on California's rocky shores and tidepools. Where wave action is heavy, large beds of mussels can be found, some of which have been estimated to hold up to one million individuals. But that's not all: tucked in among these mussel beds, large as well as small, countless other marine creatures— sponges, worms, snails, crabs—take shelter.

California mussels are typically brownish to grayish black, and their thick shells have visible ridges or ribs. Although those hard shells may stop most predators, some gull species know how to pluck up a wave-loosened mussel, fly aloft, and drop the mussel on rock or pavement to crack it open. Analysis of coastal Indian middens tells us that mussels were a staple of the coast's native people as well.

Mussels attach themselves to rocks very tightly. They do this by secreting tough strands called byssal threads, which allow them to stay put in even the roughest weather. These shellfish eat by filtering seawater for plankton and other organic bits. Mussels are quarantined in California between May 1 and October 31 because during that period they are known to consume a toxic organism, *Gonyaulax catanella,* that can cause paralysis and even death in humans.

Franklin Point

Franklin Point received its name from a sorrowful disaster: in 1865 the ship *Sir John Franklin* smashed into the rocks just offshore. Today, thankfully, joy prevails. No matter the season, this portion of the reserve is perfect for a brisk hike or an all-day adventure.

The turnout for Franklin Point is marked by an enormous chunk of driftwood planted in the ground. Please read and heed all the park rules and seasonal warnings (such as mussel and clam quarantines).

An easy ten-minute walk through coyote bush, yellow lupine, European dune grass, and wind-trimmed stands of willow takes you to a wonderful beach on the north side of the point. At low tide this stretch of sand extends between Franklin Point and the Gazos Creek beach area to the north. You're only ten minutes from Highway 1, but out here it is just you and the wild shoreline.

Looking north you can spy the Pigeon Point Lighthouse, balanced on the end of a nearly flat marine terrace. On cool days, you may see steam rising above a roadside row of cypress, inland between Gazos Creek and Pigeon Point. Not a hot spring, what you see is the Campbell (as in soup) mushroom plant, growing mushrooms for your dinner table.

Work your way south out to the point via the confusion of human and animal trails. And remember, it is always possible to see lone male elephant seals out here. If you do, stay clear! They are wild animals and can move surprisingly fast.

"*Like the sea itself, the shore fascinates us who return to it, the place of our dim ancestral beginnings. In the recurrent rhythms of tides and surf and in the varied life of the tide lines there is the obvious attraction of movement and change and beauty. There is also, I am convinced, a deeper fascination born of inner meaning and significance.*"

Rachel Carson,
The Edge of the Sea
(1955)

From the southern tip of the Atkinson Bluff Trail, just beyond the intersection with the Cascade Creek Trail, you can look south into the reserve and across a vast field of dunes, some 350 acres' worth. If the wind is up during your visit, it will probably be blowing against your back, sweeping down over the dunes. Take note of it, for that wind is slowly moving the dune field away from you, to the south. This is one of the few remaining active dune fields on the California coast.

Slowly, however, the dunes are changing because less sand is coming into the system than in years past. The reason for this lies partly in geologic history. California's large dune systems were formed thousands of years ago under different climatic conditions when more rainfall occurred and glaciers covered much of North America. Heavier rains caused more dune material—ground-up rocks from coastal streams—to be deposited in nearshore waters. Today, although we still experience heavy winter storms, there is far less stream water in coastal California compared to, say, 15,000 years ago (when present-day Seattle was under about 3,000 feet of ice and California's coastline was several miles offshore from its present location).

Also, an unnaturally abundant supply of freshwater from nearby agricultural irrigation has permitted plants normally kept in check by the austere dune environment to flourish, thus incrementally changing the face of the dunes. European dune grass, sprawling mats of wild strawberries, and deep-rooted willows have stabilized large sections of the dunes. Other bushy perennials—lupine, coyote bush—then are able to move in and augment the stabilization process. Nonetheless, these dunes are still wild, and they are alive with creatures large and small.

"There is one ocean, with coves having many names; a single sea of atmosphere, with no coves at all; a thin miracle of soil, alive and giving life; a last planet; and there is no spare."

David Brower

As you climb through the dunes, study the corridorlike blowouts, or furrows, in the sand. What do you think made them? What do they line up with?

Franklin Point should be experienced slowly and easily. It's a wild spot, so the more lightly you move about, the more you are likely to see. Work your way through the dunes carefully; don't rush. You might even want to curb your conversation and hunker down for the final approach to the point (harbor seals, if present, are very skittish). You're sure to be rewarded for your efforts.

Once there, you can look down on a series of harbor seal haul-outs, which are actually marine terraces. Cormorants line the jumble of offshore rocks—the downfall of the clipper ship *Franklin*. Cast your eyes around: not only can you revisit the view of Pigeon Point, you can also swing south and take in the main portion of the reserve. Inland the mountains rise up to about 1,500 feet, and signs of agriculture can be seen to the north.

Here, and at most points along this shoreline, you'll quickly realize that big waves can come in off this ocean with awesome power. Use common sense and don't go climbing around on the rocks.

Wildflowers at Franklin Point

European Dune Grass

European dune grass (*Ammophila arenaria*), also known as marram, was probably introduced along the West Coast to stabilize San Francisco's shifting dunes in 1869; it arrived in Monterey Bay in 1919. It has dominated central and northern California beaches ever since—as here at Franklin Point. This aggressive exotic routinely replaces native dune grasses, forming monocultures, or single-species plantings. Native dune grass species, such as wild ryes (*Elymus mollis* and *E. pacificus*), grow in clumps, which encourages variety. Like many introduced plants, European dune grass supports nitrogen-fixing bacteria, giving it a competitive advantage over most natives in the nutrient-starved sand dunes.

In addition to being bad for native plants, this exotic has been known to overrun the historic nesting sites of the endangered snowy plover, which needs open and isolated stretches of beach to nest. Perhaps more significantly, it stops dunes from doing what they are meant to do—and what native plants have adapted to—which is shift and move. Where this grass grows, unnaturally high ridges are formed, which starve dune systems of incoming sand—their lifeblood. This ability to invade and stabilize sand is why it has been introduced around development sites, highways, and other places where blowing sand is an inconvenience.

CABRILLO HIGHWAY

California's Highway 1 is also known as the Cabrillo Highway, in honor of Juan Rodriguez Cabrillo. This Portuguese navigator (his real name was João Rodrigues Cabrilho), working for the Spanish, was in charge of the first European expedition to sail along California's coastline, in 1542. The state of California adopted this name for the highway in 1957 after being petitioned by the Cabrillo Civic Clubs of California.

Wild Strawberry

As you explore the various dune systems around the bay, you'll keep coming across a familiar cherubic face: the wild strawberry (*Fragaria chiloensis*). Also known

Dune strawberries

as the sand strawberry, this wild species is the great-grandmother of those enormous strawberries you buy at the market. It has dark evergreen leaves and grows from Alaska to southern Chile. These low-growing plants spread rapidly by underground runners, forming thick mats. In the spring they explode with one-inch white flowers. The red fruits that follow are small and tasteless, though, so leave them for the dune creatures. And don't worry: plenty of cultivated strawberries are grown nearby for us sweet-toothed humans, especially around the Elkhorn Slough area.

The main entrance to Año Nuevo is on Highway 1 approximately 55 miles south of San Francisco or 27 miles south of Half Moon Bay, and 20 miles north of Santa Cruz. To find the reserve's trailhead pullouts and inland roads, head north from the main entrance and visitor center. Cascade Creek Trail is 1 mile north, on the west. Whitehouse Creek Trail and Road (across Highway 1 from each other) are approximately 2.5 miles north of the Año Nuevo entrance (there is another turnout on the north side of creek, but it is not as easy or safe as the one to the south). The Franklin Point turnout is another mile beyond Whitehouse Creek, or about 3.5 miles north of the reserve's main entrance. Gazos Creek Road is another half-mile beyond the turnout to Franklin Point. There is another signed turnout between the principal Franklin Point turnout and Gazos Creek, but parking is sparse and access to Highway 1 problematic.

Black Phoebe

The black phoebe (*Sayornis nigricans*) is a year-round resident at Año Nuevo and other shoreline sites around the bay. What appears as a friendly greeting by these soft-spoken flycatchers is really a low-key territorial maneuver. They will often fly right up to you (the "greeting"), then return to their favorite perch or move down the trail in front of you. It is trying to lead you out of its territory! Like all flycatchers, black phoebes frequently pop off their perches to chase flying insects. If you are very close and the day is calm, you can actually hear their bills snap shut around their hapless prey.

MONTEREY BAY AQUARIUM

Black phoebe

Brush Rabbit

This coastal resident has sizable ears (it is a rabbit, after all), but not nearly as large as its cousin the jackrabbit. Brush or cottontail rabbits (*Sylvilagus bachmani*) are grayish brown and sport, not surprisingly, a white, puffy tail.

Brush rabbit

Instead of ricocheting off like a jackrabbit, the cottontail moves into the underbrush just as Beatrix Potter describes, going "lippety, lippety." Watch one and you'll understand. Normally, cottontails are most active at night and twilight, when they eat grasses, leaves, twigs, and fallen fruit. But in the dunes, you can see them scampering about in daylight.

The Quiroste people lived in the Año Nuevo area seasonally to hunt, fish, and collect shellfish. Their large village here was visited by Gaspar de Portolá in 1769 as he ventured north to San Francisco Bay with his sickly band of men.

By all indications the Quiroste, a group of the Ohlone Indians, had a well-developed community and extensive knowledge of their environment. And this should come as no surprise. After all, it is believed that native peoples had lived in California for more than 10,000 years before European explorers arrived. The state was home to an estimated 1,000 to 1,400 independent groups of Indians—perhaps the densest population of native peoples in North America. Some 10,000 men, women, and children lived between San Francisco Bay and Big Sur in approximately 50 different village groups. Each group had its own territory and spoke one of eight different dialects. The Spanish called these people Costeños—people of the coast. For many years they were collectively called Costanoans. Today their descendants prefer the name Ohlone.

The Quiroste produced spear points, arrowheads, and other tools from local chert. These items have been found in sites throughout the Coast Range and the Central Valley, indicating that the Quiroste had well-established trade links with other Indians. Additionally, spear points from the eastern Sierra Nevada have been uncovered by archeologists at Año Nuevo.

"The Indians . . . received us with great affability and kindness, and, furthermore, presented us with seeds kneaded into thick pats. . . . In the middle of the village there was a large house, spherical in form and very roomy. . . . Because the large house so much surpassed the others, the village was named after it."

Miguel Costansó, with the Portolá expedition, describing the Quiroste village at Año Nuevo (1769)

Ohlone Valley

To reach the northern entrance of the reserve's fire road system (east of Highway 1), follow Gazos Creek Road. Gazos Creek Road is a beautiful route that winds along Gazos Creek with its meandering forest of red alder.

After about two miles the road to Butano State Park eases off to the left (north); to the right is the trailhead for the northern end of Old Womans Creek Road. This is a great spot for hiking, running, biking, and simply being in nature. After crossing over Old Womans Creek on an old metal bridge, you're in parkland and moving along a dirt road (a fire road, really) that follows the curves of a small side creek.

After half of a mile you pass through a towering stand of red alders. Shade providers in summer and starkly beautiful in winter, these trees are a real joy. As you move out of the alders, a road to your right crosses the creek and leads south to Ohlone Valley and Whitehouse Creek Road (also dirt).

After one mile on Old Womans Creek Road, the route begins to climb steeply, leaving the small creek far below. You move through a mixed forest of young redwoods, tan oaks, and other species. After another mile of climbing you reach the end of the road: a locked gate announces the beginning of private land. During wet weather, come prepared: these roads can become very muddy.

California newts can be seen during wet weather.

MONTEREY BAY AQUARIUM

California Newt

During the moist part of the year (fall through early spring), keep an eye out for newts crossing your path. Although several species are found in the central coast hills, you are most likely to encounter the California newt (*Taricha torosa*) en route to a breeding pond.

Dark brown above and deep yellow below, these amphibians don't move fast on land, so don't expect them to get out of your way. Instead, drop down to your hands and knees and check them out. Notice the vertically flat tail (good for swimming and coupling in those ponds), the bulbous eyes, and the fine speckling on its back. They may not fulfill your idea of beauty, but they are amazing animals, able to migrate considerable distances.

Red Alder

Red alder (*Alnus rubra*) is the largest—and perhaps most graceful—of the American alders, commonly reaching up to 130 feet in height. It is readily identified by the clusters of diminutive cones dripping off its branches (though they aren't true cones, because alders aren't conifers). Also known as the Pacific coast alder or western alder, this species ranges from southern California to Alaska. In the Northwest it is commonly used for furniture and other crafts and for firewood.

Whitehouse Creek Road

The other way to explore Ohlone Valley and other inland portions of the reserve east of Highway 1 is to venture up Whitehouse Creek Road. This dirt road was named after a house built near here by pioneer Isaac Grahm in the early 1850s; for years the house was a well-known local landmark until it burned in 1978. The entrance to the road is not obvious, but you can find it right across the highway from the shoreward trailhead to Whitehouse

ARCHEOLOGICAL SITES—DON'T MESS WITH THE MIDDENS

Finding evidence of people who came before us can be thrilling. But whether you kick over a horseshoe or an arrowhead, you must leave it where you found it and report it to a ranger or other official. All archeological sites, no matter how recent or old, no matter if on private land or public, are keys to our understanding of the past. They deserve to be researched and managed properly. On all state and federal lands, it is illegal to collect any type of artifact. Even a chip of obsidian or a cracked piece of china can tell the educated eye an entire story.

Every year there is an annual wild mussel quarantine along the California coast from approximately May through October. Mussels are filter feeders and they can accumulate high levels of a naturally occurring toxin in their tissues. This toxin is produced seasonally by certain plankton on which mussels feed heavily. Though not fatal to the mussels, the toxin can cause paralytic shellfish poisoning, or PSP, an occasionally fatal nerve affliction, in humans who eat the contaminated mollusks. If other wild shellfish—clams, oysters, and scallops—are affected, the state will post the shoreline with warnings; however, these species are not affected as commonly as mussels owing to their different habitats and feeding patterns. The toll-free Shellfish Information Line maintained by the state can give you current information; call 1-800-553-4133. The warning does not apply to commercially grown shellfish, and other marine animals, such as abalone, shrimp, crab, and fish, do not eat the toxic plankton.

Creek Trail. Look for the large ranch sign at the road's entrance; drive in and you will see some state park signs.

You can drive some three miles before the road enters private land, but consider riding your bike or walking. It is perfect country for either activity. You begin by entering low rolling hills adorned with coyote bush, yellow lupine, willows, and an impressive eucalyptus forest along Whitehouse Creek to the north. Just short of two miles the road suddenly dips and turns before entering a dense stand of Douglas fir heavily festooned with lace lichen. Scope the meadows around here and you may see the rooting areas of wild pigs.

A few more downhill bends in the road bring you to a closed metal gate on your left. It may not appear very inviting, but look closer and you will see a well-worn footpath around one end and a state park sign. This is the southern entrance to Ohlone Valley. As with Old Womans Creek Road, wet weather turns these fire roads into muddy tracks. Be prepared.

This dirt road eventually splits, and each branch circumnavigates Ohlone Valley. The valley itself has a beautiful meadow area surrounded by a Douglas fir forest on several sides and hillsides of coyote bush. An impressive buckeye forest runs through the middle of the valley. Researchers believe that dense concentrations of certain plants commonly used by the Ohlone are good indicators of past habitation by these peoples. The buckeye is one such plant. Its large seeds were eaten (after treatment) when acorn crops failed.

Lichen

Lace lichen (*Ramalina menziesii*) is a wispy gray-green adornment commonly found hanging from trees in cool coastal canyons. Not really a plant, lichen is actually two organisms: a fungus and an alga that have come together as one in a relationship known as mutualistic symbiosis. That is, each organism helps the other one make a living. The algal portion of lichen engages in photosynthesis, generating food from air, water, and sun. Fungi can't photosynthesize, but they do something algae can't: absorb minerals. It's a wonderful example of natural cooperation.

Researchers believe lace lichen is one of the most dominant species in coastal California. It survives through periods of both drought and high rainfall, growing by 30 percent every year (a far greater growth rate than that of any plant species associated with it). Lace lichen is highly nutritious, and several animals are known to eat it, particularly deer.

Many people believe lichens kill trees, but nothing could be further from the truth. Although it does grow on dead portions of trees, that is so it can maximize exposure to the sun (no leaves to block the light). In fact, lace lichen helps fertilize the tree it is growing on. Acting like a huge dry net, it captures airborne nutrients throughout the dry season; when the first rains arrive the lichen's dusting of nutrients is turned into a gooey dark liquid that trickles down the tree trunk and is absorbed by the root system.

Hastings Natural History Reservation in Carmel Valley is conducting considerable research on lace lichen. To find out more about this fascinating organism, and about other interesting coastal research topics, contact their website: http://nrs.ucop.edu/reserves/hastings/hastings. html.

Pampas Grass

Pampas grass (*Cortaderia jubata*) is scattered like so many silky-haired sentries across the grasslands of Whitehouse Creek, mostly on the northern, private side of the road. Even though pampas grass is handsome and readily catches the eye, State Parks has taken considerable pains to remove this exotic species from public lands. Why is that? Wasn't it just last year your neighbors crowed about the beautiful stand of pampas grass they'd planted in their front yard?

Pampas grass, native to South America, is used widely as an ornamental in land-scaping. There are two species: one is sterile, the other is fecund and very aggressive. The fertile species is the one growing here. Not only can it grow just about anywhere (except under redwoods), but it also out-competes most native plant species and it can invade and take over sand dune systems. It is extremely hard to eradicate, so don't help it out by innocently picking some plumes and waving them around—you might be spreading thousands of seeds.

Pampas grass is an exotic grass species found along the shoreline.

There are many ranches and farms fronting Highway 1 and smaller shoreline roads through the entire Monterey Bay region. Owners often welcome visitors for purchases of fresh produce and U-pick-'em crops. If so, the fact will be well posted out on the road or by the front gate. If you spot such a sign, feel free to drop into these ranches and farms to buy some produce and learn how these operations are run.

Whatever you do, don't wander onto private property. Otherwise friendly people may not be very understanding if they discover you standing in the middle of their herd or crop!

INFORMATION

Año Nuevo State Reserve:
650-879-2025

Recorded information:
650-879-0227 (24 hours)

Walk reservations:
800-444-4445

Website:
http://www.anonuevo.org

Shellfish Information
Hot Line: 800-553-4133

California State Parks, Bay
Area District: 415-330-6300

Loggerhead Shrike

One of the first birds to greet you moving up Whitehouse Creek Road, as well as elsewhere in the reserve, might be a loggerhead shrike (*Lanius ludovicianus*) standing guard atop a willow tree. The loggerhead shrike is a medium-sized bird looking somewhat like a mockingbird in both its coloration and size. Whereas the mockingbird is leggy and tall, though, the shrike looks like a solid bantam boxer with a roundish head and a heavy curved bill. Its gray and white body is highlighted by a distinctive black face mask—the avian equivalent of a raccoon.

Although there are several subspecies throughout the state, all shrikes like to perch on a favorite tree or bush in open country where they can keep an eye on things. It has a rather harsh call—brief, deliberate notes that are issued like a reprimand: "bzee, bzee." Its song—a longer, more complex composition—is easier on the ear, beginning with a soft "queedle-queedle" sound. Shrikes feed mostly on large insects, though small mammals and birds are occasionally eaten. It has been called the butcher bird because of its habit of impaling excess food on thorns or barbed wire for storage. In fact, its scientific name means the butcher from Louisiana!

Wild Pigs

Keep a lookout for scrambling packs of wild pigs as you explore the roads and trails of Año Nuevo and the Santa Cruz Mountains. Today's wild pigs (not to be confused with javelinas or peccaries) are either descendants of domesticated pigs gone feral—that is, reverted to a wild state by growing long hair, impressive tusks, and an ornery disposition—or the descendants of introduced European wild boars. Both are favorites of sport hunters, who enjoy a year-round open hunting season on these porkers.

If you don't see any live pigs (the odds are best in the morning and early evening), you will definitely be able to see where they have been. Large patches of grassland, marshy areas, and streambanks may look as though someone has been busy with a rototiller! The pigs' joyful rooting and wallowing around these environments can destroy native vegetation and habitat for other species. Wild pigs are also keen predators of ground-nesting birds and other small critters.

Wild pigs are a scourge around the world. Here in California they are found throughout most of the coastal regions from San Luis Obispo north, on some of the Channel Islands, and throughout the Sierra foothills.

Points North

Here is a sampler of interesting sites north of Año Nuevo State Reserve.

■ Gazos Creek Coastal Access

A large sign and parking area (with bathrooms) mark the Gazos Creek Coastal Access, across Highway 1 from Gazos Creek Road. A wheelchair-accessible path leads to the beach, a favorite spot for fishing. From the beach here you can hike south to enter the reserve by Franklin Point.

■ Campbell's Pacific Mushroom Farm

This mushroom farm has been in operation just north of Gazos Creek since 1957. It includes 96 growing houses and processing facilities. No public tours for individuals are offered.

■ Pigeon Point Historic Lighthouse

Situated on a beautiful coastal plain, this lighthouse—at 110 feet, one of the tallest in the United States—was built in 1872 and outfitted with a Fresnel lens manufactured in France. The area is open daily from dawn to dusk. Lighthouse tours are on weekends only. There is also a youth hostel here. For information, call 650-879-0633.

■ Butano State Park

This 3,200-acre park is a real gem, situated between the town of Pescadero and Gazos Creek Road, just inland from the coast. There may not be ocean vistas here, but you'll find plenty of redwoods, creeks, and trails. Both overnight camping facilities (fee) and day-use picnic areas can be found here. For information, call 650-879-2040.

SHORELINE PUBLIC TRANSPORTATION

Because the San Mateo–Santa Cruz county line is just south of Año Nuevo, two public transportation systems serve Waddell Beach. Monday through Friday, twice daily, a San Mateo Transit (SamTrans) bus leaves Half Moon Bay and works its way south to Waddell Beach, where it stops, waits, then turns back north. And every day of the week, also twice a day, a number 40 Santa Cruz Metro bus travels north to Waddell Beach, stops, waits, then turns back south. All coastal Metro buses have racks able to carry two bikes. SamTrans buses accommodate bikes only if the bus is less than 50 percent full. For information, contact Sam-Trans at 1-800-660-4287, or look for them on the web at http://www. samtrans.com. Metro can be reached at 831-425-8600 or http://www. scmtd.com—the website has detailed route information, as well as excellent links to much of the region's transportation network.

Next time you are strolling down one of the region's beaches and you come across a person fishing in the surf, ask what types of fish are biting. You will get an amazing array of common fish names thrown at you—and often in various languages—but most likely their buckets will be full of shiner perch *(Cymatogaster aggregata)*.

Some 17 species of perch thrive in the marine sanctuary, and although none are of commercial value, several are popular with surf fishermen. The shiner—named for its shimmering silver scales—can be found up and down the entire Pacific coast and has one of the largest ranges of all the perches. You might want to ask the person fishing how to prepare perch. You'll get an informal cooking lesson that typically involves some combination of butter, olive oil, and garlic. When they don't end up on the dinner plate, shiners are sometimes used as bait to attract larger fish, such as striped bass.

Perch species are favorites of people fishing from the shoreline.

Just South

Just south of the reserve's main entrance is a CalTrans pullout on the shore side of the highway, popular with surfers and people wanting to visit Cove Beach. Look for the big sign "Park Entrance .5 Miles," with an arrow pointing north. Surprisingly, the paved trail here—which leads to the reserve's trail system—is an abandoned section of Highway 1. You soon cross a 1940s-era cement bridge some 50 feet above Año Nuevo Creek, in the upper reaches of a canopy of bays and willows. A five-minute walk from your car will bring you not only to the reserve's trails, but also to a side trail down to Cove Beach and the creek's mouth. Everything south of Cove Beach is private property. Where the trail drops down toward the creek, stop and look at the bankcut. Check for the distinct layering of stream pebbles. This deposit indicates a former position and size of the creek. From the beach you have a nice view of Año Nuevo Island and bluffs both north and south.

Warning: You are in elephant seal territory here. Keep at least 20 feet away from these animals at all times.

Waddell Beach

Waddell Beach is the shoreline gateway to a region full of natural wonders, history, and recreational opportunities. It is a popular spot for windsurfers, hang gliders, and surfers.

The beach and parking area here form the westernmost portion of the 18,000-acre Big Basin Redwoods State Park. Gulls, waterfowl, and shorebirds such as marbled godwits, willets, and sanderlings overwinter here, often congregating in large flocks around the mouth of Waddell Creek. Elephant seals can be seen swimming offshore here, and occasionally they haul out to snooze on the beach. (Be sure to keep at least 20 feet away.) The beach is also the end—or beginning—of the scenic Skyline to the Sea Trail, which meanders from Castle Rock State Park through Big Basin to the coast.

Waddell Creek Marsh, an extensive wetland on the inland side of Highway 1, is in the 20-acre Theodore J. Hoover Natural Preserve. It is important habitat for many water birds. Salmon and steelhead trout can also be seen in Waddell Creek seasonally.

Waddell Bluffs

The massive bare cliffs framing the beach at its northern end are called the Waddell Bluffs. The exposed face has been slowly shedding material—in this case, Santa Cruz mudstone—into the ocean for eons. Pulverized by waves and carried south by the prevailing nearshore currents, the eroded bluffs have helped to create the region's beaches. When Highway 1 was constructed at the base of the bluffs in the 1940s, however, the bluffs lost their access to the sea. Because of this predicament, CalTrans gives some 10,000 to 20,000 cubic yards of talus a ride every year—from the bluff side of Highway 1 to the shore side. It is moved between October and December so strong winter wave action can break up the talus and take it on its way south.

"What makes a place special is the way it buries itself inside the heart, not whether it's flat or rugged, rich or austere, wet or arid, gentle or harsh, warm or cold, wild or tame. Every place, like every person, is elevated by the love and respect shown toward it, and by the way in which its bounty is received."

Richard Nelson, The Island Within (1989)

Looking north from Waddell Beach toward the Waddell Bluffs

JERRY EMORY

The Rancho del Oso Nature and History Center is situated on the southern side of Waddell Valley. In this biologically diverse area, a short walk can carry you through redwood groves, Monterey pine and hardwood forests, and open meadows, past streams, a marsh, a sandy beach, and rocky tidepools.

The center features exhibits of native plants and animals, history, and nature-oriented art work in a homey setting. It also has a small bookstore, restrooms, and a courtyard picnic area. A self-guided nature trail behind the center focuses on the ecological features of the Monterey pine forest (for more on this statuesque tree, see pp. 230–231). Call ahead (831-427-2288) to find out about guided nature hikes. The center, operated jointly by California State Parks and the nonprofit Waddell Creek Association, also has special programs on subjects ranging from wildlife, botany, and geology to Ohlone Indian lore, and it produces a quarterly newsletter.

BIG BASIN REDWOODS STATE PARK

Big Basin, established in 1902, is California's oldest state park. It is also home to the largest stand of ancient coast redwoods south of San Francisco. The park takes in 18,000 acres, and most of it is covered in redwoods (both old growth and younger) growing alongside a beautiful mix of conifers, oaks, chaparral, and streamside vegetation. Big Basin is also unique in having a large variety of facilities: family and group camp sites, tent cabins, backpack camps, and horse camps, as well as trails for equestrians, hikers, and mountain bikers. The main entrance to the park, and access to the large ancient redwoods, is on Highway 236, nine miles northwest of Boulder Creek.

Skyline to the Sea Trail

From Waddell Beach you can start at sea level and climb to over 2,000 feet within Big Basin on the Skyline to the Sea Trail (or in this case, the Sea to Skyline Trail). About a third of a mile up the paved road from the parking area just off Highway 1 is the Rancho del Oso Ranger Station and visitor center (on the north side of the creek; foot access only). From here you can cross the Marsh Trail and walk 250 yards to the Nature and History Center, on the other side of Waddell Creek. Beyond the ranger station is a parking area (for horse trailers and backpackers only), an outhouse, ranger residence, and horse camp. The trail crosses the parking area and moves up the canyon and into the heart of Big Basin.

Hikers can go all the way to Big Basin Headquarters from here, some ten and a half miles. Bikers are asked to turn around five miles up the canyon. All trails are well marked and clearly signed. Whether on foot or bike, you might be surprised to come across several private residences and agricultural fields about a mile up canyon. Don't fret; you are still in parkland. These folks are the descendants of Theodore Hoover, the person who made this part of the park possible by working with the state to preserve these lands.

The trail hugs Waddell Creek for the first couple of miles (the creek—which in wet years is more like a river

—eventually branches). The bottomlands here are very lush, vegetated with stately redwoods, pines, bays, and a mix of other tree species. At about the three-mile mark a footbridge allows hikers to negotiate the creek. When waters are high, horses and bikers are invited to use it also. It is a handsome arching metal bridge with a wooden plank path. Once you've crossed the bridge, wander into the woods; in the shadows you'll find enormous redwood stumps scattered about—quiet reminders of a once ancient forest and years of human activity.

After four miles the trail begins to climb a bit, but not too steeply, and you pull away from the rush of the creek and move through quieter woods. When you cross another metal bridge spanning a side creek of Waddell, stop to look down at the rushing water below. You are now just shy of the five-mile mark, and the turnaround for bikes. Hikers and equestrians can continue to climb into the heart of the park.

Remember that mountain lions live in this park and are seen from time to time (see page 275). Use simple safety tips when hiking here.

Coast Redwood

California's coast redwood (*Sequoia sempervirens*), which is confined to the narrow coastal-fog belt from the Big Sur area to southern Oregon, has played, and still plays, a vitally important role in the history, economy, and ecology of the central California coast. Redwoods are the tallest plant species, with some individuals reaching over 360 feet. They are also one of the oldest living things on earth: in 1933, a tree was felled that was 2,200 years old. Most redwoods, however, live around 600 years.

Continuous logging of redwoods for the past 150 years has severely reduced their numbers. Redwood lumber was prized for its strong straight grain; it is also relatively

The coast redwood is one of the oldest living species.

This chunky little sea bird is a relative of auks, murres, and puffins. Unlike its cousins, however, the marbled murrelet *(Brachyramphus marmoratus)* nests inland. In the spring, adult murrelets rise from coastal waters and fly onshore up to 30 miles to nest in old-growth trees. Only one egg is laid, typically on a moss-covered branch of a redwood or Douglas fir. After the egg hatches, the parents take turns commuting to the coast to gather fish for the youngster, which is ready to zoom to the coast itself in just four weeks to start its ocean-going life.

Murrelets nest in Big Basin Redwoods State Park and are believed to nest in other old-growth forests nearby as well. Because of logging, other habitat disruptions such as oil spills, and fishing net fatalities, murrelet populations have plummeted this century, and the bird is presently on the state endangered species list.

"We directed our course to the north-northwest, without withdrawing far from the coast, from which we were separated by some high hills very thickly covered with trees that some said were savins. They were the largest, highest, and straightest trees that we had seen up to that time; some of them were four or five yards in diameter. The wood is of a dull, dark, reddish color, very soft, brittle, and full of knots."

Miguel Costansó, with the Portolá expedition, near Monterey Bay, with first known description of a redwood tree (1769)

easy to work with, and because the wood is packed with tannins it naturally resists rot and termites. Redwood was used for everything from railroad ties to housing material and even fuel for homes and industry. Prior to the tree's exploitation by European settlers, redwood logs had been used by coastal Indians for canoes, redwood planks for housing, and the tree's fibrous roots made excellent baskets.

Plants well adapted to deep shade, such as rhododendrons, redwood sorrel, huckleberry, hazel, poison oak, and numerous flowering herb and fern species, can be found at the base of these trees. Redwoods also grow in mixed evergreen forests with Douglas fir and, in drier areas, with bays, tan oaks, and madrones. Because the soil beneath redwood forests tends to be poor owing to leaching by frequent heavy rains and occasional floods, the trees compensate by recycling the nutrients available in fallen plant material, animal waste, and other forest litter. To maximize this recycling, redwoods have developed a shallow yet broad root system that can extend some 100 feet from a tree's trunk.

Portolá Expedition of 1769

The Spaniard Sebastián Vizcaíno sailed along the California coast in 1603 and glowingly described the amazing harbor of Monterey. For the subsequent 150 years, however, interest in Alta California was less than enthusiastic as the Spanish focused their attention on other parts of the globe, including Baja California, where 13 Jesuit missions were built.

In 1767, however, the Jesuits were replaced by Franciscan missionaries, and interest in the northern territories was soon rekindled. In that year, two expeditions set out for Alta California from Baja California, one by ship and one by foot. Their goal: the legendary Monterey Bay.

WADDELL

We will never know what the Ohlone called today's Waddell Valley, but we do know several other names that have been pinned on this steep-sided entrance into the coastal mountains.

The Portolá expedition of 1769 called it Cañada de la Salud—Canyon of Health—because many of the men "miraculously" regained strength after stopping here for several days (perhaps thanks to food supplied by local Indians). During the mission era (1793–1834), grizzly bears were captured here for use in bull and bear fights; to these people, then, the region was known as Cañada de los Osos—Canyon of the Bears. Even rock-wary sailors, who stayed well off the coast if possible, had a name for this pronounced valley, which could be seen far out at sea: Arroyo Grande, or Big Gulch.

William Waddell, the pioneer lumberman whose name graces the valley today, built a mill, tramway, skid roads, and wharf here in the 1860s. He actively logged the valley's redwoods until 1875, when he was killed by a grizzly bear. In 1913 Theodore J. Hoover, a mining engineer, dean of the Stanford University School of Engineering, and brother of President Herbert Hoover, purchased 3,000 acres here. An early naturalist and conservationist, he considered his ownership of the land to be essentially a protective stewardship. The Hoovers named the property Rancho del Oso.

In 1975, California State Parks, looking for a corridor from Big Basin to the sea, acquired a major portion of the ranch from Hoover's daughters, Mildred Hoover Willis and Hulda Hoover McLean.

After meeting in San Diego, the two parties reshuffled their men and resources and set forth. By the time the group of 64 men left San Diego on July 14, 1769, it consisted of several individuals who would help shape the future of the region for decades to come and change the lives of native Californians forever: Capt. Gaspar de Portolá, Father Junípero Serra, Capt. Fernando Rivera y Moncada, Lt. Pedro Fages, Father Juan Crespí, engineer and cartographer Miguel Costansó, and Dr. Pedro Prat.

On October 20–23, 1769, Portolá and his men— believing they hadn't yet found Monterey Bay—camped at the mouth of Waddell Creek for three days to rest and treat the ill. They rapidly recovered, causing Father Crespí thankfully to name the valley Cañada de la Salud— Canyon of Health.

California quail, the state bird

California Quail

The California quail (*Callipepla californica*) is one of the best-known birds of the coast and inland regions of the state. And rightly so: it is the official state bird, after all. Its distinctive call of "ca-CA-ca" or "Chi-CA-go" is often heard in early morning or late afternoon throughout the coastal canyons and chaparral-covered hillsides. Coveys of quail may reach 100 birds, and they can make quite a spectacle as they dash across trails or take to the air for an intense and noisy short flight to safety.

The grizzly bear *(Ursus horribilis)* was once extremely common throughout most of California—just one good reason it adorns the state flag. Grizzlies were particularly abundant along the state's fertile coastal plains. Early accounts report them hunting and scavenging along beaches and throughout the dense chaparral.

Because of their size, power, speed, and temper (if surprised or defending cubs), grizzlies were a serious threat to Indians and early settlers. In 1875, for example, William Waddell was killed by a grizzly in the valley that now carries his name. These massive animals were hunted relentlessly by the Spanish and the early American settlers. It is believed that the last grizzly in the Santa Cruz Mountains was killed in 1886, although rumors of sightings continued for decades.

The grizzly's cousin, the black bear *(Ursus americanus),* has not been seen in Big Basin or the Santa Cruz Mountains for years. Southward, however, in the rough coastal mountains of Monterey County, black bears, though rare, are present.

Although both adults sport handsome plumes on top of their heads, the male is the real dandy of this nervous-looking species. With his deep reddish-brown cap, jet black bib, and chestnut sides, he makes for an especially pretty picture as he struts around the covey or stands guard over his brood while they peck for seeds or wallow in a dust bath.

Periwinkle

When exploring the shoreline and nearby hills, no matter how far away from civilization you think you are, you can almost always find a healthy stand of nonnative periwinkle *(Vinca major).* This European exotic with its purplish blue flowers—also known simply as vinca—was originally intended for the wild borders of cultivated gardens. It is successful virtually anywhere because its rooting stems spread rapidly in sun or shade, it thrives in all types of soils, and practically nothing bothers it. Periwinkle is very much at home along the Skyline to the Sea Trail, where it forms enormous mats that preclude native shrubs and flowers from growing. Though beautiful, it is also toxic to many animals. Enjoy it, but don't encourage it!

Big Creek Lumber Company

The Big Creek Lumber Company, overlooking Waddell Creek, has been a familiar sight for generations of visitors to the area. The company's longevity and prosperity are based on sound stewardship of Big Creek timberlands and the fact that the family has lived on the same land for more than 130 years.

Founded by Frank McCrary Sr., his sons Frank Jr. and Homer McCrary, and their brother-in-law Homer Trumbo, the Big Creek Lumber Company got going after World War II when the small crew, polishing up their cross-cut saws and axes, began working Mill and Scott Creeks. In 1947 they struck a deal with Theodore Hoover to buy the right to cut standing trees in most of Waddell Creek Canyon. With some surplus war machinery, ingenuity, and plenty of elbow grease, the new company kept busy for many years cutting mostly redwoods but also some Douglas firs and Monterey pines.

Big Creek now owns thousands of acres throughout the central coast. Instead of cross-cut saws, today the company, 200 employees strong, uses state-of-the-art machinery and sound harvest and replanting practices.

They are proud to say that not only are three generations of McCrarys involved in the business, but the lands they own are also a certified Well-Managed Forest according to the Scientific Certification System's Forest Conservation Program. According to the McCrarys, their land will be producing excellent timber for generations to come while also supporting a wide variety of wildlife and native vegetation.

The Bluffs: Greyhound Rock to Red, White, and Blue Beach

Between the Waddell Beach region and Wilder Ranch State Park—a distance of about 12 miles as the gull flies—the coastline is best described as high and windswept. Although some private land does remain along this section of coast (most of it dedicated to agriculture), the majority is publicly owned. (The process of acquisition is ongoing. In fact, the region just south of Scott Creek to the south side of Laguna Creek—a spectacular seven and a half miles of coastal property formerly known as Coast Dairies—was purchased for preservation as recently as late 1997.) Along the way are a series of pocket beaches and public access points, a couple of side trips, and a spectacular historic town.

Coastal bluffs typical of the northern Monterey Bay shoreline

Rancho del Oso Nature
and History Center:
831-427-2288

Rancho del Oso Ranger
Station and Visitor Center:
831-425-1218

Big Basin Headquarters:
831-338-8861

SamTrans: 1-800-660-4287
Website:
http://www.samtrans.com

Santa Cruz Metropolitan
Transit District:
831-425-8600
Website:
http://www.scmtd.com

Ride Sharing on the Coast:
831-429-POOL

Swanton Road

Swanton Road, which winds inland from Highway 1 for just over six miles, is a perfect side trip away from the shoreline. Along its route you pass a mixture of historic homes and newer dwellings, agricultural lands, and a Forest Service fire station. You also cross over no less than six tributaries of Scott Creek. Although the northern entrance to Swanton Road, just south of Big Creek Lumber, is a bit steep as it works its way through a Monterey pine forest, otherwise the road is perfect for a bike trip. Its southern junction with Highway 1 is north of Davenport.

Leeks

Casual observers may mistake a crop of leeks (*Allium ampeloprasum*) along Swanton Road, and elsewhere along the shore of Monterey Bay, for a field of garlic. The mistake is an easy one to make, at least from the ground up. But when harvest time arrives during the winter months, the confusion vanishes. Instead of a bulb plucked from the ground, the leek has an edible six- to ten-inch-long round stem up to two inches in diameter. Leeks also have wider, flatter leaves than garlic. This mild-flavored member of the onion family has been cultivated for centuries in various parts of the world. Leeks can be eaten raw or cooked and are favorites in soups, stews, and stir-fry dishes.

Greyhound Rock

Greyhound Rock is no secret to shoreline aficionados, but for first-time visitors it's easy to pass—and even easier to dismiss—as nothing but a large parking lot just south of Big Creek Lumber. Take the time to slow down, turn off, and prepare yourself for the steepest paved walkway on the coast.

Although there is a full complement of blufftop picnic tables, to really see this place, find the path by the restrooms and descend. The paved path drops down to a dramatic stretch of coast. Of course there is Greyhound Rock, a favorite of rock scramblers (at low tide), and the beach here is a great site from which to cast for rockfish and lingcod (to name just two species you might catch here). Several other isolated rocks are just beyond the waves as well.

Looking north from
Greyhound Rock

If you catch this spot at a low or medium tide, you will
be able to explore on sandy beaches southward well over
a mile, and to the north all the way to Waddell Beach.
The cliffs looming over you reach straight up at least 100
feet, so be careful not to dally too long near their base
(falling debris is serious business).

Like many public-access sites along the coast, this spot
was developed cooperatively—in this case, by Santa Cruz
County, the California Department of Fish and Game,
and the Wildlife Conservation Board.

Cattle Country

This stretch of coast may not seem like typical cattle
country, but look closer at the hills and small canyons
inland from Highway 1. You will see not only some
bovine faces gazing back at you, but also numerous loading corrals both old and new telling a story rich in cattle
lore. Much of this land has been grazed on and off for
over 200 years. Cattle were introduced here after Mission
Santa Cruz was established in 1791. Grazing has continued ever since—throughout the rancho period of the
early and mid 19th century, through early statehood, and
right up to the present day.

Scott Creek, with wild mustard in
the foreground

Scott Creek Beach

Scott Creek Beach and Creek were named for Hiram
Scott, a successful 19th-century prospector who had the
good sense to abandon the itch for gold and settle here.
There is no skirting the fact that parking for Scott Creek
Beach is dangerous, since you have to park on the shoulders of Highway 1. Be careful as you slow down and park,
and be careful again while crossing the highway.

Once you are on the beach, you will see the massive
cliffs framing Scott Creek, and several miles of shoreline
are accessible at low tide. The marine terraces to the
north are especially good sites for tidepooling—look for
sea anemones, chitons, sea urchins, surfgrass, and kelp—
and the large freshwater marsh inland of Highway 1 is
important for overwintering birds. Even at high tide,
large stretches of shoreline are open to exploration,
casual strolls, or sunbathing.

To the south, sand prevails. Crossing the creek may
look easy enough, but use good judgment. This creek
(like Waddell to the north) moves like a small, swift river
much of the year—just one of the reasons salmon and
steelhead are found here.

Waddell Beach, the Skyline to the Sea Trail, the Rancho del Oso Ranger Station, and the Rancho del Oso Nature and History Center are all situated around the mouth of Waddell Creek, approximately 29 miles south of Half Moon Bay, or 2.5 miles south of the main entrance to Año Nuevo. From the south, the creek is about 16 miles north of Santa Cruz city limits. The parking lot, trail, and ranger station are on the north side of the creek, the Nature and History Center and its trail system are on the south (look for the small sign on the southern, inland, side of the bridge over the creek). The main entrance to Big Basin Redwoods State Park is off of Highway 236, north of Boulder Creek.

Snowy Plover

Many beaches along the bay's shoreline are home to the snowy plover (*Charadrius alexandrinus nivosus*), a diminutive shorebird that can blend in perfectly with drifts of sand thanks to its cryptic, or well-camouflaged, coloring. From March to September snowy plovers build their nests and raise their young along dry stretches of beach.

Tragically, this bird faces extinction. A majority of plover breeding sites have been destroyed in recent years owing to a variety of human activities, including development, trampling by walkers, joggers, running pets, horses, and off-road vehicles, and beach raking by large vehicles. The invasion of exotic plant species, such as European dune grass, also harms plover nesting sites.

The snowy plover, an endangered species, nests on sandy beaches.

Here at Scott Creek Beach—and elsewhere around the shoreline—you may see fenced exclosures on the beach helping to protect the birds' fragile eggs, a joint effort of Santa Cruz County and the State Coastal Conservancy. Similar efforts are under way in Monterey County. Please stay away from these exclosures. Disturbances by people and dogs are the leading causes for nest failures.

Coast Dairies Property

In late 1997 an enormous swath of coastal lands between Scott Creek and Laguna Creek was purchased by the San Francisco–based Save the Redwoods League. The property, formerly the land of Coast Dairies, takes in some 7,500 acres along seven and a half miles of shoreline, with the city of Davenport nestled right in the middle of it all.

STEELHEAD AND SALMON

Steelhead *(Salmo gaird-neri)*, coho salmon *(Oncorhynchus kisutch)*, and chinook or king salmon *(O. tshawytscha)* once crowded California's estuaries, streams, and rivers. Not so anymore. Generations of human tinkering have polluted some spawning areas, while upstream dams and water diversions have affected others. Development has also diminished the extent of coastal marshes and lagoons, which serve as nurseries for ocean-bound fish. Today, despite the efforts of fish hatcheries and conservation programs, the populations of these fish continue to decline.

Coho, chinook, and steelhead (actually oceangoing rainbow trout) are anadromous —that is, they are capable of moving from fresh to salt water and back again by means of a complicated physiological process. In the case of salmon, this movement is a necessary aspect of their life

Many populations of steelhead trout, which spawn in coastal streams, are now endangered.

cycle. Some rainbows, however, never venture out to sea—though all steelhead eventually return to freshwater to spawn.

Steelhead range from the Kamchatka Peninsula in the North Pacific down the coast of North America to Malibu Creek in southern California. Although they have an amazing array of life histories because they live in a wide range of habitats, most steelheads migrate to the sea when they are about two years old, then return after another two years at sea to spawn and die.

Several populations of Pacific coast steelhead (from specific watersheds) have been officially designated endangered by the federal government. The population along California's central coast is considered threatened, which means it is likely to move onto the endangered list in the near future.

Coho salmon can be found in the North Pacific Ocean from Baja California to Alaska, the Aleutian Islands, and down into Japanese waters. Along this vast stretch of shoreline Coho salmon hatch upstream between January and May, depending on conditions. The young can spend up to a year in their stream before venturing downstream in late winter or early spring. After reaching the Pacific, they hug the nearby shoreline before ranging up and down the coast for hundreds of miles. Cohos appear dark metallic blue or blue-green along their backs and silvery on their sides and belly.

After a couple of years in the Pacific, they reenter their stream of birth, spawn (producing up to 3,500 eggs), then die.

Chinook salmon are found from northern Alaska to central California and from the Bering Sea to northern Japan. Even though cohos can weigh just over 30 pounds, if you snag a salmon that size it will more than likely be a chinook. The principal distinguishing feature between coho and chinook is the color of their gums! Chinooks have blackish gums, while cohos have white. Also, chinooks have far more black spots on their tail fins.

Although chinook salmon once spawned in local streams and rivers, today they are confined to the Sacramento–San Joaquin River system. Nonetheless, they are found off the coast here as they travel the shoreline for up to four years before returning inland to spawn. The Sacramento–San Joaquin is the only river system in the world that supports four separate races, or runs, of chinook: fall, late-fall, winter, and spring runs. The total population, however, has declined more than 97 percent over a period of less than 20 years despite numerous conservation measures. In 1993, only 341 fish returned from the winter-run population. That race is now an endangered species. Today, attempts are being made to restore key spawning areas and ensure adequate water levels and temperatures in salmon rivers and streams throughout interior California.

After the Hearst Corporation's San Simeon, the Coast Dairies property is the largest single parcel of oceanfront property between San Francisco and the Mexican border. Although it was once slated for development, today the land will be managed to help restore native grasslands, improve salmon habitat, and protect threatened and endangered species.

A project of this scope could not be accomplished without considerable cooperative effort, as is true of many of the protected areas of this shoreline. In order to secure the deal, the Save the Redwoods League had help from the Trust for Public Land, Peninsula Open Space Trust, Santa Cruz Land Trust, and the Nature Conservancy. Funding came from several anonymous donors, the David and Lucile Packard Foundation, the State Coastal Conservancy, and other state and county agencies.

Issues of protection and public access are still being decided for the property, but areas presently in livestock grazing or agriculture will continue to be leased for those uses into the foreseeable future.

Davenport Landing

Davenport Landing was founded in the late 1860s by Captain John P. Davenport and his wife, Ellen, at the mouth of the Agua Puerca Creek, just south of El Jarro Point. This small cove was used primarily for loading local products such as lumber, dairy goods, grain, and lime onto ships. Some whaling also took place from the landing.

The Davenports built a 450-foot wharf here, and the town sported two hotels, a post office, shops, a small shipyard, and a scattering of homes. By the late 19th century, however, the wharf was in disrepair and commerce had waned. In 1915 fire (one of several) destroyed most of Davenport Landing, which by then was a poor cousin to the new town of Davenport up on the bluff.

More recently, Davenport Landing has received a facelift—or at least its beach access area has. Parking is ample, and a creekside walkway leads visitors down to a mile-long beach. At low tide, you can squeak around both ends of this beach and venture farther north and south (but keep an eye on the tide!).

Davenport

Most travelers on Highway 1 are in too much of a hurry to stop at Davenport. But make the time: you'll be glad you did. Not only is this town filled with history, but it is also a convenient place to stretch your legs, have a bite to

WILDLIFE CONSERVATION BOARD

Who and what is the Wildlife Conservation Board (WCB)? Good question. In short, it is a separately funded branch of the California Department of Fish and Game. It consists of some 15 members: the director of Fish and Game, the president of the Fish and Game Commission, the director of the Department of Finance, and a bipartisan Legislative Advisory Committee. The board has been working on wildlife conservation and public recreation projects in all of the state's 58 counties since 1947.

In its early days the WCB focused on stream restoration projects and the construction of fish hatcheries, boat ramps, and fishing piers, including almost 50 coastal piers. More recently, the board has become active in the preservation of habitat for fish and wildlife species; it already has succeeded in setting aside over 300,000 acres of prime habitat.

I f a beach or wildlife area is signed for no dogs, or dogs on leash only, it is for a good reason. Every time your dog runs wild down the beach and scares a flock of shorebirds into flight, it is disturbing their feeding and resting activities. Dogs can also trample a variety of shoreline nests and attack wildlife. On some popular stretches of beach this happens countless time a day. Be especially careful near wildlife reserves and snowy plover beaches. What seems like a joyful romp by your pooch can be very harmful to the plants and animals that live there.

Around Monterey Bay several locations are designated as off-leash zones for dogs: Lighthouse Field State Beach in Santa Cruz (specific hours), Carmel City Beach, and Garland Ranch Regional Park (Carmel Valley). Although no leash is required, be sure your animal can be controlled by voice if necessary.

eat, or do a little shopping. In addition, it's a great place for a bit of shoreline exploration, and it looks out over a sizable portion of the National Marine Sanctuary. And as if those weren't sufficient reasons to stop, the people of Davenport are downright friendly.

The town of Davenport was—and still is, after a fashion —a company town. When the Santa Cruz Portland Cement Company began operations here in 1906, the town quickly followed. The site flourished, in part, thanks to the San Francisco earthquake and fire: cement from the plant helped rebuild the city.

Today the plant is owned by RMC Lonestar and still produces cement. The town, however, has changed considerably. Several fires over the years destroyed much of historic Davenport, but a few old buildings still stand, such as Forresters Hall, the jail (now a museum), and the Church of Saint Vincent de Paul. A stroll through the back streets of town reveals several blocks of nicely kept houses with well-tended coastal gardens.

To the north of the cement plant is another section of town, referred to by some as New Town. When the cement plant moved into full and constant production, locals soon realized the prevailing winds were carrying the plant's dust right over town. Some sixteen cottages were therefore built upwind, in New Town. Since then, several more streets have been added, and more modern houses constructed.

There are about a dozen businesses in Davenport today. You can stop here to take care of an appetite, stock up for the road, or buy unique arts and crafts and other handmade items. Or you can simply park and look for whales. For a "virtual tour," visit the town's website at http://www.swanton.com.

Davenport Beach

To the immediate south of the commercial building on the bluff side of Highway 1, a well-worn footpath crosses the railroad tracks, leading to a nice beach. If you can't find it, ask anybody in town for directions. The crescent-shaped beach is just under half of a mile long and ringed by massive cliffs. At its southern end waves slam into the angled marine terraces during rough and even moderate seas, then bounce back out to sea, creating spectacular confrontations with incoming swells. Keep an eye open for signs of this area's history: metal rings driven into the marine terraces, old cables disappearing into the surf, bleached lumber stacked in a cove.

Rather than walking down to the beach, you can work

Davenport's coastal bluffs, looking north, with the RMC Lonestar facility on the right

your way through the wild mustard, dill, and blackberries out to the bluff overlooking the beach's southern end. If you turn north you'll see an old pier jutting out into the water. This is the skeletal remains of a steel pier built in 1934 by Santa Cruz Portland Cement. Today it is a favorite nesting and roosting area for cormorants.

Beyond the pier the northward vista is composed of an impressive line of bluffs. Marine terraces buttress the cliff faces from below, like a grand construction project in progress—or decay. Please use caution atop these cliffs. You can take in all the sights there are to see while staying well back from the edge.

Davenport Cement Plant

While exploring the Monterey Bay shoreline you will come across two coastside industrial sites that are visible for miles. One is the Moss Landing power plant, at the mouth of Elkhorn Slough (see page 151). The other impressive structure is the Davenport cement plant, next to the hamlet of Davenport. When the earthquake and fire of April 18, 1906, hit San Francisco, the Santa Cruz Portland Cement plant had been under construction for only six months. Two more years of planned construction was completed in less than one so the plant could begin producing cement and help rebuild San Francisco.

In fact, the product from this plant has a distinct historical link to many of the great construction projects of

STATE COASTAL CONSERVANCY

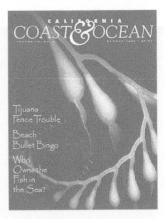

The California State Coastal Conservancy is an Oakland-based state agency working to preserve, improve, and restore public access and natural resources along California's coast and on San Francisco Bay. The conservancy undertakes various projects in partnership with nonprofit organizations, landowners, local governments, and other public agencies. It also publishes *California Coast & Ocean,* an informative magazine exploring coastal issues up and down the state. To find out more about the Coastal Conservancy or subscribe to *Coast & Ocean,* call 510-286-1015, or visit their website at http://www.coastalconservancy.ca.gov.

this century, not only at home but around the world. Cement from this facility helped build the Panama Canal, Pearl Harbor, the San Francisco–Oakland Bay Bridge, the Golden Gate Bridge, various defense structures during World War II, and the Bay Area Rapid Transit system, to name but a few.

Today, the facility is owned and operated by RMC Lonestar. Gone are the quarry picks, numerous kilns, and belching smokestacks of the plant's early years. Instead, cement is now produced by people adept with computers and high-tech machinery. Except for quarrying and shipping, the production process operates around the clock and is completely automated.

JERRY EMORY

Historic Davenport Jail

Davenport Jail

The Davenport Jail was built in 1914 out of . . . you got it: portland cement! Apparently the jail didn't see much action in this peace-loving town. When a new jail opened in Santa Cruz in 1936, this concrete block of a building stop being used altogether. Today it has been refurbished and serves as a quaint museum packed with information about Davenport and nearby coastal areas.

Lime

The quarrying of lime to make plaster, mortar, and cement was one of the most important industries in this region. Companies located here supplied most of the lime used in California during the 1850s and 1860s (before it was discovered here, lime was shipped from the East Coast via

Cape Horn). Limestone to make the lime was abundant and of high quality. In addition, the large stands of redwood provided a ready source of fuel for the lime kilns, where the limestone was baked at high temperatures for several days prior to being crushed into lime. Most of the lime was shipped by schooner to San Francisco. By 1880, 95 percent of the lime used in San Francisco was coming from the greater Santa Cruz area.

The production of what was referred to as "natural cement"—a rough mixture of naturally occurring lime and clay—faded away when portland cement began to be produced throughout the United States in the late 19th century. This new product—a precisely proportioned mixture of materials found in limestone and clay—was invented and patented in 1824 by an English bricklayer.

Bonny Doon Winery

Those people expecting to drive into Bonny Doon for a leisurely stroll around downtown and perhaps a snack are in for a surprise. To borrow a phrase from Gertrude Stein, There is no there, there! Limestone quarries have been active in these hills since the late 19th century, and some interesting and unique plant species can be found in the Bonny Doon area, but there's no town, just a loose assemblage of houses.

The first—and only—establishment to greet you as you motor in to town is the Bonny Doon Winery. Even if you aren't in the mood for tasting, park and go in for a chat with the friendly staff in their beautiful tasting room. Founded in 1983 by Randall Grahm and his family, the winery takes pride in its reputation for being somewhat different. They produce mostly Rhône varietals (their mantra is "Anything but Chardonnay") and decorate their bottles with original—and somewhat irreverent—labels. Bonny Doon Road twists uphill for about three miles before reaching the winery.

Santa Cruz Wallflower and the
Bonny Doon Ecological Reserve

The Santa Cruz wallflower (*Erysimum teretifolium*) is one of the unique—and endangered—species that survive in the rare habitat found around Bonny Doon, which is characterized by deep, coarse, poorly developed soils influenced by the humid marine climate. A member of the mustard family, this flower is tall and rather simple looking, with orange to yellow flowers. The Santa Cruz wallflower was probably never very abundant, so the

BONNY DOON BEACH

South of Davenport, the Bonny Doon Road indicates two options for the shoreline explorer: venture up the road to Bonny Doon, or park here and get your feet wet.

Just up over the railroad tracks from the new large parking area, a big crescent-shaped cove greets you. It is always a bit of a surprise along this stretch of coast to park your car out of sight of the shore, climb a little ridge, and have the ocean open up before you.

Liddell Creek flows right out of the cliff face here, thanks to some human engineering, then meanders across the beach to the ocean. This makes for a nice bird-watching spot, since many land birds and shorebirds congregate here to drink and bathe. A trail on the southern bluff looks inviting, but it crosses agricultural lands and is off-limits. Although some maps show picnic tables and other amenities at the beach, this spot has no facilities besides the nice parking lot.

California's coastal sage scrub is both beautiful and fragrant.

impact of humans (especially mining, logging, and trampling) has been particularly hard on the species.

Although tracts of wallflower habitat have been purchased in these hills by the California Department of Fish and Game, the plant's future is still tenuous. The largest piece of preserved habitat is the Bonny Doon Ecological Reserve, which takes in some 525 acres of unique ponderosa pine sandlands and protects several endangered plant and animal species in addition to the wallflower. Although the reserve is presently closed to visitors, it will be opened to the public in the near future. For information about the reserve, contact the Department of Fish and Game's Monterey office at 831-649-2870.

Coastal Sage Scrub

This plant community is well represented along the shores of Monterey Bay. A version of its inland cousin, chaparral, out here on the coast this mix of plants has adapted to a moister climate thanks to frequent foggy days. Because it doesn't grow as tall as inland chaparral, or as tough, some call this coastal community "soft chaparral."

The most ubiquitous member of the coastal sage scrub community is coyote bush (*Baccharis pilularis*), an evergreen shrub that may grow close to the ground in windy areas or rise over your head in more protected spots. Coyote bush has a light pungent smell to its leaves when crushed. During the autumn flowering season these bushes become a mass of swarming insects. (The name, according to one story, comes from its appearance when it's flowering: it looks like coyotes have brushed past it and left small tufts of fur.) Ceanothus (*Ceanothus* spp.), bush monkeyflower (*Mimulus aurantiacus*), California sage (*Artemesia californica*), and Indian paintbrush (*Castillejia* spp.) are also typical—and beautiful— members of the coastal sage scrub assembly.

In some regions of the state, local versions of this plant community have become endangered because of intense coastal development. Indeed, as a habitat it tends to be neglected; scruffy looking and dried out most of the time, it simply doesn't draw one's attention like a giant stand of redwoods or a field ablaze with poppies. But take the time to visit these areas in the spring and you'll be amazed at the variety of flowers, insects, birds, animals,

CALIFORNIA GRAY
WHALE WATCHING

One of the most spectacular ways to view California gray whales *(Eschrichtius robustus)*—and numerous other marine species—is to hop on a whale-watching boat in Santa Cruz or Monterey and motor out into the marine sanctuary. But for a topside, distant view of these 30- to 50-foot beauties, park across the street from Davenport's commercial area, get out of your car, strap on some binoculars, and start looking.

From late November through January patient observers here (and from coastal bluffs all along the bay's shore) can see the tell-tale spouts of grays—and even their tails, or flukes. Unlike some other whales, grays don't have pronounced dorsal fins. Instead, look for a series of small humps along their arching back (near the tail) as they swim by and then sound (dive down).

During these winter months the grays are migrating south, often just beyond the surf zone, from their feeding grounds in the Bering Sea to their birthing and breeding grounds off Baja California—a short swim of some 5,000 to 7,000 miles . . . one way! Pregnant females come by first, heading for the warm waters of Baja's lagoons to deliver their 1,500- to 2,000-pound calves. When the grays return north in the spring they

Gray whales can be seen offshore during their southward migration each fall and winter.

swim farther offshore and are less likely to be seen.

Gray whales are actually more black than gray, but a coating of hitchhiking white barnacles, orange whale lice, and pale scars (from scraping against the ocean floor and rocks while feeding) lighten them up.

Grays feed on amphipods—small crustaceans—that live in the mud of the ocean floor. They also eat plankton, microscopic plants and animals that float in the open water. Instead of having teeth (like sperm whales, for example), they have comblike plates in their mouths called baleen. When feeding, gray whales scoop up muck from the ocean floor, or close their mouth around a mass of plankton, then they use their gargantuan tongues to press the water out through the baleen. The amphipods and

plankton stay behind. Gulp: big meal! It sounds improbable, but their diet of these minuscule pieces of food helps them attain an adult weight of some 40 tons.

Once there were three populations of gray whales. A North Atlantic population is now extinct, probably because of overhunting. A western North Pacific, or Korean, population is still in existence, but very few whales remain. The population off California's coast—the eastern North Pacific stock—was hunted to near extinction in the late 19th century. In 1947, however, this population was given full protection by the International Whaling Commission, and it has since rebounded to some 23,000 individuals, close to its original size. (For more about whales and whaling, see pp. 155–157.)

RED-TAILED HAWK

The common yet nonetheless striking red-tailed hawk *(Buteo jamaicencis)* is typically seen soaring high in the sky, where sunlight frequently illuminates its amber-red tail feathers. When aloft, the red-tail often calls out repeatedly with a high-pitched, down-turning scream—"keee-r-r, keee-r-r"— while being harassed by ravens, crows, smaller hawks, and even hummingbirds! Steller's jays are great imitators of the red-tail's call, so don't be fooled: look twice. When not soaring, red-tails can be spotted along Highway 1 and side roads perched on telephone poles or fenceposts as they scan the countryside for prey.

Laguna Creek Beach and agricultural lands

and overall color. After a winter rain in coastal sage scrub, or during late summer and early fall following an evening of dense fog, the smells off these plants are intense. It is as though someone lifted the top off a giant simmering kettle, tickling your nose with hints of mint, sage, thyme, and even a bit of celery.

Yellowbank Beach and Laguna Creek Beach

Just over two miles south of Davenport, on the shoreline side of Highway 1, a dirt pullout leads to Yellowbank Beach. (As always, be careful exiting and entering the highway.) Once you are parked, you'll see the trail. It is a steep climb down to the beach, but once there, you'll be impressed. The beach, though only about 100 yards wide, is beautiful. Look for the old marine terraces sticking right up out of the sand. This turnout and the beach have no formal facilities.

About another half mile south of this site is Laguna Creek Beach (also with no formal facilities). Look for the parking area next to Laguna Road, on the east side of the highway. Crossing the highway here is extremely dangerous, so again, proceed with great caution. Once on the shore side of the highway, you have to cross the railroad tracks, then follow a dirt road for about half a mile. The beach is about half a mile long and rimmed by agricultural fields. Laguna Creek makes a nice little marsh here, active with songbirds.

Davenport website:
http://www.swanton.com/
index.html

Davenport Jail Museum:
831-429-1964

Bonny Doon Winery:
831-425-3625

Bonny Doon Ecological
Reserve, Department
of Fish and Game:
831-649-2870

CalTrans District 05:
805-549-3111

Bike map website:
http://www.dot.ca.gov/dist
05/planning/bikemap.htm

California State
Coastal Conservancy:
Website: http://www.
coastalconservancy.ca.gov

California Coast & Ocean
magazine: 510-286-0934

Santa Cruz County
Regional Transportation
Commission: 831-460-3200

Red, White, and Blue Beach

About three miles south of Bonny Doon Beach is Red, White, and Blue Beach, just off Scaroni Road. Look for the red, white, and blue mailbox and telephone pole along Highway 1. This is a clothing-optional beach, and because the access point is privately held, it costs to get in. If nude sunbathing is your thing, then this is your spot.

If not, the short drive down the C-shaped Scaroni Road is worth it anyway, just for a glance at the large white house perched above the road on the north side of the low valley. This house is owned by the proprietors of the access point, and it is famous among haunted-house aficionados as a certified possessed palace. Both the owners and local residents will tell you all about it, or you can pick up one of many books on haunted houses at your local library and read about it there. The tale starts with a late-19th-century sea captain, who built the house and then proceeded to torment his family there until his death. Where it ends is still up in the air—literally, if you believe the stories.

Wilder Ranch, Long Marine Lab, and Natural Bridges

After the long stretch of bluffs, agricultural lands, and the Coast Dairies property to the north, Wilder Ranch State Park marks another area of extensive public lands. Just south of the park is one of the bay's many marine-oriented research facilities, Long Marine Lab, a facility of the University of California, Santa Cruz. And next door to the marine lab is more parkland, in the form of Natural Bridges State Beach.

BRUSSELS SPROUTS

Twelve percent of the nation's commercial production of brussels sprouts comes from Wilder Ranch. These odd-looking (some would say odoriferous, if not downright unpalatable) plants are named after the capital of Belgium, a country where they've been grown for over four centuries. The plant, a relative of cauliflower, broccoli, kale, and collards, thrives in the cool coastal climate of Monterey Bay.

The portions of this plant that are edible (at least according to brussels sprouts enthusiasts) are the small buds—walnut-sized heads that grow along the stem. During a good year, one acre of farmland can produce about three and a half tons of sprouts. For Wilder Ranch, which has 500 acres under cultivation, that means 1,750 tons of brussels sprouts!

Wilder Ranch State Park

It is easy to drive by the main entrance to 6,000-acre Wilder Ranch, just north of Santa Cruz, largely because no obvious break occurs in the surrounding patterns on the land. The Wilder family operated a dairy for nearly 100 years on these lands, and many of the original buildings still stand. In fact, a portion of the park, which was dedicated in 1974, is a cultural preserve—a designation that helps maintain this ranch's dairy past through displays and living-history demonstrations. The park also leases out some 500 acres of coastal benchlands for brussels sprout production.

Before the Wilders, many others lived on and worked these lands. Rancho del Matadero was established by Mission Santa Cruz in 1791, and Ohlone village sites throughout the park tell of an even earlier use. Though not all Wilder-era buildings (and a Mexican-era adobe) are yet open for visitation, many are, and the friendly staff and tiny bookstore will help you plan your visit. On weekends, staff and volunteers dress in period costumes and demonstrate baking, blacksmithing, and other ranch-related activities.

Behind the historic buildings is a nice picnic area with tables, and animals that kids can watch. Old pieces of machinery scattered about serve as educational tools. Look them over and try to figure out what they were used for. Just beyond the picnic area a tunnel leads under Highway 1 to the park's backcountry, comprising some 5,000 acres.

The park has a multiuse trail system consisting of more than 35 miles of dirt trails. Trails are open to hikers, bicyclists, and horseback riders, though horseback riders are restricted to the inland side of Highway 1.

Wilder Ranch State Park

The northern entrance to Swanton Road is on Highway 1 just south of Waddell Creek, and its southern entrance is about 1.5 miles north of Davenport. Greyhound Rock is a few hundred yards south of Swanton Road's north entrance. Scott Creek is about 5 miles south of Waddell, or 2.5 miles north of Davenport. Davenport Landing is on Davenport Landing Road, just north of Davenport. Davenport itself is 9 miles north of the last stoplight (Western Drive) as you leave Santa Cruz, or some 36 miles south of Half Moon Bay. Bonny Doon Beach is 1.5 miles south of Davenport, and 7.5 miles north of Western Drive; the turnoff to Bonny Doon proper is here also. Red, White, and Blue Beach is 4 miles south of Davenport, and 5 miles north of Western Drive.

Coastal Bluff Trail

Wilder's coastal bluff trail is truly one of the most spectacular attractions on Monterey Bay's shoreline. Part of its allure comes from the fact that to reach the blufftop portion of the trail from park headquarters—or from the roadside turnouts leading to Three Mile Beach and Four Mile Beach, north of the park's main entrance—you have to zig and zag through half of a mile of brussels sprout fields. The southern section of this trail is called the Old Cove Landing Trail, while the north half is called the Ohlone Bluff Trail.

From the park's main parking lot next to the headquarters, you reach an overlook after just half a mile on the trail. It affords a nice view of Wilder Beach, a natural preserve closed to the public. Among other benefits, this closure allows a small number of snowy plovers to nest here every year.

Once past the sprouts, out on the bluff, it's just you and the Pacific. Waves smash into a series of marine terraces at the base of the cliffs, and hidden beaches entice you to scramble down and walk about.

Overhead, gulls and hawks work the bluff-created updrafts, while from the bushes white-crowned sparrows and meadowlarks serenade your passage. You can follow this trail for several miles to reach Four Mile Beach (where there are restrooms).

At the northern end of the bluff trail—where it turns to a footpath and meanders down a bluff to Four Mile Beach—a large pond behind the beach is usually packed with waterbirds. Although the shoreline of the pond is inaccessible, from above you can engage in some nifty topside birding. Look for pied-billed grebes, cormorants, marsh wrens, mergansers, and seasonal vagrants stopping by for a rest and a bite to eat.

As you explore this blufftop trail, stop and study the marine terraces below you. Some are so flat that wave-

MARINE TERRACES

As you walk Wilder's bluff trail or drive along Highway 1 north of Santa Cruz, you will notice a certain aspect to the landscape. Basically, you are moving through a series of flat areas separated by valleys. The flat areas are marine terraces—ancient seafloors. The valleys were created by creeks and streams that have cut down through the marine terraces.

It is not always easy to determine the location of a former shoreline by looking at marine terraces. Not only has the sea level fluctuated over thousands of years—rising and falling, thus erasing old terraces and creating new ones—but the terraces, after being planed flat by wave action, have also been lifted up and twisted around thanks to Earth's internal forces. It is believed that the marine terraces at the base of the cliffs along this section of shoreline were part of the seafloor some 10,000 years ago.

Wilder Ranch's coastal bluffs
and marine terraces

JERRY EMORY

borne waters seem to hesitate for a split second before deciding which side to spill over. Once the decision has been made, a cascade of foaming sea water rejoins the incoming swells.

Now turn your back on the water and look out over the fields of brussels sprouts to the coastal bluffs on the other side of Highway 1. Let your mind wander back to a time when the shoreline here was very different. Take in the sweep of the land and its gentle contours; soon ancient marine terraces will jump out at you from the familiar landscape—flat-topped ridges or mini-mesas, often covered in grass and standing out from the surrounding coastal scrub and redwoods. Of course, they were there all along, but you probably never thought to look for them.

Two more sites accessible from the bluff trail are the Fern Grotto and Old Landing Cove (nicely explained back at the park's main parking lot).

Poison Oak

Poison oak (*Toxicodendron diversilobum*) may look pretty at certain times of the year, but don't touch it! Make sure to learn—and to teach your children and friends—all about poison oak. Most of the potential irritation can be avoided if after a hike you wash immediately with soap and water (or with commercial products available at pharmacies), though that isn't always feasible.

Remember that poison oak can look like a bush, it can crawl along the ground, or it may pretend it's a vine and climb trees. And it is deciduous, so in the winter it loses its leaves—but not its toxicity: a scramble through a leafless poison oak patch can be just as painful, eventually, as if you crushed an oily leaf against your skin. Also, dogs that have run loose through poison oak can spread it to humans.

The Backcountry

Wilder's backcountry is very popular with hikers, bikers, and equestrians. Countless habitat types can be found across the park's 5,000 acres of backcountry: redwood forests, grass-covered hillsides, coastal sage scrub, and

As you near the Santa Cruz city limits you'll notice more and more bicyclists zooming along Highway 1. This section of highway is part of the Pacific Coast Bicycle Route. (CalTrans signs read "Pacific Coast Bike Route.") In addition, Santa Cruz County is just beginning to plan and develop a Class I bike path (separate from the main road) on the ocean side of Highway 1 from Shaffer Road in Santa Cruz to Wilder Ranch State Park, to be completed by the end of 1999. (Class II paths are on roads, but within a bike lane. Class III paths are routes on the shoulder of the road.)

To receive a free bicycle route map from CalTrans District 05 for the Monterey Bay region, contact them at 805-549-3111 or order one via their website, http://www. dot.ca.gov/dist05/planning/ bikemap.htm. Not only is there a route that hugs the shoreline as closely as possible, but a series of side routes also penetrates the mountains to the east, opening up endless possibilities for cyclists. The Santa Cruz County Regional Transportation Commission also produces a nice bicycle map, which shows all these bikeways, including the Pacific Coast Bicycle Route. Contact them at 831-460-3200 to receive a free copy.

mixed evergreen forests. If you are ambitious enough to reach one of the backcountry's ridgeline trails, the views of the bay are phenomenal.

With the 1997 addition of the Gray Whale Ranch property to the park, visitors can now explore from Wilder to UC Santa Cruz's parklands, then on to the Pogonip Open Space Preserve and even Henry Cowell Redwoods State Park.

Granite Rock Company

Granite Rock, located just across Highway 1 from Wilder Ranch, is the largest American-owned construction materials supplier in northern California. The company was founded in 1900 and today operates in fifteen different locations in a six-county area of northern California ranging from San Francisco to Monterey. Granite Rock produces rock, sand, gravel, concrete, and other materials.

Long Marine Lab

You can learn all about marine science research—and a lot more—by stopping for a visit at the new facilities of the Joseph M. Long Marine Laboratory. Part of the University of California, Santa Cruz, the lab, which is situated on 40 acres of coastal bluff overlooking the marine sanctuary, was dedicated in 1978; it has since become distinguished for its marine mammal, invertebrate, and toxicology research. Visitors are invited to view marine mammals and have a hands-on experience in touch tanks

Mountain biking is popular in the Wilder Ranch backcountry.

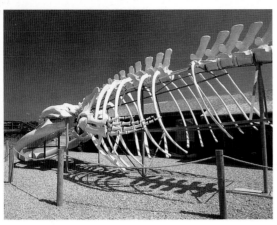

Blue whale skeleton
at the Long Marine Lab

chock full of fascinating critters. Outside, the 85-foot blue whale skeleton will leave you shaking your head in awe. (Blue whale skeletons are a rare commodity because typically when these largest of all animals die, they sink to the ocean floor.)

A good supply of friendly docents is always on hand to answer questions and lead tours. The bookstore is packed with all sorts of educational materials to help you teach young ones (and perhaps older ones as well) about the ocean and marine resources. For information about visiting Long Marine Lab, and about its annual open house (usually held the second Sunday in October), call 831-459-4308.

Also in the complex of new buildings scattered across the coastal bluff is the Oiled Wildlife Veterinary Care and Research Center, operated by the California Department of Fish and Game. It is the largest and most modern facility of its kind. In the case of a marine disaster, the 18,000-square-foot building and staff here can handle up to 125 sea otters, 100 birds at a time, and larger marine mammals. When not in use during emergencies, the facility will help local scientists with ongoing marine research.

Across the road from the wildlife center, the National Marine Fisheries Laboratory is constructing an array of buildings and transferring their staff from the building they've occupied in Tiburon since 1961. This lab studies many marine fish species and their habitats, though the emphasis is on two commercially important groups of fish: salmon species and "groundfish" (including the many rockfish species found in Monterey Bay and along the Pacific coast).

GETTING AROUND

The main entrance to Wilder Ranch is approximately 2 miles north of the stoplight at Western Drive in Santa Cruz, directly across the road from the Granite Rock sign. Long Marine Lab and Natural Bridges State Beach can both be found by turning shoreward at either Western Drive or Swift Street. The lab is at the northern end of Delaware Avenue, while park access can be had at the terminus of either Natural Bridges Drive (walk-in entrance) or Swanton Boulevard, both off of Delaware.

Natural Bridges State Beach

Although Natural Bridges State Beach is slowly losing its natural bridges to erosion, the park has a lot more to offer than mere scenery. A large sandy cove here is perfect for a midday snooze or a game of frisbee. When the waters are low, tidepools unveil themselves for light-handed exploration. And if you are really into waves, the north point of the park is a popular spot with surfers. Do what they do: just grab your board, run across the beach, wade through the creek, scramble across the marine terrace, hug your board for dear life, then jump into the surf between swells. Kowabunga!

If you look carefully, as you move down a smooth beach or coastal trail, the signs of who came before you are all around. But first, some tracking terminology:

Print: The impression made by one paw or hoof.

Track: A series of prints.

Straddle: The width of the track.

Stride: The distance between prints.

Leap: The distance between sets of prints made by hoppers or bounders.

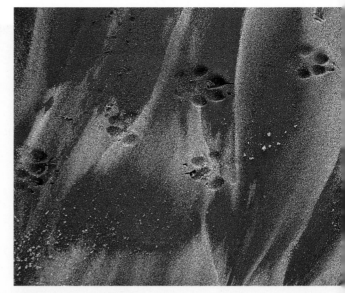

Coyote tracks on the beach

Print size and stride will vary a little within a single species, just as with humans, all of whose feet and walks aren't the same. Also, prints look different when pressed into sand versus mud or dust.

If the track makes a more or less straight line, and the animal is placing its hind feet almost exactly into the prints made by the front feet, then it is probably a member of the dog (coyote) or cat (bobcat) family. Animals with hoofs (deer) are also straight-line walkers. Prints that don't cover each other and form a zigzag pattern with a wide straddle are from relatively heavyset critters like raccoons, skunks, and opossums. If the prints are regularly spaced and in pairs or groups, the track was probably made by someone in the weasel family. Sets of two small and two large prints tell you a rabbit dashed by: they land on both front feet, then swing their hind feet around and in front of their front ones.

Even frogs, lizards, snakes, beetles, and crickets leave tracks. If the creature looks like it is sliding or crawling in its tracks, or if it leaves pinprick tracks, it's probably one of these guys.

■ More Clues: Scat

Scat is animal droppings, and it's a good indication of what animals are around and what they're eating. Scat is often deposited right in the middle of trails to maximize exposure: animals want other animals to know they've been there. If scat is packed with fur, bones, and feathers, it probably came from an animal in the dog, cat, or weasel family. If it looks like rounded dark pellets of sawdust or dry plant material, deer or rabbits may have visited last night.

Wildlife biologists always collect scat, and there are even scat specialists—known, logically enough, as scatologists. Scat is usually dry and harmless to handle, much like the one-to-two-inch fur-, bone-, and tooth-packed pellets that owls regurgitate periodically. But if it grosses you out to pick at scat, use twigs to break it apart, and wash your hands when you've finished your examinations.

■ Twigs, Limbs, and Bones

Many animals chew on twigs, limbs, and bones for food and to sharpen their teeth. They also leave prints with their teeth. Miniature gnaw marks on wood or bone mean mice have been working. Rabbit marks are less than an eighth of an inch wide. Larger chew marks on trunks are beaver. Tree trunks are used by bears and mountain lions for scratching (vertical lines), and by deer for rubbing the velvet off their antlers (shredded bark three to four feet up the trunk).

Large congregations of monarch butterflies spend the winter at Natural Bridges State Beach.

INFORMATION

Wilder Ranch State Park
  Visitor Center:
  831-426-0505

Long Marine Lab:
  831-459-4308

Natural Bridges State Beach:
  831-423-4609

Santa Cruz Metro:
  831-425-8600
  Website:
  http://www.scmtd.com

San Trans:
  1-800-660-4287
  Website:
  http://www.samtrans.com

No board? Okay, then find the visitor's center by the upper parking lot and learn all about the area's natural wonders. Throughout the upper portion of the park, too, picnic tables and barbecue stands nestle among the towering eucalyptuses, inviting shady relaxation.

You may object to having eucalyptus, an exotic tree, in a state park, but the tens of thousands of monarch butterflies that overwinter in them sure don't. In fact, they depend on them for shelter. Although many people associate Pacific Grove with monarchs, and rightly so, this grove of eucalyptus trees shelters one of the densest and most accessible concentrations of monarchs along the Pacific coast. A monarch trail winds through the grove and allows you to see the butterflies up close from several angles. (The trail accommodates most wheelchairs.)

In many ways, this park is like an urban park. Starlings and pigeons share the beach with gulls and shorebirds, and housing has crept up to the park on three sides, which means parking can be tough at times. Natural Bridges is a real gem, though—not just for the people of Santa Cruz, but for everyone. Walking through the park's monarch groves puts you very close to some deceptively awesome creatures. Winter storms off the Pacific can reveal the astounding fury of the ocean. The tidepools are brimming with life, and there is also a nice interpretive trail through a wetlands area.

SANTA CRUZ MUDSTONE

Most of the shoreline covered in this chapter is made from Santa Cruz mudstone. Formed millions of years ago, it is composed of fine particles of silts and clays from coastal streams, mixed with the tiny shells of diatoms —one-celled marine plants. These components were mixed and turned into stone over a very long period of time. The bridges at Natural Bridges State Beach are made of this mudstone. Where once there were three bridges, now only one remains. But that was predictable, according to geologists. Bridges like these eventually erode, and the span collapses. In their place another feature is formed, the solitary sea stack.

Circling the bay are other rock types, variously able to resist erosion. Near Aptos, for example, the bluffs are made of a sedimentary rock similar to Santa Cruz mudstone, part of what is called the Purisima formation. The Purisima material, however, is far more erodible than the Santa Cruz mudstone, in part because it contains less silica (a strong glasslike binding material). By contrast, much of the Monterey Peninsula is ringed by granite, which is very resistant to erosion.

Natural Bridges State Beach

The park has a very dedicated staff that helps host the annual Migration Festival, celebrating migrations of all types (second Saturday of February), and Welcome Back Monarchs Day (second Sunday of October) and maintains an active natural history program year round. The park also has restrooms with showers for rinsing off after a wild ride in the waves.

2

Santa Cruz to New Brighton State Beach

Natural Bridges State Beach is the ideal spot to begin an exploration of the shoreline between Santa Cruz and New Brighton State Beach. This section of the bay's shore is graced with numerous parks, blufftop pathways, beautiful beaches both large and small, and some of the world's most popular surfing spots.

And although generations of humans have left their marks on the shoreline here, there are ample opportunities for recreation, sightseeing, rest, and seclusion. You can pursue plenty of natural history activities here—bird-watching, botanizing, tidepooling, hiking. When you're done with that, or to take a break from the shore, you can stop for a cappuccino, study the arts, ponder local history, or seek out architectural gems. If you're more inclined to cardiovascular activity, then dust off those roller blades, go for a run, or hit the waves and surf, windsurf, or body surf. The adventurous soul can pedal or walk the entire 13 or so miles between northern Santa Cruz and New Brighton State Beach in a day, losing sight of the bay for only a few minutes during that whole stretch. Or you might want to think like a harbor seal: find a secluded stretch of beach, stretch out, and bask in the sun until you are warm and completely content.

West Cliff Drive and Downtown Santa Cruz

West Cliff Drive is one half of Santa Cruz's shoreline circulation system. The other half is East Cliff Drive (which segues into Opal Cliff Drive as you approach Capitola). Combine the two and you have an amazing union of roads and pathways that hug the entire shoreline. A few brief deviations stray briefly from the sight and sound of the Pacific, but essentially you are directly above or alongside the bay all the way from Natural Bridges State Beach to New Brighton State Beach.

Along the way, numerous pocket beaches can be reached from the blufftop. You'll also find countless benches—as well as emergency telephones and lifesaving stations. There are cliff warnings everywhere, and for good reason. Not only can you fall considerable

◄ Walking down the sand on one of Monterey Bay's many beaches

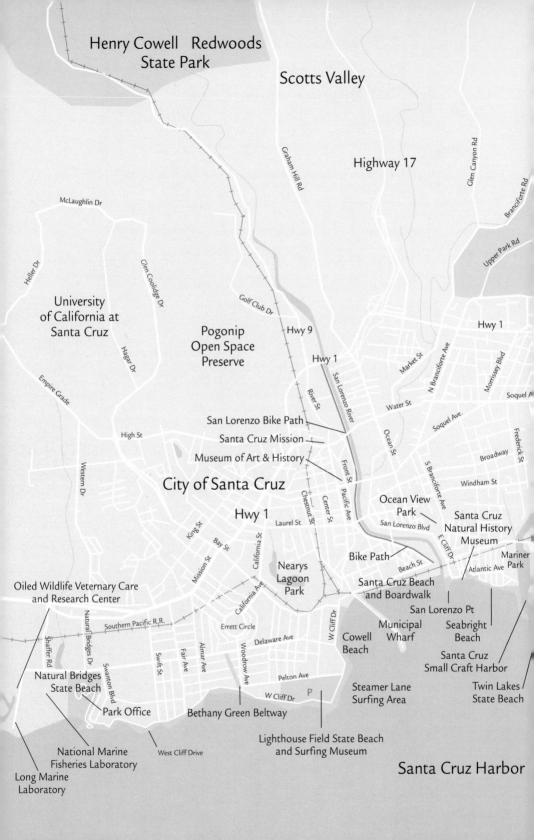

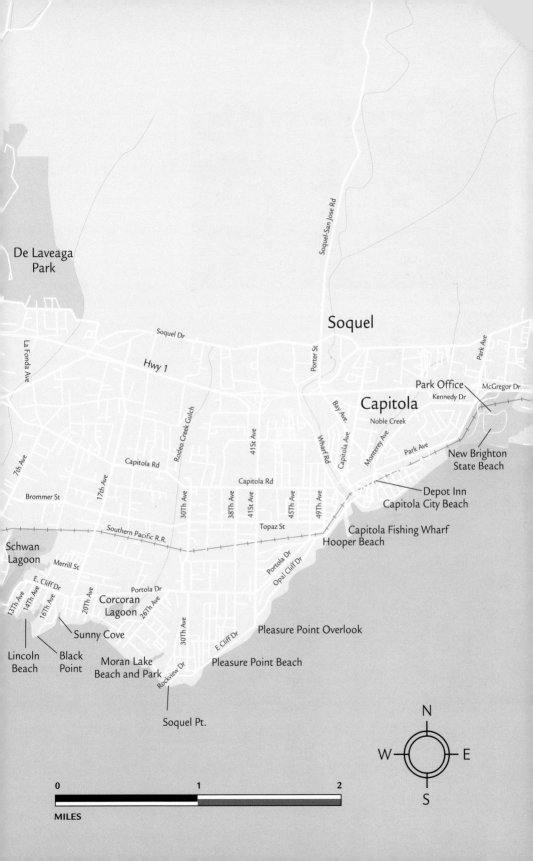

De Laveaga
Park

Soquel

Soquel-San Jose Rd

La Fonda Ave

Soquel Dr

Hwy 1

Porter St

Park Ave

Park Office

Kennedy Dr

McGregor Dr.

Capitola

Bay Ave.

Noble Creek

7th Ave

17th Ave

Capitola Rd

Rodeo Creek Gulch

30th Ave

38th Ave

41St Ave

41St Ave

Capitola Rd

45th Ave

49th Ave

Wharf Rd

Capitola Ave

Monterey Ave

Park Ave

New Brighton
State Beach

Brommer St

Depot Inn
Capitola City Beach

Topaz St

Southern Pacific R.R.

Schwan
Lagoon

Merrill St

Portola Dr

Opal Cliff Dr

Capitola Fishing Wharf

Hooper Beach

13Th Ave

14Th Ave

16Th Ave

20Th Ave

26Th Ave

30Th Ave

E Cliff Dr

E. Cliff Dr

Portola Dr

Corcoran
Lagoon

Pleasure Point Overlook

Sunny Cove

Lincoln
Beach

Black
Point

Moran Lake
Beach and Park

Rockview Dr

Pleasure Point Beach

Soquel Pt.

N

W   E

S

0   1   2

MILES

The rugged yet accessible shore of West Cliff Drive

distances if you are not careful, but sneaker waves can easily pick you off the rocks if you venture too far out. But don't let wave paranoia ruin your visit; simply use common sense: don't go out onto slippery rocks at the water's edge, and stay clear of the surf during storms or high winds (unless you are a seasoned surfer).

Parking along the shore can be tricky on busy weekends. Your best bet is to find a spot at either end of this shoreline path-and-roadway system, then simply start working west or east (*not* north or south, as you might imagine—a good map, a compass, or a nice sunset will quickly help you get your bearings along this curving coast). Another option is to park inland several blocks, then head toward the water. Either way, once you reach the shore, you'll be amazed at the natural beauty, and at the parade of locals, visitors, and watchful gulls on the prowl for handouts.

Bethany Green Beltway

About a dozen blocks—and several small coves—east of Natural Bridges State Beach you'll spy a little creek on the inland side of the road that leads into a verdant passageway between two houses. This is Bethany Green Beltway, and it can be a welcome break from the glare off the ocean on hot, still days. As it winds away from the shore for five blocks, the pathway takes you past nicely kept grass areas and shade trees—a great place for a cool picnic before heading back to Lighthouse Trail or the beach. It is open sunrise to sunset. Dogs must be leashed, and bikes may not be ridden on the path.

Lighthouse Field State Beach

Next door to the Bethany Green Beltway is Lighthouse Field State Beach, about one and a half miles from Natural Bridges. At first glance the land portion of the park may look like a big empty field ringed by private homes and public parking, but as the park's literature states, "There is more to lighthouse field than meets the eye."

POOCH ON THE LOOSE

The only officially sanctioned leash-free park along the shoreline within the city limits of Santa Cruz (and most of the county) is Lighthouse Field State Beach. Your dog can be off leash before 10 A.M. and after 4 P.M. Between those hours, though, leashes are required.

Lighthouse Field State Beach and surfing museum

In 1869 a two-story lighthouse—the nation's twelfth federal lighthouse—was built on the bluffs of Point Santa Cruz to help passenger and cargo ships steer clear of the point and Seal Rock offshore. In 1879 the lighthouse was moved 300 feet inland, to Lighthouse Field, because of fears that sea caves forming under Point Santa Cruz might cause the bluffs to fall into the water and destroy the structure. During its years of operation, just three lighthouse keepers ran the facility. Adna Hecox, a Santa Cruz pioneer, worked here from 1870 to 1883; his daughter Laura served as keeper until 1916; and Arthur Anderson ran the operation until the Coast Guard took over in 1939 and removed the beacon, hooked it up to an automatic timer, and placed it on a wooden tower in front of the lighthouse. The lighthouse itself was torn down in 1948.

Today's park, some 36 acres in extent, is much larger than the 10 acres given over to the original lighthouse. The additional land was once part of an estate owned by San Franciscan James Phelan, who purchased it in 1887. Phelan, a former mayor of San Francisco and later a state senator, was a renowned patron of the arts. His Santa Cruz getaway, which he often shared with artists and writers, boasted an impressive residence, extensive gardens, and pathways adorned with statuary.

In 1960 the entire site was cleared (except for some of the larger trees) in preparation for an extensive development, but intense opposition from the neighborhood eventually stopped the proposal. California State Parks purchased the land in 1977, and it has been one of Santa Cruz's only coastside open spaces ever since. Although most of the park's vegetation is nonnative, plans call for more planting of native species. Even so, because of the proximity to the shore, a type of "edge effect" occurs here, where several habitats merge to support an impressive

PEDAL POWER ALONG THE SHORELINE

From Natural Bridges State Beach to the Municipal Pier and Boardwalk area you can travel on the Lighthouse Trail, a Class I bike path that also accommodates pedestrians, roller bladers, and skateboarders. From the pier to New Brighton State Beach, follow the Pacific Coast Route signs, which will take you along the coastline for much of the distance, on a combination of Class I, II, and III bikeways.

In the name of expediency, the official CalTrans bike route takes you away from the shore, diverging from West and East Cliff Drives and the Lighthouse Trail. Still, it is a nice ride—in fact, the view of the bay from sections of Soquel Drive is spectacular—and you re-emerge near the coast just past Rio Del Mar. For bike maps of Santa Cruz County, contact the Santa Cruz County Regional Transportation Commission at 831-460-3200 and CalTrans District 05 at 805-549-3111.

While you're exploring the beach here, or snooping around for local surf hangouts, take a moment to look at your feet. Along the bay where rocks can be found, you might spot the purple shore crab (Hemigrapsus nudus), a busy little creature that spends much of its time scraping the rocks for a meal or nibbling on green algae.

The crab's main body part—its carapace, or shell—is about two inches wide and smooth.

MONTEREY BAY AQUARIUM

The purple shore crab is found most commonly along rocky shores.

Although it's called purple, its color can range from purple to greenish yellow to red brown. However, it does sport reddish-purple spots on its claws. Purple shore crabs breed in winter, and some females may produce over 36,000 eggs in a season! A common neighbor, the striped shore crab (see page 228), is thinner than the purple and has distinctive transverse stripes across its back.

variety of wildlife. For example, some 120 bird species have been recorded at Lighthouse Field.

Across the street you can step down to a small beach to watch surfers or continue your nature observations. California sea lions are often seen—and heard—on the rocks here. Otters snooze in the kelp forests offshore, and gray whales can be spotted seasonally. Gulls and other shorebirds cruise the shoreline and bluffs. You might also want to mosey over to the Surf Museum on Point Santa Cruz or check out Steamer Lane.

Eventually the park will have additional areas for nature watching, more trails, and other amenities. Parking is relatively trouble-free here, and you'll find restrooms with showers at the east end of the field (toward the Surf Museum).

Monarch Watch

Lighthouse Field, like Natural Bridges State Beach, is another spot along the Monterey Bay shoreline where you can watch overwintering monarch butterflies. In a good year, patient observers may see thousands of these amazing creatures clinging to the field's eucalyptus trees. They were first noticed here, and recorded, by James Phelan in the late 19th century.

Santa Cruz Surfing Museum

The Santa Cruz Surfing Museum was established in 1986 inside the Mark Abbott Memorial Lighthouse. The lighthouse was built in 1965 by the Abbott family in memory of their son Mark, who died in a body surfing accident nearby. The building was eventually donated to the city of Santa Cruz.

Inside the small brick building, the history of surfing is told through historic photographs, home movies from the 1930s and 1940s, contemporary surf videos, and a wonderful collection

A surfer working a wave at Steamer Lane

of surfboards. One old redwood board is over 10 feet long and weighs some 120 pounds. A portion of the museum is dedicated to Duke Kahanamoku, the "Father of Surfing" (and Hawaii's 1912 Olympic swimming champion). Kahanamoku visited Santa Cruz in the 1930s and showed the locals how to surf. Although some believe that surfing was first introduced here in 1885 by two visiting Hawaiian princes, it was the Duke who taught the first generation in the current lineage of Santa Cruz surfers.

The staff and volunteers of the museum are extremely nice and full of information. There is also a gift shop with books, posters, cards, some clothing, and more. (For virtual surfing, go to the museum's website at http://www.cruzio.com/arts/scva/surf.html.) Outside, you can enjoy a spectacular view of Santa Cruz and the Monterey Bay while overlooking Steamer Lane, one of the world's premier surfing spots.

Steamer Lane

You may think that the lingo and attire popular with surfers are an indication of the archetypal laid-back California lifestyle. After all, what does it take to surf? Some water and a board, right? Surfers just sit out there bobbing up and down waiting for a big wave that practically surfs for them. Be that as it may—and all joking aside—surfing is serious business.

WAVES

The Monterey Bay National Marine Sanctuary is a diverse and fascinating stretch of the Pacific Ocean. We might tend to think of it as a collection of habitats and species, but it is also a place of winds, fog, tides, and currents. Something else the sanctuary serves up all along the coast is waves.

In a nutshell, waves are generated by wind. Visit the coast after a big storm, and you'll see huge waves. Basically, waves are of two kinds: sea waves and swells. Sea waves are created by local winds and storms; they come in all sizes and reach the shore in irregular patterns. Swells are the result of distant storms. They, too, can vary, but typically they are long and smooth, similar in size, and arrive onshore in regular patterns. Swell waves travel across the oceans for thousands of miles. Some of the swells breaking on the shores here come from immense storms in the Gulf of Alaska and the Sea of Japan.

Surfing statue on West Cliff Drive pathway

If you stroll the promenade outside the surfing museum and work your way toward the bevy of surfers who are sure to be there studying Steamer Lane—the birthplace of mainland American surfing—you'll quickly realize that these dudes and dudettes aren't joking around. Flippant attitudes can result in serious injuries, even death. Talk and observation are sober before these athletes enter the water, and it's all business when they're out working the waves. Once the rides are over, good times are had reviewing the session and drying off: "They were, like, killer waves, dude . . . high, outside, and gnarly."

Surf Cams

In Santa Cruz two cameras presently satisfy the need-to-know of surfing and windsurfing aficionados who also are adept at surfing the web. One is pointed at Cowell Beach; the other provides several views of Steamer Lane. The Surfin' Santa Cruz website (http://www2.cruzio.com/~rls/surfnSantaCruz.html) has links to these surf cams and to other local surfing-related websites. There's no shortage of information on the web, including surfing history, surfing photographs, and information on weather, shops, equipment, lessons, and surf camps.

More of West Cliff Drive

From Point Santa Cruz and the Surfing Museum, West Cliff Drive continues to Cowell Beach and the Santa Cruz Municipal Pier. It is a great road to drive, though the cliff-hugging Lighthouse Trail is even better, for a casual walk or bike ride with benches, memorial overlooks, and stunning views.

Cowell Beach

If you are inspired by the intensity and joy of the surfers at Steamer Lane and want to give the sport a try, then venture down the shore to Cowell Beach. Lessons are offered here by several companies operating out of the wharf area. An impressive set of stairs works down the cliff face near the intersection of West Cliff Drive with Manor Avenue and Monterey Street. The stairs, though very steep, are fun. They lead down to the southern end of Cowell Beach. The beach then continues northward all the way to the Santa Cruz Boardwalk. On the east side of the boardwalk is a handicap access ramp to the beach.

After rough seas, Cowell Beach and shallow waters here are often riddled with large clumps of seaweed, of interest to shorebirds and kids alike. Beach lifeguard service is provided from Cowell Beach to the San Lorenzo River during spring break, spring and fall weekends, and daily in summer months.

Nearys Lagoon Park

Just a few blocks inland from Cowell Beach is Nearys Lagoon Park, a 44-acre open space preserving a 14-acre freshwater marsh. Some believe this lagoon was once an oxbow bend of the San Lorenzo River that, after being severed and abandoned by the meandering river, remained a water catchment. The lagoon also once covered most of the surrounding neighborhood. In the 1870s, however, the Nearys purchased this land and converted a portion of the lagoon to farmlands.

Today the park and de facto wildlife preserve—which is also part of the city's flood control system—has a fantastic interpretive trail around its perimeter (about one mile in length). You can access the park at one of three entrances. The principal entrance is at the end of Chestnut Street. There you'll find trail pamphlets, tables, a basketball court, and the start of the boardwalk portion of the trail. Bathrooms can be found throughout the park. The west side of the park, along Bay Street, is home to a large wastewater treatment facility, so that entrance can be rather busy at times with truck traffic.

After dallying along the shoreline, you'll notice the difference a bit of freshwater can make. At Nearys Lagoon, instead of pickleweed and saltgrass, you find yourself peering into tules and cattails. But birds aren't particular. You'll discover herons, coots, willets, and other shorebirds at the lagoon, as well as mallards and wood ducks

It might be hard to remember at times—like on a brilliantly sunny day when the beach here is packed with a fun-loving crowd and surfers are parading into and out of the water—but seashore life is all around you. Take a closer look at some of the rocks near the base of the cliffs at Cowell Beach, in the high and middle intertidal zone. You may be surprised at what you find.

One common animal of this habitat is the owl limpet (*Lottia gigantea*), a three- to four-inch long snail with a cap-shaped shell. Owl limpets are sandy brown with a rough shell (often dotted with smaller limpets and barnacles). These algae farmers act like miniature bulldozers to clear their rock of fellow limpets and other crustose creatures. Once cleared, the rocks can grow algae more quickly, on which the limpet grazes under cover of darkness. Limpets' teeth are capped with iron, so they can grind right into the rock to quarry out an indentation that is an exact fit for their shell. During low tide, the limpet retreats to its scar, hunkers down, and waits until the next high tide to move about. Large owl limpets were once eaten by coastal Indians, and the shells can be found in middens. There was also a booming commercial harvest of limpets earlier this century.

COWELL

Following the arrival of Europeans, many pioneering families played prominent roles along the shores of Monterey Bay. Some present-day residents can trace their lineage back to the first Spanish settlers, or to the mid-19th century during the American period. One surname that stands out in the greater Santa Cruz area is Cowell. A quick look at the Cowell family history provides an insight into the region's history of commerce, ranching, education, and land preservation.

Not only is there Cowell Beach, Cowell Street (above the beach), and Henry Cowell Redwoods State Park (inland toward Ben Lomond off Highway 9), but there was also the family home, Cowell Ranch, donated lands from which helped create the University of California, Santa Cruz. Remnants of the ranch's buildings are still standing by the main entrance to the campus. Not surprisingly, there is a Cowell College at UCSC. Farther afield, the Cowell name is on a theater in San Francisco and countless university health

SPECIAL COLLECTIONS, UNIVERSITY LIBRARY, UC SANTA CRUZ

Henry Cowell helped to shape Santa Cruz from the late 1800s into the early 20th century.

clinics and halls throughout California.

Henry Cowell (1819–1903) and his brother, John, came to California from Massachusetts in 1848 during the gold rush. Within two years they owned a drayage (transportation) and storage business in San Francisco. In 1865 Henry was the head of a very successful waterfront business, but he decided to sell his business and move his family to Santa Cruz, where he bought into the Jordan Davis lime operation. When Davis, who was Santa Cruz's pioneer lime merchant, died in 1888, Cowell bought the balance of the business. By 1897 the Henry

Cowell Lime and Cement Company employed 175 men and had a payroll of over $100,000 annually. At the time of his death it is estimated that, in addition to his business holdings and sizable ranch, Henry Cowell held title to some 82,000 acres throughout central coastal California, with a few holdings outside of the state as well.

Although Henry Cowell had six children (one died as an infant), they did not produce any heirs. Therefore, when the last of Henry Cowell's children, S. Harry Cowell, died in 1955, the San Francisco-based S. H. Cowell Foundation was formed to handle the family's considerable fortune. It was the foundation that gave the acreage to begin UC Santa Cruz. And before his death, Harry donated the land for Henry Cowell Redwoods State Park, in memory of his father.

SPECIAL COLLECTIONS, UNIVERSITY LIBRARY, UC SANTA CRUZ

At Cowell Ranch, oxen were used to haul limestone.

and a cross-section of songbirds absent from the shore. Look down, and you may even see some freshwater fish—including some huge carp.

To find out more about Santa Cruz City parks and museums, check out the city's website, http://santacruz parksandrec.com.

Common Tule

Wherever fresh or brackish water can be found along the coast, you might encounter tules (also called bulrush). There are nine species of tule in coastal California, and 17 statewide. The round stems of common tule (*Scirpus acutus*) can grow up to 15 feet in length, and they produce impressive flower clusters. For Indians living here and throughout the state, tule had many uses. The plant's roots and seeds were eaten, and its leaves and stalk were used to make baskets, mats, roofs, and boats known as balsas. Today, scientists have found yet another benefit: tule removes metals (copper, zinc, lead) from marsh waters and retains them in its roots, making marsh habitats safer for both wildlife and humans.

Common tules (and cattails) are so good at monopolizing marshlands that little else grows where they do. However, they provide food and shelter for wildlife. Marsh wrens and red-winged blackbirds use tules as high-rise apartment complexes. Coots, pied-billed grebes, and various ducks nest in them at water level. Below the water's surface, fish, crustaceans, and insects thrive among the roots. As evening falls, the night shift kicks in as huge flocks of European starlings, red-winged blackbirds, Brewer's blackbirds, and brown-headed cowbirds descend to roost, sounding the wake-up call for the black-crowned night herons who are just about to start their day.

DON'T GET GOOSED

The resident goose population at Nearys Lagoon can be a rough bunch. They have been known to be a bit aggressive at times, so don't give them handouts, and if necessary, chase them before they chase you! Just pretend you are another goose when approaching a trail-blocking gang of geese: be loud and wave your arms.

Howe Truss Bridge

The Howe Truss Bridge is a relic from a bygone era. It stands where the county's first wagon bridge was constructed, at the bottom of West Cliff Drive where the busy routes of Beach and Front Streets converge. The original bridge was built in 1849 so wagons could reach a wharf located at the end of Bay Street, owned by Santa Cruz pioneer Elihu Anthony. Since those days the Howe Truss Bridge has seen many modifications. Today it is being considered for renovation. It is already recognized as a local landmark, and it may one day be eligible for inclusion in the National Register of Historic Places.

Santa Cruz Municipal Wharf

Santa Cruz Municipal Wharf

The half-mile-long Santa Cruz Municipal Wharf is a destination in its own right—even though it happens to be next door to the ever-popular Santa Cruz Beach Boardwalk. The wharf is packed with all the things you might expect—seafood restaurants, souvenir stores, and typically some local characters hanging around. You can also find rental outlets for boats and kayaks, whale-watching businesses, and nice informational kiosks about the National Marine Sanctuary and local marine life. Although the wharf is hopping on summer weekends, it is always an enjoyable place for a walk or a casual bike ride.

The wharf has been here in one version or another since 1914. Until the early 1960s it was a working wharf for local fishermen. Today it is a tourist attraction, but fishing still takes place here: the end of the wharf is a mecca for those who love to drop a line into the surf. There are also fishing spots, with cleaning sinks, about midway along the wharf. You can catch a wide variety of species here, including flounder, bonito, striped bass, blue shark, lingcod, halibut, and crab. Or take a minute to peek down through viewing windows cut into the wharf's planks to get a topside view of the sea lions that cavort in the water under the wharf.

You can drive right onto the wharf (there is a minimal fee for parking), and there are restrooms along its length.

Santa Cruz Beach Boardwalk

The entire shore stretching from Santa Cruz down to the Aptos and Rio Del Mar area has hosted generations of summer visitors for over 130 years. Summer cottages, hotels, and bathhouses dotted the coast near sandy

STRIPED BASS

Striped bass is a very popular sport fish.

One of the most popular sport fishes in California's waters—fresh, brackish, or salty—is the striped bass (*Morone saxatilis*). One of the first railcars to arrive in Martinez, California, from the East Coast in 1879 carried live young striped bass. They were immediately released into the Carquinez Strait in the northeastern portion of San Francisco Bay. More shipments followed. The West Coast's entire striped bass population evolved from these early introductions. That's right, this popular game fish is not a true native, but what some biologists call a "new native"—an introduced species that has survived here long enough to become established. The same is true of brown trout, largemouth bass, and kokanee salmon.

Stripers (as aficionados call them) can grow to four feet in length, weigh 90 pounds or more, and live for over 20 years. Most pier catches, however, are in the less-than-five-pounds category. Striped bass are anadromous, like salmon and steelhead—they spend part of their lives in freshwater, and part in saltwater. Each winter they migrate from the open ocean and from the salty waters of San Francisco Bay into the brackish San Joaquin Delta. They spawn the next spring, then return to saltwater. The approximate

West Coast range of stripers is from Los Angeles north to the Columbia River.

Stripers may be tough—they are renowned fighters on the line—but they're in trouble. State biologists believe legal stripers (over 18 inches long) numbered just under two million in the early 1970s. Today, owing to pollution and freshwater diversions in the delta, the population has plummeted to about half a million fish. Present efforts to save the striper include complicated diversion pump screens and hatchery programs.

beaches, and warm-weather tents and bungalows hid under towering redwoods in inland valleys. However, if one place—one name—put the region on the tourism map for all of northern California (and beyond), it was the spectacular Santa Cruz Beach Boardwalk.

Even before the boardwalk came into existence in 1907, this lengthy beach had been home to public bathhouses, a casino, and a smaller boardwalk resembling Coney Island. After a fire destroyed most of these structures in 1906, the new boardwalk was designed, complete with a fresh casino building, indoor pool, boardwalk, pleasure pier, and more. Today, in addition to cotton candy, bags of roasted peanuts, and industrial-strength hot dogs, perhaps the most recognized items of the boardwalk are the merry-go-round and the roller coaster—and rightly so: they are classics.

The boardwalk's famous merry-go-round is a rare Looff carousel, which has been in operation since it was

Summer volleyball tournament in front of the Santa Cruz Beach Boardwalk

delivered in 1911 by its creator, the Danish woodcarver Charles Looff (his first was in Coney Island in 1875). The Giant Dipper roller coaster has thrilled millions of visitors since it was built by Arthur Looff, Charles's son, in 1924. Both structures are registered National Historic Landmarks, and the entire boardwalk complex and adjoining Coconut Grove are state Historical Landmarks.

In addition to these two old-timers—which are fully upgraded and modern (inspectors walk the Dipper's tracks every two hours)—you can go crazy on 20 major rides, arcades with everything from pinball machines to computer games, and some 40 snack bars, restaurants, and gift shops. Bowling enthusiasts can even bowl at the Surf Bowl Bowling Center.

In addition to all the indoor activities, and rides both inside and out, there is a lot to do on the beaches surrounding the complex. The west side of the boardwalk (between the Casino Fun Center and the wharf) is the site of numerous volleyball nets. It's a hopping place on the weekends. There is also wheelchair beach access located here. Also, both here and on the Cowell Beach side of the wharf, stores will rent you just about anything you could possibly need for the beach or the waves. You can even sign up for surfing lessons at several spots.

Santa Cruz Big Trees & Pacific Railway and Roaring Camp & Big Trees Narrow Gauge Railroads

After you've played yourself silly at the Santa Cruz Beach and Boardwalk, why not slow down and relax: go for a train ride behind a century-old steam locomotive. If you do, the sounds, smells, and sights of times gone by will surround you. That's right: you can catch a train—the Suntan Special, run by Santa Cruz Big Trees & Pacific

Perhaps the first railroad to grace Santa Cruz County was a horse-drawn rail car operated by the Jordan and Davis Lime Company in the 1850s to haul processed lime from the hills behind the town of Santa Cruz to their wharf. Since that early adventure with rails dozens of different railroads have operated throughout the county.

Prior to passenger rail service between the Santa Cruz coast and San Francisco, via San Jose, people had to endure a two-day stagecoach journey through San Juan Bautista and Alviso or an overnight steamship ride up the coast. So when the first passenger train left the town of Pajaro (just over the southern Santa Cruz County line) for San Francisco in 1871, there was no turning back. Soon, a confusion of rail lines snaked across the land, often at cross-purposes: in some cases their gauges were different, which meant the trains couldn't move from one set of tracks to another.

Reliable service from Santa Cruz and Monterey to San Francisco became a reality in the following decades. For a brief period in the 1880s, merchants could ship and receive goods via a rail line that ran through the mountains behind Santa Cruz directly to Los Gatos (somewhat like today's Highway 17).

By 1900 big plans were under way for a rail connection straight up the coast from Santa Cruz to San Francisco. The project was well developed on paper, and competition for contracts was fierce. But the 1906 San Francisco earthquake and fire put an end to it all. Even so, just prior to the arrival of the first gas-powered vehicle in the early 1920s, some 18 passenger and six freight trains pulled into downtown Santa Cruz daily.

Soon the automobile, bus, and truck took the place of the train. Increasingly, people were relying on vehicles for travel, pleasure, and work. Also, government funds helped make bigger and better roads. In spite of the car, rail service to the coast experienced a brief revival with Southern Pacific's Suntan Special, which ran between San Jose and Santa Cruz on weekends for about 20 years starting in the late 1920s. Although wildly popular, even this service succumbed to America's love affair with the car, and eventually all rail passenger service to Santa Cruz ended. Somewhat ironically, today there is talk of reviving some of these old rail lines for commerce, pleasure, and to ease congestion on the highways.

Railroad—right at the boardwalk and head off on a one-hour ride to Roaring Camp, in Felton off of Highway 9.

Once in Felton you can switch trains and hop onto the Roaring Camp & Big Trees Narrow Gauge Railroad for a 75-minute trip through the redwood forests of the encircling Santa Cruz Mountains. These trains were originally employed to haul logs to mills. Today they haul people while traversing some of the steepest, most crooked grades of any narrow-gauge railroad in North America. The trains stop occasionally, so you can stretch your legs if you wish. You can even disembark, picnic, and be picked up later by the next train coming down the tracks.

The Big Trees Narrow Gauge Railroad runs year-round. The Suntan Special—which makes a stop at Henry Cowell Redwoods State Park as well—is seasonal (usually from May through October). Call 831-335-4400 for schedules.

El Rio San Lorenzo

> "At the distance of two leagues from El Rosario we forded a river considerably swollen; the water reached to the girths of the animals. The descent to the river, and the ascent after we forded it, gave the pioneers much work in clearing and opening a way through a thicket that covered the river bottom . . . We pitched our camp on the right bank of the river, which was named San Lorenzo."
>
> *Miguel Costansó, with the Portolá expedition, 1769*

When Gaspar de Portolá named this river in 1769 it was a lush corridor leading to the bay. Towering maples, willows, alders, laurels, elms, oaks, and redwoods outlined a sinuous path downriver. The canopy of trees cooled the waters of the San Lorenzo, producing an ideal habitat for steelhead and salmon. In the spring the trees filled with nesting songbirds, while shorebirds bathed and fed at the river's wide and fertile mouth.

The river remained much the same for almost two more centuries—despite the fact that during the late 19th century at least three tanneries and one gunpowder factory dumped their waste directly into the San Lorenzo. Additionally, the river's mouth was routinely dammed to accommodate elaborate river festivals and seasonal events: local politicians wanted Santa Cruz to be known as the "Florence of the West." In fact, early tourists were drawn to the river just as much, if not more, than they were to the beach, and it was known as a premier fishing spot well into this century.

As the city of Santa Cruz grew, however, pollution increased, and riverside tree cutting became commonplace. The last two miles of the river—from today's Highway 1 to the bay—slowly changed. After a series of devastating floods in the 1950s, the U.S. Army Corps of

San Lorenzo River

Engineers stepped in, cut down the riparian forest, and channelized the lower stretch of the San Lorenzo. Some locals believe it has looked like a large drainage ditch ever since. It certainly has never been the same.

But now the Corps, along with other government and citizen groups, have reappeared to help restore the river's lower portions. Plans call for massive revegetation of native plants, grasses, and shrubs along the inner bank of the river and on top of the levees. The project, which will take many years to take hold, is going to use the resident steelhead trout as an indicator species: when their population rebounds to a healthy level, that will be one important sign that the river is making a comeback.

Not only will the restoration efforts help local and resident wildlife species, but people will benefit too. Plans call for tree planting, new benches, improved bike paths, and additional access areas along the lower stretch of the San Lorenzo.

But don't wait until the restoration is complete to explore the San Lorenzo. Today, though plans are just beginning to unfold, visitors can enjoy the river fully. From the river's mouth you can follow a paved path for just under two miles atop the western levee; it dead-ends at Highway 1. (There is a trail on the eastern portion also, but it is not complete.) On the way back, you might want to turn off at the train trellis at the river's mouth, either moving west to the boardwalk or crossing the trellis on a bike path and continuing east toward Seabright Beach and beyond. It is a true joy to bike along the levee on a sunny but crisp coastal day. (However, it is presently not recommended to explore the levees after dark.)

If you'd like to find out how to help with the restoration efforts, contact the San Lorenzo River Institute, at 831-426-0156. The institute also maintains a nice website (http://www.cruzio.com/~slriver/pd) for both adults and children.

Santa Cruz Circle Trail

In 1995 Santa Cruz inaugurated the Santa Cruz Circle Trail in a ceremony at Lighthouse Field. The trail is a pedestrian and bike route covering almost 30 miles over public roads and pathways, including some of the city's most popular jogging, in-line skating, cycling, and walking routes. In addition to covering a good length of the shoreline west and east of the San Lorenzo River, it moves inland and takes you through redwood groves, oak woodlands, meadows, and streamside forests. The San Lorenzo River is a great place to begin your

SPORT FISHING

There is more than one way to catch a fish along the Monterey Bay shoreline. The options include ever-popular pier fishing, poke-pole fishing in tidepools (especially useful for eels), shore fishing, and heading out onto the beautiful Pacific in a boat for some trolling or deep sea fishing.

Steelhead trout, salmon, striped bass, and lingcod are the perennial favorites along this section of coast, although halibut, rockfish, and surfperch are in close competition. To go after these fish you need a state fishing license if you are 16 years of age or older (this is also true for the take of any mollusk, invertebrate, amphibian, or crustacean in California). The only exception is if you are angling from one of the numerous public piers: there, no license is required. Licenses remain valid for a full year, although nonresidents and vacationers can purchase licenses good for a single day. They can be obtained just about anywhere along the coast: bait and tackle shops, sporting goods stores, and diving shops. For more information about sport fishing along the shoreline here—or elsewhere in the state—contact the Department of Fish and Game's 24-hour recording, 916-227-2244.

Downtown Santa Cruz near the
Museum of Art and History

explorations of the Circle Trail—which actually consists
of two circles that meet on the pedestrian bridge over the
river. A map and description of the trail, in both words
and pictures, is available on the web at http://www.
ecotopia.org/trail/index.html. Or contact the Santa Cruz
Circle Trail Committee at 831-469-3384 to obtain a nice
little guide (for a modest fee).

DON'T GET GOOSED

From Riverside Avenue
downstream there is
another healthy resi-
dent population of geese.
They are a mixed lot of characters, but all can be rather
aggressive. They've even been
known to chase bike riders.
But don't fear—just pretend
you're another goose when
approaching one of these
trail-blocking gangs: be loud,
wave your arms, and don't
feed them.

Downtown Santa Cruz

The location for downtown Santa Cruz was determined
over 200 years ago by the intrepid Portolá party. What
they were actually claiming when, in 1769, they planted
a cross on the banks of the San Lorenzo River was a site
for a mission, which would follow 22 years later. The
mission's plaza soon became the focal point for conducting business, keeping up with the news, and socializing
along this stretch of coast. When California came under
American influence in the mid-1840s, the city of Santa
Cruz slowly grew up around the old mission as Ameri-
cans and immigrants arrived bringing new skills, interests, and needs.

Today, instead of finding thriving businesses in tallow,
cow hides, lime, and lumber, you will discover a downtown that is thoroughly modern—and completely rebuilt.
After the devastating 1989 Loma Prieta earthquake, Santa

Cruz rebuilt its downtown and surrounding neighborhoods with enthusiasm and imagination. Downtown now
has something for everyone. Not only are there special
late-night shopping hours during part of the week, but
other events include a weekly farmers' market, outdoor
antique fairs, and other events every month of the year.
For more information about downtown Santa Cruz, contact the Downtown Information Center at 831-459-9486,
the Santa Cruz Downtown Association at 831-429-8433,
or search the website of the Santa Cruz County Conference and Visitors Council, http://www.scccvc.org.

Museum of Art and History

A visit to downtown Santa Cruz isn't complete unless you
pause at the Museum of Art and History. Housed in the
McPherson Center for Art and History on Front Street,
the museum has both permanent and changing exhibits.
The historic Octagon Gallery—once the Hall of Records,
built in 1882—is now the museum's bookstore.

The museum strives to interpret local history through
a variety of programs and activities, including educational tours, lectures, and special events. Emphasis is
also placed on art education for all ages. In the art arena,
the museum offers docent-led tours, children's art workshops, films and lectures, and tours of local studios, galleries, and other museums. Call 831-429-1964 for hours,
exhibits, and upcoming events, or search their website,
http://www.infopoint.com/sc/mcpherson/musevent.html.
The museum also manages the Davenport Jail Museum
and Evergreen Cemetery.

Santa Cruz Mission State Historic Park

Mission Santa Cruz was the 12th mission built in the
21-mission system (1769–1823), which stretched from
San Diego north to Sonoma. (There are also earlier, Jesuit
missions in Baja California, with fascinating histories of
their own.)

Originally constructed in 1791, the Mission La
Exaltación de la Santa Cruz was taken apart and moved
upslope away from the San Lorenzo River two years later.
Today, a visit to the park verifies that their second site
was well chosen: not only is there a commanding view of
downtown Santa Cruz and beyond to Monterey Bay, but
the site is also safe from the meandering, flood-prone
river and very defensible.

TUNE IN AND FIND OUT

For traveler information,
turn your car's AM dial
to 1610 (the signal is
clearest around the immediate Santa Cruz area). The
recorded message will give
you directions to the Santa
Cruz County Conference and
Visitors Council, as well as
traffic and weather conditions. If you are arriving by car
via Highway 17, stop at the
summit at the Visitor Center's
satellite office. It is staffed
most of the time, but if it is
closed you will find brochures
and other free materials outside, plus the latest weather
report and events calendar
written on a message board.

EVERGREEN CEMETERY

Cemeteries can be fas-
cinating places to
visit, and Evergreen
is no exception. Located off
Mission Street by Harvey West
Municipal Park, this State
Point of Historical Interest is
one of the earliest Protestant
cemeteries in California, dat-
ing back to 1850. People from
all social, economic, and eth-
nic backgrounds are buried
here—quiet legacies to the eth-
nic diversity in 19th-century
Santa Cruz. The cemetery is
managed by the Museum of
Art and History.

"Chappa," circa 1882: an Indian woman from the Santa Cruz region born in the late 18th century

The original complex consisted, in part, of a church, priests' quarters, mission guard headquarters, and row houses for "new citizens" (that is, converted Indians). In all, 32 buildings were erected. A devastating earthquake in 1857 destroyed the mission (by then in need of serious repair), and thereafter many other buildings fell to ruin. Today, the original mission site is occupied by a Catholic church built in 1889. Across the street, a half-size replica of the mission church was erected in 1931.

The park's museum is in an adobe structure built in 1822 to house the Indians who worked at the mission. Because the mission depended more on livestock than agriculture, many of the Indians became early cowboys. The adobe is the only authentically restored Indian residence in the California mission system chain, as well as the oldest building in Santa Cruz County. Seven rooms have been preserved alongside one another showing how Spaniards, then Indians, then Californios (a mixture of Mexican, Indian, and American), and eventually an Irish family lived in this building. A fascinating cutaway through a portion of the adobe wall shows how consecutive generations of adobe inhabitants improved and modified the structure. You will also find a scale model of the entire mission complex as it looked in the early 1820s.

Future plans for the park include the construction of a historic garden and more outdoor activities. Down the street from the museum building is the Santa Cruz Mission Plaza, a nice place to stretch out on a lawn and rest.

FRIENDS OF SANTA CRUZ STATE PARKS

Friends of Santa Cruz State Parks is a not-for-profit organization dedicated to preserving local state park resources—history, traditions, and natural beauty —for generations to come. By working closely with California State Parks employees, members help to fund and support interpretive activities, teacher and student activities, and recreation. To find out more about their work and about local state parks, give them a call at 831-429-1840.

Soap Plant

It is commonly believed that an area's previous occupants are best studied by digging up artifacts long since buried underground. In the case of the Ohlone, however, you can leave your shovel at home. Instead, look for some ordinary plants—soap plants (*Chlorogalum pomeridianum*), to be specific—to learn something of how the local Indians lived. You see, Ohlones used soap plant— also known as *amole*—for many things, and they may have encouraged its cultivation. Some researchers believe that dense stands of soap plant may indicate previous use of an area by Indians.

The Ohlone had many uses for the soap plant, which typically grows in grassland areas. The Indians used the coarse brown fibers around the palm-sized bulb to make an acorn-processing brush. Crushed bulbs, known to contain compounds that stupefy fish, were thrown into streams so fish could be caught by hand. And as the plant's name indicates, the bulb was also used as soap.

A walk through the remaining adobe of the Santa Cruz mission can be humbling, inspiring, and thought-provoking all at once. The mission, its grounds, and its history are impressive when you consider how the first Europeans survived in this wilderness. Their dedication, innovation, and persistence are motivating, even by today's standards. However, the human toll exacted here—and throughout the mission system—is cause for somber contemplation.

The arrival of the Spanish was the beginning of the end for California's native peoples. The two groups' worldviews, social systems, and cultures were simply too different to be able to prosper side by side. Certainly some native Califor-

nians survived under Spanish rule, but historians now know that the mission way of life, at least for the native peoples, more likely led to malnourishment and early death than to prosperity and longevity.

Within several decades of their arrival in Ohlone territory the Spanish had built seven missions, two forts, and two towns. By 1810, hundreds of Ohlones had been baptized and brought to the Santa Cruz mission, where they lost touch with their native culture, came in contact with European diseases, and died in great numbers. The life expectancy of infant Indians born at the mission was less than three years. Each generation saw a 95 percent drop in its population numbers.

Distrust and revolt were inevitable. In 1793 the mission was attacked and partially

burned by a group of Quiroste tired of being held like slaves. Ironically, it had been the Quiroste, an Año Nuevo group of Ohlones, who so kindly greeted Gaspar de Portolá in 1769 (see Chapter 1).

After local Indian populations had either died off or fled, the Spanish mounted expeditions to capture Yokuts from the distant San Joaquin Valley. Abducted and brought to Santa Cruz, these people eventually fled and joined other Indians who had escaped, learned to ride horses, and become raiders. Spanish soldiers routinely hunted these Indians down, killing the horse thieves and attempting to return whomever was left to the missions. It was a system and mentality on the outskirts of the Spanish Empire that were doomed to failure.

As a bonus, the soap plant produces an elegant stalk with a spray of branchlets tipped with pure white flowers that open from late afternoon into the early evening throughout the late spring and early summer. The brilliant little flowers appear ethereal, as though they are floating in the air.

Pogonip Open Space Preserve

Tucked between the University of California campus and Highway 9 is the 614-acre Pogonip Open Space Preserve. Even though it's several miles away from the shoreline, if you're exploring downtown Santa Cruz or the campus, it is a must-see place.

The origin of Pogonip's name is rather unclear. It could come from an Indian word for icy fog (the term is used by Indians elsewhere in the state, such as the Mono Basin, for that phenomenon). A less serious suggestion is that it is

Harvey West Park is a 50-acre municipal park situated adjacent to the intersection of Highways 1, 9, and 17. This park has something for everyone: hiking trails, swimming pools, six ball fields, a clubhouse you can rent for events, and picnic areas with barbecue pits.

The official mascot of the University of California, Santa Cruz, is a bright yellow, slimy, shell-less mollusk called a banana slug (this is one of those "Only in Santa Cruz" items). You've probably seen these six- to ten-inch creatures lying torpid in redwood forests, or other damp places. When the campus opened in 1965, the banana slug immediately became the unofficial mascot —appropriately enough for a school that did not take athletics quite as seriously as certain other universities. In 1981, however, the powers-that-be decided it was time to settle on an official mascot. You can imagine the uproar that erupted when a sea lion was chosen! After a five-year fight, the students finally prevailed, and the banana slug was picked. (But never, ever try to pick one *up*.) You do wonder, though, how students yell encouragement to their teams . . . "Go slime 'em!"?

The open, welcoming campus of the University of California, Santa Cruz

an acronym for "POlo, GOlf, and take a NIP." Although questionable, this explanation does say something about this land's previous uses. There *was* a short-lived golf course here early in the century, followed by a polo field. And of course, after-event drinking is often associated with both endeavors.

Although the park has endured these uses, as well as extensive logging in the 1850s, it has survived to the present in spectacular shape. Several old-growth stands of redwoods that survived the loggers' axes can be discovered here. But Pogonip is about more than just impressive redwoods: it's a showcase of diversity, a great place to explore the various habitats of these coastal hills. You can stroll through open grasslands (watch the edges for coyotes or bobcats in the morning and evening), hike within cool forests, ford creeks, and scratch your way through chaparral. Enter the preserve from the university or off Highway 9 (known as River Street near Santa Cruz).

Note: The railroad tracks cutting through the preserve are used regularly by trains. Don't use them as a trail.

University of California, Santa Cruz

Even if you're not into academics, the University of California's campus in Santa Cruz is a spectacular spot for panoramic views, hiking trails, and history. Just one mile up Bay Street from Mission Street you'll come across an information booth that is staffed most of the year. You can pick up a map there that will help you tour the campus, or call ahead and request one from the university's Public Information Office, 831-459-2495.

Santa Cruz County Regional Transportation Commission: 831-460-3200

CalTrans District 05: 805-549-3111

Bike map website: http://www.dot.ca.gov/dist05/planning/bikemap.htm

Santa Cruz Surfing Museum: 831-429-3429

Beach Lifeguard Service Headquarters, Boardwalk Area: 831-429-3747

Santa Cruz Weather and Surf Conditions: 831-429-3460

Santa Cruz Beach Boardwalk: 831-426-7433

Website: http://www.beachboardwalk.com

Santa Cruz Metropolitan Transit District: 831-425-8600 Website: http://www.scmtd.com

Santa Cruz Big Trees & Pacific Railway and Roaring Camp Railroad: 831-335-4400

Department of Fish and Game Fish recorded information: 916-227-2244 (24-hour)

The Santa Cruz Circle Trail website: http://www.ecotopia.org

San Lorenzo River Institute: 831-426-0156 Website: http://www.cruzio.com/~slriver/pd

Downtown Information Center: 831-459-9486

Santa Cruz Downtown Association: 831-429-8433

Santa Cruz County Conference and Visitors' Council: 831-425-1234

Museum of Art and History, and Evergreen Cemetery: 831-429-1964

Santa Cruz Mission State Historic Park: 831-425-5849

Friends of Santa Cruz State Parks: 831-429-1840

University of California Santa Cruz Information: 831-459-2495

California State Parks, Santa Cruz District Office: 831-429-2850

To reach the western end of West Cliff Drive from Natural Bridges State Beach, stick to the coast. From Highway 1, take Western Drive toward the ocean. Turn right on Mission Street, then left on Natural Bridges Drive (toward the ocean). Natural Bridges T's into Delaware; go left, then right on Swanton Boulevard. Continue to West Cliff.

From West Cliff Drive, you can head down the coast to the San Lorenzo River and downtown Santa Cruz. To find downtown, take Front Street and move inland until either Soquel Avenue or River Street. The Santa Cruz Mission is a nice walk from downtown (uphill) on School Street, off of Water Street.

To reach the university, turn inland onto Bay Street from Mission Street; Bay becomes Glenn Coolidge Drive on the campus. Pogonip preserve can be found off Coolidge (it is well signed) or at the end of Golf Club Drive off Highway 9 (River Street becomes Highway 9). Harvey West Park and the Evergreen Cemetery are next to each other off of Coral Street (reached via Highway 9).

One of the first things you'll notice at the entrance kiosk is a set of historic lime kilns and a blacksmith shop off the left side of the road. This 2,000-acre campus was once part of the sprawling Cowell Ranch (see page 70). In 1965 the University of California opened the first college on the campus, Cowell College. Today, a total of eight colleges (minicampuses within the larger campus) make up UC Santa Cruz.

From the neighborhood of Seabright, East Cliff Drive meanders to, and around, Soquel Point (with a break at the harbor), then gets a new name at 41st Avenue—Opal Cliff Drive—en route to downtown Capitola. It's a great bike route, and a nice drive.

The campus has some 25 miles of trails, all of which are open to the public. Take a drive—or better yet, walk or bike—up and around Glen Coolidge Drive (Pogonip Open Space will be on your right, to the east), cut over to Hagar Drive, then mosey back toward the entrance kiosk. If it is a clear day, you'll want to stop and take in the view from Hagar: it's stupendous. You can see across the entire bay, and in the right light the Monterey Peninsula appears close enough to touch.

Seabright to Moran Lake Beach

This section of the Santa Cruz coast is definitely less hectic than the colorful cavalcade of humanity along West Cliff Drive and the Boardwalk area. You'll find yourself moving through some older neighborhoods to access the beautiful beaches here. Throughout, historic Victorian houses rub shoulders with eclectic bungalows. At the Santa Cruz Harbor you can sit and watch the boats—everything from yachts to commercial trollers—or stroll down the beach. Farther along, a series of embayments add a bit of contour to the shoreline while creating habitats different from the nearby sandy beaches.

Pueblo de Branciforte

In the upland neighborhood of Seabright, even the trained eye would have difficulty telling that much of this area was once a Spanish town. Branciforte was one of three pueblos—civilian towns —organized in California by the Spanish in the late 18th century. (The other two were Los Angeles and San Jose.) Although it never became the frontier fortress it was envisioned as— insufficient provisions, lack of discipline, and external historical events changed those plans —Branciforte, it is believed, played a vital, if brief, role fostering Mexico's independence from Spain in the early 19th century.

If you'd like to find out more about Branciforte, visit the Santa Cruz Art and History

Seabright Beach and sailboats

Museum. You can also venture to the Branciforte Elementary School, at the corner of North Branciforte Avenue and Water Street, where you will find an informative historical marker in front.

De Laveaga Park

Although it might seem a bit far from the shore, if you want to check out one of the largest city parks around—some 565 acres—move inland on Branciforte Avenue, pass over Highway 1, and you'll enter De Laveaga Park. The Mexican-born José Vincente De Laveaga, a successful San Francisco businessman, built a vacation hacienda on this land in the 1880s. The property, willed to the city of Santa Cruz by Mr. De Laveaga, became a park in 1900.

Seabright State Beach

When East Cliff Drive reaches the coast, after following the San Lorenzo River, it veers downcoast toward Alhambra and Pilkington Avenues. Where it veers there is a nice parking area. From here, you can access a neat little walkway that goes out to a sliver of land called San Lorenzo Point. From the tip of the point you can look west to the boardwalk, the wharf, and out to Steamer Lane, or east down Seabright State Beach, which lines out for a couple of miles. The main entrance to the beach, just beyond the Natural History Museum, has a place to lock bikes. For a long time this beach was called Castle Beach after the castlelike Scholl Mar Hotel, which graced the shore here until the bluff was undercut so heavily that the building fell into the sea.

Continuing past the entrance to the beach, East Cliff Drive moves up a slight rise to Seabright Avenue (one-way moving inland). Walk down Seabright toward the water to continue on East Cliff—or drive to 1st Avenue (one block further) and park—to discover a great public walkway and a collection of nice gardens nestled in between the last row of houses fronting the avenues and the shoreline bluff. (East Cliff Drive becomes a series of disconnected blocks here, not open to vehicular traffic.) The walkway only lasts four blocks (from 1st to 4th Avenue), but it makes for a good little stroll (no bikes: the walkway is very narrow). You can see how much the bluff has been eroded here, and you'll immediately understand why the "castle" didn't last too long perched as it was over the water.

The Santa Cruz Natural History Museum is a wonderful place to visit, on your own or with your family. Tucked away in a quiet neighborhood, it is housed in the old Seabright Branch Library (look for the open book stonework above the front entrance). The museum is packed with great exhibits interpreting local cultural and natural history. The Ohlone people are featured in one exhibit, and there is an impressive collection of pre-mission-era artifacts. You'll also find information on fossils (be sure to check out the sea cow fossil), minerals, archeology, local fauna, chaparral flora, and geology. The museum also maintains a tidepool touch tank—popular with kids of all ages—and a seashell collection. Outdoors, the grounds make for a nice place to picnic or stretch out on the lawn. There is also a life-size sculpture of a California gray whale, perfect for climbing on. For information about museum hours and special programs, call 831-429-3773, or visit the city's website, http://santacruz parksandrec.com.

Santa Cruz Small Craft Harbor

The Santa Cruz Small Craft Harbor (or as locals call it, "the yacht harbor") was built in 1964 on the site of Woods Lagoon and extending back into Arana Gulch. Hundreds of boats of all kinds call this harbor home. It is easy to explore because there is a trail all the way around it with fantastic interpretive signs explaining nautical terms, the different types of boats you are looking at, and local wildlife.

Pick up the trail in Mariner Park, on the west side of the harbor. Or you can walk out to the west jetty and watch the boats come and go. The east side of the trail has some picnic benches for folks interested in observing the hustle and bustle of a working harbor. Throughout, monumental staircases bring people to and from the neighboring streets overlooking the harbor.

The harbor master's office and commercial buildings are on the east side of the harbor, by 5th Avenue and East Cliff. Restaurants, stores, more interpretive signs, and the offices of Save Our Shores can be found next to the large parking area. You can climb out on the other jetty here as well, across large cement chunks of rip-rap that look like enormous jacks. In front of the commercial area, en route to the southern jetty, there is a nice strip of beach with a well-maintained volleyball court.

Twin Lakes State Beach and Lake

Around the corner from the harbor is Twin Lakes State Beach. The beach here—touted as one of the area's warmer strips of sand—is a continuation of the beach you can access in front of the harbor's business area.

Twin Lakes State Beach

HOW, AND WHY, DO SHOREBIRDS BATHE?

Just imagine being a bird living on or next to the ocean, eating meals in the surf zone or diving head first into the water to grab your dinner. You're in and out of the saltwater all day, from before sunup to after sundown. Wouldn't you be a huge cake of salt after a few days? Of course! That's why seabirds and shorebirds need to take baths in fresh and brackish water—to rinse all that salt out of their feathers. Any place you have freshwater running into the ocean, you'll find coastal birds rinsing their plumage.

But then, why do some coastal birds bathe in the ocean? One reason may be that, whether the water is salty or fresh, splashing about—and the ritual of preening afterward—is critical for maintaining the condition of feathers, it keeps itching to a minimum, and it helps remove parasites. When a seabird needs to remove salt buildup in its feathers, it will specifically seek out freshwater.

Parking here is rather scarce, so you might want to park back on 7th Avenue and walk down, or simply amble down from the harbor jetty.

Originally, Woods Lagoon and Schwan Lake—situated on the inland side of East Cliff Drive—constituted the two "lakes" of Twin Lakes. Today, of course, Woods Lagoon has been taken over by the yacht harbor. And Schwan Lake, once brackish and open to tidal action, is now a freshwater lake, with saltwater inflow regulated by a tide gate next to the road. Its diverse vegetation, however—everything from cattails to oak trees and eucalyptus—and its proximity to the beach still make it a valuable resting, feeding, and bathing spot for both waterfowl and land birds.

Gulls, for example, can be seen bathing in the lake, then lifting up and over the road to congregate on the beach. You can also scope out numerous resident and migratory songbirds, watch the acrobatics of several species of swallows as they skim above the lake's surface gathering insects, or marvel at the precision of a belted

Schwan Lake and geese

Santa Cruz Natural History
Museum: 831-429-3773

Santa Cruz Small Craft
Harbor: 831-475-6161

Save Our Shores:
831-462-5660

kingfisher's fish-catching dive. Around the parking lot area, a less impressive, but nonetheless entertaining, mixed flock of geese watch the traffic and provide a continuous banter of commentary to pedestrians. The lake's various habitats also shelter many mammals, amphibians, and reptiles, so keep your eyes open. State Parks plans to develop access off 17th Avenue to the interior land portion of Schwan Lake in the near future.

Avenue Accesses: Bonita Lagoon and Lincoln Beach

Between Schwan Lake and the beach at Sunny Cove you will find several small access points at the end of the avenues. Twelfth, 13th, and 14th Avenues all have stairs down to the beach, but parking is very limited because these are residential areas. Please respect residents' driveways and signs. Between 13th and 14th Avenues, on the beach, is Bonita Lagoon, a small freshwater body frequented by waterfowl and other birds. The beach fronting the lagoon is Lincoln Beach. This stretch is collectively labeled by Santa Cruz County as the Live Oak Beaches.

Sunny Cove Beach

Sunny Cove Beach is aptly named. Because the sand extends inland a bit and is sheltered by higher land on either side, this place can really warm up on a clear day. Weekends find the cove packed with sun lovers, volleyball players, and body surfers. At low tide, a walk up the beach (west) toward the tip of land called Black Point can be interesting. Some rocky areas make for good exploration of intertidal life.

Sunny Cove Beach

Avenue Accesses and Corcoran Lagoon

Another set of access points can be found between Sunny Cove and Corcoran Lagoon, at 20th and 21st Avenues where they dead-end at the shore. Again, parking is tight, so use common sense and courtesy.

Corcoran Lagoon, situated between 21st and 23d Avenues, is the catchment basin for Rodeo Creek (once much larger and more lush), which originates in the coastal hills. Named after a family of early settlers in the adjacent neighborhood, this body of water has an ever-changing salt concentration. Because it can hold fresh, brackish, and salty water all at once (depending on the season and the tides), it nourishes an interesting mix of animal and plant species. For example, you can find both saltwater mussels and western pond turtles here. There is no parking at the lagoon; to reach the beach here you must park elsewhere and walk in.

26th Avenue Park

This park consists of a set of stairs leading to the beach. From here you can stroll all the way to Moran Lake Beach, or turn back upcoast toward Sunny Cove Beach.

Moran Lake Beach and Park

Moran Lake is another small body of water just back from a wide sandy beach. A bike path works up the east side of the lake, then drops you back on East Cliff Drive by Chesterfield. A maintained dirt path runs up the west side of the waterway for about half of a mile before ending in a grove of eucalyptus. You will find parking here, bathrooms (wheelchair accessible), and picnic tables. The

SAVE OUR SHORES

Save Our Shores, a not-for-profit organization dedicated to preserving the coastal and marine environment of the Monterey Bay National Marine Sanctuary, has an office in the harbor's business area. This organization works on a wide range of issues along the coast, coordinating volunteers for environmental projects and education and attempting to find creative solutions to coastal issues in cooperation with businesses, government agencies, and the public. To find out more about their work, and the marine sanctuary, stop by their offices at the harbor, or call 831-462-5660.

GETTING AROUND

Except for a break in the Seabright neighborhood and the harbor area, you can stay on East Cliff Drive all the way to Moran Lake. At Moran Lake, move onto Lake Avenue to swing around and hook back up with East Cliff. East Cliff is discontinuous by the bluffside walkway in the Seabright neighborhood, so to venture ahead to the harbor, use Atlantic Avenue. It will take you right down into Mariner Park on the west side of the harbor. After you work along Murray and Eaton Streets, East Cliff picks back up on the east side of the harbor. As you move down the coast, be sure to turn off of East Cliff (by Sunny Cove, near 16th Avenue) before it becomes Portolá Drive; by doing so you'll stay closer to the shore. Sunny Cove Beach is accessible off East Cliff from Johans Beach Drive, Geoffroy Drive (off 16th Avenue), and Sunny Cove Drive.

lake's eucalyptus groves are nice retreats on hot, windless days. Although the lake has occasional problems with inadequate circulation and flushing, it's an interesting place to explore, and it's home to monarchs during the winter months.

Soquel Point, Capitola, and Beyond

The section of coast from Soquel Point to Soquel Creek and downtown Capitola is configured like the stretch of shoreline from Lighthouse Point to the San Lorenzo River. Because of this geographic similarity, it is a great spot for surfing, and it has much the same feel as West Cliff Drive but is not as crowded. There are no large state, county, or city beaches here, but keep your eyes open and you'll find plenty of small gems along the bluff-dominated shore. Capitola is a nice little community with a beautiful beach. It is also the side door to New Brighton State Beach and great camping.

Soquel Point and Rockview County Park

If you follow Rockview Drive or Pleasure Point Road off of East Cliff you will discover a small park called Rockview. Frequented by locals and surfers, the shore is basi-

Capitola's colorful beach and wharf during the annual sand sculpture contest

cally rip-rap and rocks, with great wave action offshore. The main entrance to the shore here is at the terminus of Rockview, but if you look carefully along the shoreward side of Pleasure Point you'll notice a little path between two houses. Follow it down, and hang out with the surfers.

Pleasure Point Parkway and Beyond

Between 32d and 41st Avenues you'll find a handful of small parks and staircases along this bluff-dominated portion of shore. Severe erosion over the years has been eating away at some of these areas—like that around narrow Paradise Park—but there are still plenty of benches and overlooks for ocean viewing.

There is a set of tables and benches in a triangular park at the corner of East Cliff and 32d, several staircases at the foot of 35th and 38th Avenues, and a larger park at 41st where East Cliff becomes Opal Cliff. You won't find any wide sandy beaches here. In fact, the staircases lead down to a rocky shore popular chiefly with surfers. Only at low tide can you sit on a sliver of sand, or you might take the opportunity to do some tidepool exploration. All along the bluffs, the views of the bay are spectacular.

The 41st Avenue Park is great for views out to the bay and back toward Capitola. It is also a favorite with surfers because you can work down the bluff here via a set of stairs and dive into some prime surfing waves. Moving toward Capitola, now on Opal Cliff Drive, you'll see another beach access near the intersection with Court. This access, the Opal Cliff Recreation District Public Access Park and Beach, charges a fee for entrance (it's owned by the local homeowners) and it's behind a very tall locked gate.

Capitola might seem like the quiet little sister city to big ol' Santa Cruz, but in fact Capitola was one of the first seaside resorts in the young state of California. In 1869 a vacation spot, known as Camp Capitola, was established here along the banks of Soquel Creek by lumberman Frederick Hihn. The town of Capitola grew up around the resort and, in 1949, was incorporated with some 2,000 residents.

Although the population of Capitola has grown a bit since its incorporation, the feel of the town has stayed much the same. This is small-town California. You can walk all of downtown in the time it would take you to polish off a coffee-to-go. But Capitola isn't all quaint houses and quiet seaside living. This town knows how to entertain and celebrate. Scattered along the seafront and

Tidewater gobies *(Eucyclogobius newberri)* are unique little fish of California's coastal lagoons and estuaries. Measuring only two to two and a half inches long, tidewater gobies prefer brackish waters in the upper portions of lagoons where freshwater inflows keep salinity down. Here at Soquel Creek they are found upstream where the tidal influence keeps the freshwater salty enough for their liking.

Gobies seek out clean sandy bottoms where the male digs a vertical nest-burrow about one foot straight down. Females then fight among themselves for the mating rights with the male. Once eggs are deposited in the burrows, the male guards them until they hatch. In these areas the gobies also seek out their favorite prey: small shrimp and other crustaceans, and midge fly larvae.

Because their preferred habitat coincides with heavily populated and well-used portions of the coast, this species is officially listed as endangered by the federal government. Threats to gobies include freshwater diversions, habitat disruption due to dredging and sand removal, and the introduction of predatory bass.

Capitola's annual Begonia
Festival on Soquel Creek

through downtown are numerous restaurants, specialty stores, and galleries. The city's well-maintained beachside park has bathrooms, showers, benches, and information-packed interpretive signs.

Every year the town's calendar is crammed with events. The famous Begonia Festival, held each September, features boat races, aquatic shows, and a parade of begonia-covered floats on Soquel Creek. There are also sidewalk fairs, the Art and Wine Festival, kite flying contests, and assorted beach events. Volleyball nets are on the beach all summer. For more information about Capitola and scheduled events, call the Chamber of Commerce at 831-475-6522.

If you are visiting on a weekend and the crowds are thick, walk up Cliff Drive to the parking turnout above town and check out the view. All of Capitola is spread out before you, and you can enjoy a gull's-eye view of this portion of the bay. The first turnout you come to before the parking lot also has a set of stairs that wind down to the beach, so you can return to town via the strand.

Before moving on along the coast, be sure to look for the historic "Six Sisters": six Victorian houses set along the Esplanade behind Capitola Beach. The old railroad station (most recently an inn) can be viewed at the corner of Monterey Avenue and Escalona Drive.

Soquel Creek

Soquel Creek is a perennial stream—a small river, really —that has retained much of its luxuriant streamside vegetation. In fact, it is one of the best examples of streamside flora on this section of coast, despite the fact that the surrounding area has been steadily occupied for more than a century. Willows, black cottonwoods, bigleaf maples, redwoods, and scores of bushes and shrubs make for a cool outing if you explore the streamside trail that winds through the neighborhood. The creek also supports steelhead trout and a wide variety of other native wildlife.

Start your visit with the creek just upstream from the bridge next to downtown. Look upriver, where little summer cabins line the banks and the steel railroad bridge arches overhead, and you are sent back in time. There are nice interpretive signs on both sides of the creek. The west side of the creek has a short footpath that ends at a bench.

On the east side of the creek (the bank closest to downtown), a narrow pathway passes in front of some historic buildings and cottages, continuing for about three blocks. If you shift over to Riverview Avenue and keep going up that road, you'll reach the intersection with Center Street in less than one mile. There you will find a bicycle and pedestrian access trail and bridge across the creek to Wharf Road. The little park by the bridge is called Peery Park. Stop on the bridge and take in the cool midstream view some 50 feet above Soquel Creek—the upper reaches of oaks, buckeyes, willows, and bays will fill your view. Once on Wharf Road, double back and meander down toward the shore. The entire circuit makes for about a two-mile trek.

Capitola Wharf

A wharf has graced this coastal site since the late 1850s. And mirroring the region's history, the Capitola Wharf has had many different looks and functions. Not surprisingly, it began as a commercial pier to load lumber and farm goods from Soquel Valley onto ships headed to San Francisco. When the railroad arrived several decades later, taking business away from the wharf, it began to cater to the increasing number of summer residents and tourists attracted to Capitola. Today, the wharf has interpretive signs describing the Monterey Bay National Marine Sanctuary, snack stands, observation areas, supplies for fishing, and restrooms.

Fronting the wharf and Capitola Beach is a unique-looking set of stucco structures. Collectively they are called the Venetian Court, a 1920s-era set of buildings still in use and nicely maintained. The public beach on the other side of the wharf, toward Santa Cruz, is called Hooper Beach.

Capitola Community Center

Just inland from the shore is the Capitola Community Center. It has a nice large lawn, so you might want to stop by here to throw some frisbee or take a rest. There is a great community garden here, restrooms, tennis courts, kids' playground, and a soccer field.

A GANG OF GULLS

At least nine species of gulls can commonly be found at Capitola Beach and along the greater Monterey Bay shoreline. A total of 16 gull species have been recorded along California's central coast. Each species has unique plumage, characteristics, and behaviors.

Gulls seem to be everywhere along the shore. You can't miss them soaring overhead, resting on old pier pilings, scavenging around garbage cans, creeping up on an unattended beach picnic, or harassing other birds for their food.

With a few minor exceptions, gulls are supreme scavengers—kind of like small, dressed-up versions of turkey vultures. And just as do turkey vultures, gulls help clean up our environment. Gulls chow down on human garbage, dead fish, and marine mammal carcasses that wash up on shore. They also eat live prey—everything from fish and crabs to worms and rodents. Several species have even perfected

the art of dropping mollusks from on high to crack their shells and expose the hapless critter within. Unlike other aquatic birds, gulls can eat in any position—flying, swimming, swooping, or walking.

For basic gull identification it's best to concentrate on adult birds, because young gulls take two to four years to mature, changing plumage, bill, and leg color the entire while. Here are some of the most common gulls along the Monterey Bay shoreline.

MONTEREY BAY AQUARIUM

Western gull

■ Western gull
(Larus occidentalis)

This year-round resident is one of the largest gulls on the shore, measuring some 27 inches from bill to tail, and it's the only gull that nests locally. You'll see it walking up

and down beaches and in great flocks near garbage dumps. The adult has a white head, yellow eyes, a yellow bill with a red dot on the lower mandible near the tip, a dark back and wings with white spots at the ends, and pink legs and feet. Western gulls nest on the ground and can be viewed during late spring and early summer building their nests and raising young on offshore rocks. In a good year, some 30,000 western gulls have been recorded nesting on the Farallon Islands due west of the Golden Gate.

■ California gull
(Larus californicus)

Another permanent resident (though there are fewer in summer, when they are nesting inland), the California gull looks like a slightly smaller version of the western gull, except that it has dark eyes, the wings are lighter gray, and the legs and feet are greenish. It ranges throughout the interior of the western United States and Canada, nesting on islands in freshwater, alkaline, and salt lakes, such as Mono Lake on the

Depot Hill Loop

For an exceptional twilight or early evening walk, try the one-mile-plus Depot Hill loop. As you move up Monterey Avenue past the Capitola Theater, you'll see Depot Hill looming above you on the right (to the east). Where Monterey levels off before Park Avenue, two small roads from the Depot Hill neighborhood merge into Monterey. Go right onto Escalona Drive, and step back in time.

The first hint that you are going to be wandering past some historic buildings is right on the corner, in the form of the beautifully restored Southern Pacific Depot, which

California gulls, seen here at Mono Lake

eastern slope of the Sierra Nevada.

■ Bonaparte's gull
(Larus philadelphia)

A very small gull, measuring about 14 inches, the Bonaparte's has a distinctive black bill and red-pink legs and feet. Its head, all black in summer (when it is rarely seen here), is white with conspicuous black dots behind each eye the rest of the year. When present, these birds can be found resting on beaches in flocks.

■ Glaucous-winged gull
(Larus glaucescens)

This gull is abundant around harbors, particularly during the wintertime (it nests in the Pacific Northwest). It is one of the lighter-colored gull species, with light gray wings and dark spots on the wingtips. It has dark eyes, an orange spot on its lower beak, and its legs and feet are pink.

■ Ring-billed gull
(Larus delawarensis)

This is one of the smaller gulls along the shore, measuring about 18 inches from bill to tail. It is most common in the winter months. Its yellow bill has a black ring around its tip, and it has yellow legs and feet.

■ Heermann's gull
(Larus heermanni)

Next to the Bonaparte's, this gull is one of the easiest to identify because the adults have white heads, red bills, dark gray bodies, and black legs and feet. It can bee seen along Monterey Bay during the summer and fall. Unlike most visiting gull species, which nest to the north or inland, the Heermann's nests to the south, off Baja California and in the Sea of Cortez.

■ Mew gull
(Larus canus)

This gull is another winter visitor from nesting grounds in Alaska and northern Canada. Its name comes from its call, which sounds like a low mewing (unlike the raucous calls of the larger gulls). The mew gull is a small bird, only 16 inches long; the adult has a white head, short and plain yellow bill, white spots on black wingtips, and yellow legs and feet.

Heermann's gull

gives this neighborhood its name. It is now privately owned (currently serving as an inn), but that won't prevent you from admiring it.

Continue along Escalona to Hollister Avenue. At the end of Hollister, a narrow public path begins and moves along the bluff back toward town, in front of a row of houses. (Remember, you're in a neighborhood; if you've driven to this spot, please respect parking regulations.) Look on the other side of the railing and you'll see evidence that the cliff here once extended farther out, seaward. Chunks of pavement and brickwork dangle from the lip of the bluff. Now, ignore the dangling rip-rap, and take in the spectacular view.

At Depot Hill you are only about one mile away from New Brighton State Beach. While moving between Capitola and New Brighton on Park Avenue you'll emerge from a large eucalyptus forest, and suddenly the entire southeastern coast will spread out before you. Stop for a moment, view the scene, and contemplate the miles of shoreline you have yet to explore.

The path continues for three beautiful blocks. There are benches throughout, and the private gardens are well maintained. The path leads to Grand Avenue, overlooking Capitola. You can follow Grand around to a series of short streets—Cliff Way, Fairview, and Central—and return to the depot (the end of the one-mile loop). Or take the stairs and drop down about three stories to the Capitola Theater. There is another set of stairs at Cliff and Fairview, by the diminutive Hihn Park, named after the founder of Camp Capitola. Throughout Depot Hill, keep your eyes peeled for historic homes, many of which have historic plaques (especially along Grand looking over downtown).

New Brighton State Beach

New Brighton State Beach has a little bit of everything: forested picnic areas, camping sites, coastal bluffs, trails, and, of course, a beach. All this, and it's only a mile or so from downtown Capitola.

There are 112 campsites in this 68-acre park, all spread out across the wooded bluff overlooking the beach. The campsites closest to the bluff's edge even have ready access to showers in the bathrooms. The forest here consists of Monterey pines and healthy stands of eucalyptus. To reach the beach, follow the well-signed trails downslope. During the winter months massive amounts of driftwood pile up along the beach; by summertime what remains has usually been engineered into sun and wind shelters and miniature forts.

Sunrise at New Brighton State Beach, looking southeast toward Seacliff State Beach

Raccoons

Of all our native mammals, the raccoon (*Procyon lotor*) has adapted to living around and with humans more vigorously—and more ingeniously—than any of their ilk. With their black facial masks and thick ringed tails, raccoons are often seen around creeks, wetlands, and human habitations, including storm drains. Raccoons are omnivorous: they'll eat anything, from garbage-can leftovers to fast-moving crayfish. The name raccoon comes from the Algonquian Indian language, and it means "he who scratches with his hands." Watch a raccoon foraging or feeding, and you'll see why. Their long-fingered front paws probe every nook and cranny where edible morsels might be hiding. They turn their food over in their sensitive paws, then, if water is nearby, clean it by dipping it repeatedly.

In the spring, mother raccoons give birth to litters ranging from four to seven young. Within a month or so the young can be seen out and about with mom learning raccoon tricks. These animals are very vocal, and mothers chatter constantly to keep their children in line (a nocturnal shoreline noise you might hear from your tent). During the mating season, or when they are fighting, raccoons may growl and snarl very loudly.

Although raccoons move about mostly at night, they can also be seen in the early morning hours and just after sunset. Adults weigh up to 35 pounds, about as much as a medium-sized dog. They might look cute, but they are wild animals with formidable teeth: don't encourage them around your campground or picnic table.

Raccoon, a common campsite visitor along the shore

China Camp

Chinese immigrants during the 19th century were an incredible lot. Throughout the Americas, Chinese arrived by sea—either in their own hand-built boats or as passengers—to start a new life in a land culturally and linguistically very different from their own. Go to a port city anywhere in the Americas, from Buenos Aires to Vancouver, and you'll find the descendants of these 19th-century Chinese voyagers.

INFORMATION

Capitola Museum:
831-464-0322

Boat and Bait, for Capitola Wharf fishing and weather reports (business hours only): 831-462-2208

Capitola Chamber of Commerce: 831-475-6522

New Brighton State Park:
831-464-6330

Santa Cruz Mountains Wine Growers Association: 831-479-9463

Websites: http://wines.com/
santa_cruz_mountains/
schome.html; http://
webwinery.com/scmwa

SAND DOLLARS

DAVID WROBEL / MONTEREY BAY AQUARIUM

Sand dollars

You might not consider wave-wrought sand dollars *(Dendraster excentricus)* as living creatures, but they are . . . or at least, they once were. The typical sand dollar collected by the beachcomber and placed on the mantel at home, or tossed like a miniature natural frisbee back into the waves, appears to be composed of pressed sand or weathered bone. That object is actually the "shell" of the once-living animal.

Live sand dollars look very different, for they are covered with a thin purple, red, brown, or gray fuzz. That coating is actually tightly packed short spines, which typically are scraped off when the sand dollar dies, is tumbled in the waves, and washes on shore.

Sand dollars live upright, half buried in the sand just beyond the surf zone. They form dense beds paralleling the beach, with possibly hundreds of sand dollars thriving in a square yard of sand. During calm weather, most of the bed can be exposed. From this position they feed on plankton and other small organic material in the water or on the sand. During stormy weather, they dig in.

Though not appetizing to humans, sand dollars are tasty treats for predacious sea stars and fish such as the starry flounder. Other creatures can also be found where sand dollars congregate—cancer crabs, wolf eels, and olive snails, to name but a few. The next time you find a bleached-out sand dollar on the beach, look seaward, just beyond the waves, and imagine an undulating bed of fuzzy purple disks dancing lightly on the sand as they filter the water for a meal.

Where the beach at New Brighton ends at the soaring bluffs, Chinese fishermen and their families once maintained an active fishing village, known as China Camp.

Turn-of-the-century China Camp near today's city of Capitola

SPECIAL COLLECTIONS, UNIVERSITY LIBRARY, UC SANTA CRUZ

If you've studied California history, of course, you'll know that China Camps abound in this state. The name, though ubiquitous, was nevertheless descriptive. Most of the Chinese immigrants to our part of the coast, moreover, were from a single region: coastal Canton (Guangdong), near Hong Kong.

Beginning in 1882, California exclusion laws

From Soquel Point (just beyond Moran Lake), you can stay on East Cliff Drive until 41st Avenue. However, between 32nd and 41st, East Cliff is one-way downcoast (i.e., to the northeast, or away from Santa Cruz). At 41st, take Opal Cliff Drive and continue all the way to downtown Capitola. The Capitola Community Center is just off 47th Avenue and Jade Street. Depot Hill can be explored by leaving downtown Capitola on Monterey Avenue and turning right on Escalona by the old Southern Pacific depot. To reach New Brighton State Beach, turn off of Monterey onto Park Avenue and continue until the frontage road (McGregor Drive) just before Highway 1; turn right on McGregor and you'll see the signs for New Brighton almost immediately.

attempted to put a stop to Chinese immigration and to deny Chinese residents the right to become citizens and own property. The Chinese—it seemed to some—were simply too successful. Unfortunately, the laws were effective. By the early 1900s restrictive legislation and outright hatred had brought an end to many Chinese fishing villages throughout the state. Although some Chinese returned to their native land, others stayed—and endured.

Cabrillo College

Cabrillo College, named for the 16th-century navigator Juan Rodriguez Cabrillo, is a two-year community college spread out across some 125 acres on the other side of Highway 1 from New Brighton. In addition to offering a wide range of classes for students, it hosts the local farmers' market every Saturday, as well as numerous other civic events. The college's tennis courts and track are open to the public. A bike path runs through the middle of the campus on Soquel Drive..

Wine Growers in Santa Cruz County

Premium wines have flowed from Santa Cruz County since the late 1800s. Today, some 40 small, family-owned wineries can be found nestled throughout the Santa Cruz Mountains. The region's winegrowers association sponsors several events throughout the year—providing the perfect excuse for a weekend of shoreline exploration. Contact them at 831-479-9463 for more information, or go to one of these websites: http://wines.com/santa_cruz_mountains/schome.html or http://webwinery.com/scmwa.

RED-SHOULDERED HAWK

Red-shouldered hawks *(Buteo lineatus)* spend a lot of time calling frantically as they fly above the treetops at New Brighton. When not making a commotion overhead, they perch quietly scanning for prey: rodents, small birds, even insects. Red-shoulders are much smaller than the more common red-tailed hawk. And when they are both talkative, there is no confusing the two. Red-tails let out a single high, faint scream; red-shoulders emit a series of high-pitched, irritated squeals.

Red-shouldered hawks also have a distinctive look: a beautiful, deep rust-colored front, black wings with white spots, and very visible black and white tail bars.

3

Seacliff State Beach to Moss Landing State Beach

If you love miles and miles of beaches, then this portion of the Monterey Bay shoreline is for you. Unlike the coast around the city of Santa Cruz, where you are almost always within sight of the shore, here the roadway is slightly inland and you must turn toward the sea to reach the shoreline. It is estimated that more than six million people visit these shoreline parks and beaches every year. That might sound like a recipe for crowds, but don't worry. Even if you seek out one of these spots on a hot summer weekend, all you have to do is walk a short distance from the stairway access or the parking lot, and the crowds quickly diminish. During the winter months it's common to have entire beaches all to yourself.

Consider a longer walk—a *much* longer walk—and you can hike from Seacliff State Beach (due south of New Brighton State Beach) all the way to Moss Landing State Beach, a distance of some 15 miles. Pack along some gear, and you can camp at several state parks along the way. Amazing! There are not many places in the United States where the public has such complete access to the shoreline. Your biggest challenge would be fording the Pajaro River into Monterey County, something recommended only during periods of low river water.

Seacliff State Beach to Manresa State Beach

Between Seacliff and Manresa, beach aficionados can find countless opportunities for exploration, swimming, and relaxation. No matter which beach you stop at, you are never more than a few minutes away from a small downtown and all its amenities: the towns of Aptos, Rio Del Mar, Seascape, and La Selva Beach are all close by. Only as you approach Manresa State Beach does the landscape become increasingly open and agricultural.

Seacliff State Beach

Seacliff State Beach is fully equipped. Not only does it have a beautiful beach, a pier, and an extensive picnic area with covered shelters and barbecue stands, but the

◀ Sunset State Beach

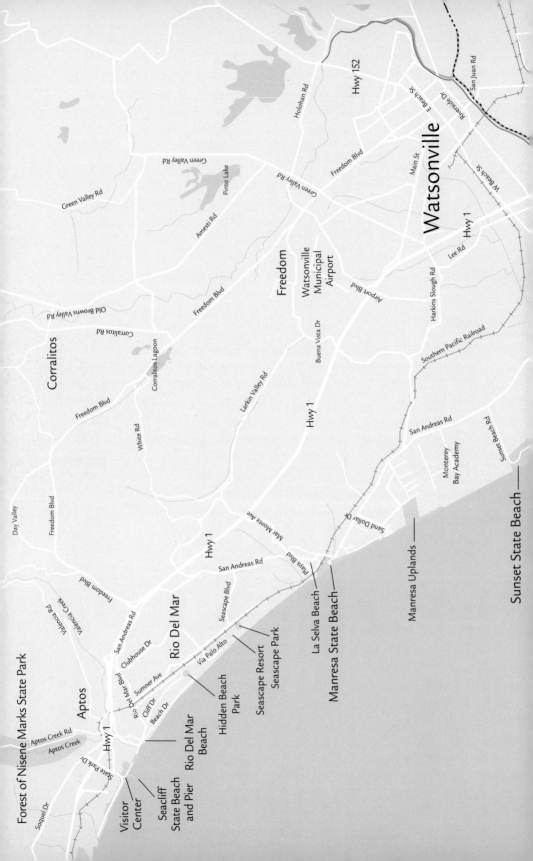

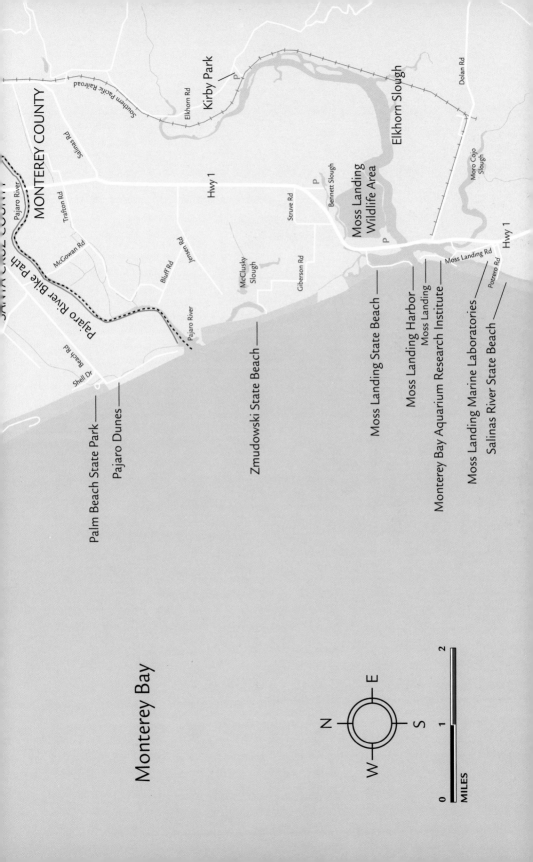

Seacliff State Beach and the *Palo Alto* cement boat

park is also home to one of the nicest little natural history museums on the coast.

As you move down State Park Drive toward the park's entrance kiosk, notice the expansive parking area on the bluff. This is spillover parking for busy days, but it is a nice place to stop and admire the view—of a cement boat from above and the entire bay beyond. You can also walk down the stairs here to the beach below.

After paying your admission fee, meander down the road to the beach. To your right is the RV section of the park, some 26 slots for self-contained vehicles. On a sunny day it's interesting to stroll down the sidewalk in front of these homes-on-wheels, where you might find everything from knickknacks to hot and cold drinks for sale. If you travel with an RV, make reservations well in advance. This park is extremely popular year round.

To your immediate left, at the base of the hill, is the Natural History Museum and Visitor Center, as well as the road leading to the pier and picnic grounds. The compact nature center is a great place to bone up on local history, both human and natural. Detailed information can be found on Chinese fishing camps along the coast here, the history of the *Palo Alto* (the cement boat mentioned above), and a fascinating array of local wildlife—both land and marine species. The large historical photographs are spectacular. The center also maintains a very popular touch tank packed with aquatic species found along the shore.

Beyond the visitor center is the *Palo Alto* and an extensive picnic area. This picnic spot is without rival along the entire Monterey Bay shoreline. If you are hoping to find the most tables, barbecue stands, and sheltered group areas per square foot, look no further. There are also bathrooms and showers here. Just beyond the picnic grounds the road, which soon becomes a pathway, leads over Aptos Creek and on to Rio Del Mar, Rio Del Mar State Beach, and Aptos (just inland).

Cement Boat

That ancient boatlike thing now used as a pier in Seacliff State Beach really is a boat—its name is the *Palo Alto* and it really is made of cement. Because building materials were scarce during World War I, in 1918 the U.S. government ordered that eight ships be built of concrete in an

BY-THE-WIND SAILORS

Have you ever walked down the beach and come across wind-blown rows of small, purplish, plastic-looking things scattered about the beach? They are stranded by-the-wind sailors *(Velella velella)*, fascinating marine animals that are actually a small colony unto themselves. Not only can these relatives of jellyfish lay claim to one of the nicest common names of all marine organisms, but even their scientific name is beautiful.

The feeding habits, life cycle, and reproductive strategy of these two- to three-inch creatures are rather complicated. Basically, the individuals you come across on the beach are actually small colonies of reproductive bodies that have gathered together under a collectively spun raft of intense purple blue, on top of which a transparent sail is attached. In the open ocean—just offshore from this coast—millions of velella come together to sail about and feed on minute marine animals, which they catch with their dangling tentacles.

The velellas' sails allow these unique life forms to roam the open seas, but the

By-the-wind sailor

sails can also be their downfall. Because they drift at the mercy of the winds—think of a fully rigged sailboat without a captain—strong spring storms can beach these creatures by the millions. In fact, if you find one velella on a beach, you're soon likely to find more than you can possibly count.

Oakland shipyard (the feasibility of such a ship was proven earlier by a Norwegian shipbuilder). The war ended before the *Palo Alto* could be commissioned, so it sat in the shipyard for just over a decade before it was purchased by the Cal and Nevada Stock Company. The company towed it to Seacliff, flooded it so the boat would rest on the sand, then converted it into a casino complete with a dance floor, café, and a 50-foot pool. When the company went belly up shortly thereafter, the *Palo Alto* was stripped, and since the late 1930s it has served as a very popular fishing pier. The park's natural history museum contains some entertaining photographs of the *Palo Alto* during its heyday.

Jays

Not all shorebirds come from the sea. Take, for example, the scrub jay *(Aphelocoma coerulescens)*, a resident of Seacliff State Beach and the entire Monterey Bay coast. This rather aggressive bird is a land bird, but it is perfectly at home along the coastal bluffs and beach strand, where it hunts for just about anything.

Although the scrub jay is commonly referred to as a blue jay, there are actually two species of jays in coastal California: the scrub and the Steller's jay *(Cyanocitta stelleri)*. When seen side by side—a common enough occurrence—there can be no mistaking the two. Scrub jays are

Steller's jay

The entire shoreline is serviced
by the Santa Cruz Metropolitan Transit District (Metro).
You can ride buses all the way
from New Brighton State
Beach to downtown Wat-
sonville. In Watsonville you
can link up with Monterey-
Salinas Transit and continue
to Monterey and beyond, or
go to Salinas and catch an
Amtrak train. For bus numbers and schedules, contact
Metro at 831-425-8600, or
visit their website at http://
www.scmtd. com.

light blue over most of their body; their chest can be light
gray, and they often have black markings around the eyes.
Steller's jays are dark blue over their entire body, and they
sport a prominent crest of head feathers. Stellers are commonly seen around campsites but less frequently near
beaches. Both are in the Corvidae family, which also takes
in crows and ravens. Anthropomorphism aside, this is
a family of exceedingly smart—and smart-aleck—birds.

Both jays are true generalists when it comes to food.
They eat everything from insects, to the young of other
birds, to peanuts out of a bag. At campsites along the
coast they know human patterns well, so don't leave any
food unattended, and don't feed them. Nothing can ruin
a picnic or camp dinner as quickly as a gang of wily jays.
It is especially important to keep your eye on the scrub
jays, which are a bit more aggressive than their cousins
the Stellers. Also, keep an ear tuned when the Stellers are
in camp: they are excellent mimickers of other birds, and
their vocal repertoire includes an odd variety of seem-
ingly unnatural sounds as well, ranging from electrical
buzzing to beepers.

Forest of Nisene Marks State Park

The Forest of Nisene Marks State Park is a true treasure
and not very far from the shore. It is also dark and cool
compared to the open shoreline. Deer and banana slugs
roam this landscape instead of sea lions and sand crabs.
Aptos Creek runs through the heart of the park, and
miles of trails crisscross the rugged terrain. If you enjoy
hiking, running, or mountain biking, this is definitely
a park worth visiting.

The entrance kiosk is about one mile in from Soquel
Drive. From the kiosk you have another two miles of
road ahead of you—and one nice bridge—before you
reach a gate and a large parking area at the Porter Picnic
Area (just beyond the Mary Easton Picnic Area). All
along the main road there are well-signed trailheads.

Beyond the gate, you can continue by foot or bike on
the fire road and climb 2,500 feet onto Santa Rosalia
Ridge. One fascinating side trail off the fire road is the
Loma Prieta Grade, a former narrow-gauge rail bed that
leads past several historic building sites. Another is the
Big Slide Trail, which runs close to the epicenter of the
devastating October 17, 1989, Loma Prieta earthquake.
They say that if you look around carefully you can still
find large cracks in the ground. But don't stop there,
because across this park's 10,000-plus acres more than 30
miles of trails await you. There are also several primitive
campsites at West Ridge Trail Camp.

Most of the forest lands within the park were clear-cut more than a century ago. There was a mill site here, and steam engines hauled logs down off the mountains. Hiking through today's towering redwoods, you might find it's hard to imagine the area's earlier appearance.

The Forest of Nisene Marks State Park exists thanks to a generous gift. Nisene Marks was a successful immigrant farmer and rancher from Monterey County. She and her children became very wealthy through hard work and investments in real estate, and in the early 1950s they purchased the holdings of the old Loma Prieta Lumber Company. By 1963 the property had been turned over to the state for a park.

Aptos Creek

Aptos Creek originates in the Forest of Nisene Marks State Park and spills into the Pacific between Rio Del Mar and Seacliff State Beach. Immediately upstream from Rio Del Mar beach the creek supports healthy stands of alder and maple. The creek once fed a lagoon (long since filled) here, and it also supplied the water for a large swimming pool constructed on the creek. Before the pool and lagoon were filled in, a wharf extended well into the bay on the west side of the creek near a site called Aptos Landing. The wharf was built in the 1850s by Rafael Castro, the grantee of Rancho Aptos.

APTOS AND SOQUEL

The names Aptos and Soquel are believed to originate from coastal Indian words. Although their meaning is lost to us today, they may have been the names of village sites, distinct natural features, or prominent people in the tribe. In any case, they illustrate how names are easily turned around and their meanings lost with time. Aptos, for example, was recorded by the Santa Cruz Mission as Aptos, Abtos, and Avtos, while maps from the 19th century show it variously as Outos, Otas, Atos, and Ortos.

Rio Del Mar and Aptos Creek

HIDDEN BEACH PARK

What was once an area with a narrow dirt trail skirting an odoriferous wastewater treatment plant en route to the beach is now a beautiful park with picnic tables and a playground, with no wastewater tanks visible (they were moved underground). True to its name, Hidden Beach Park is sequestered away at the end of Cliff Drive. You can also park on Sumner Avenue by Los Altos Drive and walk about a quarter of a mile on a nice dirt path through eucalyptus and under a train trellis to the park.

Rio Del Mar State Beach

The pathway from Seacliff State Beach continues southeast over Aptos Creek, past the little downtown of Rio Del Mar, and on to Rio Del Mar State Beach. You might miss this beach if you don't look carefully. At the terminus of Beach Drive is a very large parking lot, beyond which the beach stretches out of sight. This state beach is another excellent access point for the shoreline generally, and it also has bathrooms, showers, and benches. Because of the parking lot's proximity to the beach, it is a good choice for less mobile people.

Rancho Aptos

Rancho Aptos was granted to Rafael Castro in 1833, when he was 30 years old. Castro was part of a large and powerful family that first arrived in Monterey in 1776. Collectively the Castros were granted eight different ranchos in the Santa Cruz area, which took in tens of thousands of acres. Rafael Castro's rancho spread out across more than 6,000 acres along an impressive section of the coast—from today's New Brighton State Beach to the town of La Selva Beach. His property was bounded by three other ranchos, two of which were in his family.

Rafael Castro and his wife reportedly had 12 children. Legal challenges and family problems over several decades—as Spanish rule gave way to Mexican and then U.S. rule in relatively quick order—ended in the 1870s when Claus Spreckels (the "Sugar King") purchased nearly all of Castro's holdings. Some local historians mark the arrival of Spreckels (and other wealthy businessmen like him) as the end of the region's Indian-Spanish-Mexican period and the beginning of the area's Americanization.

Beach Access and Viewpoint

If you're traveling by car or bike, the next public access point south of Aptos is on Via Palo Alto off of Club House Drive. (If you're walking to Moss Landing along the shore, the trek from Hidden Beach is about 10 miles long and passes several beachfront developments.) This is a residential area, but look carefully: about halfway along Via Palo Alto between two houses you'll see a path that leads to an impressive set of stairs. The stairs drop down to the beach with several bench turnouts along the way. The benches are great spots to stop, rest, and gaze out over the

SOOTY SHEARWATER
SPECTACULAR

Perhaps the most phe-
nomenal display of
nature a shoreline
observer can experience is the
annual arrival of tens of thousands of sooty shearwaters
(*Puffinis griseus*) to Monterey
Bay each spring and, especially, fall. (Their world population is estimated at close to
a billion.) Mere words cannot
describe the spectacular scene
of thousands of sooties, in a
line that stretches for miles,
circling the bay in the late
afternoon on stiffly beating
wings in pursuit of their
favored food items: market
squid, anchovies, juvenile
rockfish, sardines, surfperch,
and smelt. You can sit and
watch these gull-sized birds
stream by just offshore for an
hour or more—there are that
many!

Occasionally, when a
school of fish is spotted, a
section of the shearwater
parade peels off and begins to
circle above a spot on the
water. Pandemonium soon
breaks out: shearwaters dive
into the water so abundantly
the surface appears to boil;
brown pelicans arrive hoping
to get a part of the action;
and gulls hover above it
all keeping an eye out for
dropped morsels. Eventually,
the prey move on, and the line
of shearwaters re-forms and
continues on its way.

Sooty shearwaters (which
not surprisingly are sooty in
color) are pelagic birds—that
is, birds of the open ocean.

Sooty shearwaters feeding in the bay

The only land they seek out is
on remote islands in the
southern reaches of Australia,
New Zealand, and South
America, and then just for
breeding. The rest of the year
they spend flying a huge
figure-eight route around the
Pacific Ocean, resting at night
on the surface of the sea.

Shearwaters, like their
cousins the albatrosses,
storm petrels, and fulmar, are
among a group of birds called
tubenoses because their nos-
trils extend onto the top of
their bill in short tubes. One
purpose for these nostril
tubes is to help these birds
eject excess salt from their
system, since they have virtually no access to freshwater.
As a result, they always
appear to have runny noses.

Recent studies have shown
a severe decrease—perhaps
as much as 90 percent—in
sooty numbers when local
coastal waters warm during
El Niño episodes. These warm,
nutrient-poor waters reduce
the number of fish the birds
can feed on, either by killing
the fish or by forcing them
into colder waters. Other
studies show that a contri-
buting factor to the decline
in sooties may be the gill nets
that are strung out across
the North Pacific, which kill
large numbers of the birds—
hundreds of thousands, by
some estimates. Overall,
however, the prognosis for
this species is improving—
so make a spring or fall visit
to the shore, sit back, and
enjoy the show.

SEASONS OF THE BAY

Monterey Bay and the surrounding Pacific Ocean have distinct oceanic seasons, which, like California's terrestrial seasons, change throughout the year and are noticeably different. We can identify three distinct cycles (as opposed to the four farther inland): the upwelling season, the oceanic season, and the Davidson Current season.

The upwelling season along this portion of California's coast occurs from March through July. Northwesterly winds serve as the engine, driving surface water away from the shore and drawing cold, nutrient-rich waters up from considerable depths. Cold, rich water is also moved south from northern latitudes along the south-moving California Current. During these months surface temperatures are at their lowest, generally

between 50°F and 55°F. This is the most productive time of the year in the bay: with more daylight during the summer months and abundant nutrients, blooms of phytoplankton (microscopic drifting plant life) occur throughout the bay, which in turn feed larger zooplankton (drifting animal life), which feed filter-feeding invertebrates— as well as a few filter-feeding vertebrates, such as humpbacks and blue whales—and on up the food web.

Summer fog is directly connected to the upwelling season. When relatively warm, moisture-laden air travels across the Pacific on the northwesterlies and moves over the cold California Current and cold upwelling waters near the coast, water vapor precipitates out as fog. Hot interior temperatures then help to suck the marine air in off the ocean.

The oceanic season occurs during late summer and early

fall (September and October, typically), when relatively warm oceanic waters flow into the bay as the northwesterlies subside. Surface temperatures during these months can rise to 60°F. These clear blue waters often carry plankton and marine species normally seen far offshore, such as leatherback sea turtles and ocean sunfish. This season is often the nicest time at the beach: no fog, relatively warm water and air temperatures, and the midsummer crowds have dwindled.

The Davidson Current season—typically November through February—kicks in when warm waters from the south move north up the coast in a reversal of the California Current. This is also normally the rainy season hereabouts. Coastal waters become well mixed, and it is often the time of lowest salinity in the bay.

bay. Depending on the season, the lucky observer can catch views of gray whales, bottlenose dolphins in the nearshore waves, or thousands of sooty shearwaters streaming across the waters at sunset. Once down on the beach, the shore toward Moss Landing is relatively undeveloped and very inviting.

Seascape: A Resort, a Park, and Beach Access

Seascape, one of Monterey Bay's newer communities, offers the shoreline explorer several options for accessing the water. From the corner of Country Club Drive and Sumner Avenue, move down the coast toward Seascape Avenue. In less than one mile you will arrive at a sizable train trellis. Stop and check it out: a path here, accessed

EL NIÑO

MONTEREY BAY AQUARIUM

Albacore tuna become more common in Monterey Bay during El Niño events.

Periodically the Pacific Ocean experiences a dramatic change in its normal seasonal fluctuations, caused when a vast wedge of warm water moves east across the southern Pacific and piles up against the shore of South America. (Since this warm water typically arrives down south around Christmastime, the phenomenon has been dubbed "El Niño"—the Christ child.) The warm water then moves down and up the Pacific coast, reaching well into California. During an El Niño year, winter water temperatures here can increase some 5°F to 10°F above their normal level.

El Niño waters often trigger radically different weather patterns up and down the Pacific coast, including torrential rains and flooding here in California. The last major El Niño events, during the winters of 1982, 1987, and 1998, caused hundreds of deaths and billions of dollars worth of damage up and down the eastern Pacific. Warm waters do not allow the very bottom of the food web to thrive because nutrients—food— become scarce due to a lack of upwelling. Therefore, the upper reaches of the web suffer heavily: fisheries can collapse, and whole colonies of birds and seals can starve to death. In the Galápagos Islands during the 1982 El Niño event, an estimated 80 percent of the coral reefs died. Locally, El Niño-fueled storms have wiped some beaches clean of their sand, eroded large sections of coastal bluffs, and spawned mudslides in the Santa Cruz Mountains and across northern Monterey County.

During these times, too, nearshore waters are invaded by marine species normally found in the warm waters off Baja California—bonito, marlin, and barracuda, to name a few—while species seasonally abundant in Monterey Bay shift far to the north.

by some wooden stairs and maintained by the County of Santa Cruz, will find you softly crunching across sand and staring down miles of beach after only a ten-minute walk.

The Seascape Resort is a popular vacation and conference facility with over 150 rooms. Drive through the resort's gate and turn left. Continue past the front entrance; you will see a small beach access sign by some parking spaces. A trail from here leads down to the beach.

Just beyond this trail access is Seascape County Park, directly on a bluff overlooking the bay. You can also park on Sumner Avenue (by Via Soderini) and follow a path over the railroad tracks to get to the park, which has nice picnic tables, a children's playground, restrooms, and a short walkway that leads along the edge of the bluff.

Yet another beach access can be found on the south side of Seascape Park, off Sumner Avenue, but be careful: the trail is rather steep and subject to washouts after heavy rains. If there is a serious problem with the trail the county will post a warning or temporarily close it.

The town of La Selva Beach is safely situated high above Monterey Bay on a bluff. However, lower-lying areas may not be so safe if a powerful—albeit rare—oceanic phenomenon hits the bay's shoreline: tsunami.

Tsunami (pronounced tsoo-nah-mee) is a Japanese word for the series of massive waves—up to 75 feet high and traveling at more than 400 miles per hour across the open ocean—that undersea earthquakes, landslides, and volcanic eruptions can trigger. The results are often startling and devastating.

California is relatively safe from tsunamis because of the extensive continental shelf off most of our coast, which would help remove energy from marauding waves. Nonetheless, a 1964 earthquake in Alaska sent 12-foot waves smashing across Crescent City, California, some 15 hours after the earthquake took place; the waves destroyed the downtown area as they traveled inland some 1,600 feet. Other events around the world have not been so tame. For a detailed and spine-tingling account of a massive 1835 Chilean tsunami, seek out a copy of Charles Darwin's classic, *The Voyage of the Beagle*.

Santa Cruz Long-toed Salamander

It is a challenge to be an efficient shoreline explorer . . . there is simply so much to see, and so many places to look. You may have to be out in the middle of the night in December to see something truly rare, but occasionally you get lucky.

One important direction to keep glancing is downward, at the ground beneath your feet. If you do, and you happen to be slightly inland from the coastal bluffs, you might be fortunate enough to see the Santa Cruz long-toed salamander (*Ambystoma macrodactylum croceum*). This diminutive, bug-eyed little salamander is a beautiful animal: it is black over most of its body, with prominent irregular yellow spots topside.

It has been a federally listed endangered species since 1967. The reasons for its decline are many, but habitat loss is the most important. Then too, this salamander probably never maintained an enormous population— it is a relic of sorts.

When the rains start in the fall, adult salamanders emerge from their subterranean burrows and migrate to nearby ponds. After pairing up and mating, eggs are attached to submerged branches and aquatic plants. Soon polliwoglike larvae are swimming around in their aquatic environment. When they change into miniature versions of their parents, they will emerge from the water and begin the land portion of their life.

Locally, both the state and federal governments have purchased lands in and around two sites—Valencia Lagoon and Ellicot Slough—in an attempt to maintain the long-toed salamander population. Valencia Lagoon is visible adjacent to Highway 1, immediately south of Rio Del Mar Boulevard. In 1975 the Ellicot Slough National Wildlife Refuge was established farther south between San Andreas Road and Highway 1. Unlike other refuges, the public is not allowed on these sites. The salamanders and their habitat are simply too fragile.

La Selva Beach

The community of La Selva Beach is one of the smallest towns along the greater Monterey Bay shoreline. And yet there is a real downtown here. It consists of a half block of businesses (one grocery store and a couple of realtors), a fire station, a library, a school, a church, and a few other ventures. The rest of sleepy La Selva Beach, which has a population of some 2,000, comprises nicely kept homes and some vacation houses. Stop in at the grocery store

Every now and again you will come across a road that is a magnet for bicyclists. It is typically a small two-lane road with diverse topography, beautiful landscapes and vistas, and preferably a bike lane. San Andreas Road is such a road. For its entire length from Highway 1 near Seascape in the north to Beach Road by Pajaro Dunes in the south—some nine miles—this road almost always has cyclists, alone or in groups, enjoying its undulating bike lane.

As nice as San Andreas is, many more biking options are available along this section of coast. Basically, there are two more or less parallel routes, with many opportunities for moving from one to the other. On the inland side of Highway 1 you can bike on Soquel Drive from Cabrillo College all the way to Freedom Boulevard—an official portion of the Pacific Coast Bicycle Route. At Freedom you have two options: you can cross over the highway to Bonita and San Andreas (see below), or you can continue inland and ride all the way to Watsonville, about nine miles. From Watsonville you can move shoreward once again on either Beach Street or the Pajaro River bike path. Or you can ride down Main Street, crossing the river to the town of Pajaro, then continue on Salinas Road to Elkhorn Road; this will lead to Elkhorn Slough.

The shoreline route leaves New Brighton State Beach on McGregor Drive and moves southeast to State Park Drive, where you can fly down the hill to Seacliff State Beach and ride the shoreline path over to Rio Del Mar. In Rio Del Mar you can either puff up Rio Del Mar Boulevard inland to connect to Soquel Drive or turn southeast on Sumner (about half of a mile up the boulevard) and stay near the coast; take Sumner to Seascape Boulevard (about two miles) and continue on to San Andreas Road.

Back at the intersection of Freedom and Highway 1, you can move toward the shore over the highway and ride on Bonita Drive until it merges with San Andreas, the continuation of the Pacific Coast Bicycle Route. San Andreas continues for approximately nine miles until it dead-ends at Beach Road. At Beach Road, turn right and you'll end up at Palm Beach State Park and the Pajaro Dunes condominium complex. If you turn left on Beach Road (which continues to Watsonville), you can immediately turn off on Thurwatcher, cross the river (the Monterey–Santa Cruz County line), continue on McGowan, then turn right on Trafton to Bluff to Jensen. This is the Pajaro River agricultural loop. When Jensen dead-ends at Highway 1, your only option is to continue south on the highway (two lanes here, and rather busy) to Struve Road and Zmudowski State Beach or to Moss Landing State Beach on Jetty Road.

Biking information on this and other sections of the Santa Cruz County coast is available from Santa Cruz County's Regional Transportation Commission (831-460-3200) and CalTrans's District 05 office (805-549-3111).

and talk with Mike, the town's unofficial mayor and historian. He owns the store and has lived here for decades.

You can also drive to the end of Playa Boulevard and park (daylight hours only) atop the bluff on Vista Drive overlooking the train tracks and the beach below. Even though you might see some young surfer dudes and dudettes climbing down the bluffs here, don't try it yourself: it is very dangerous. Instead, continue down Vista to Anita, where you'll see a small public path disappearing between two houses. This leads over the train tracks, across the parking lot at Manresa State Beach, and to the shore.

INFORMATION

Santa Cruz Metropolitan
  Transit District:
  831-425-8600
  Website:
  http://www.scmtd.com

Forest of Nisene Marks and
  West Ridge Trail Camp:
  831-763-7063

Santa Cruz County Regional
  Transportation Commis-
  sion: 831-460-3200

CalTrans District 05:
  805-549-3111

Bike map website:
  http://www.dot.ca.gov/dist
  05/planning/bikemap.htm

Rio Del Mar State Beach:
  831-685-6500

Manresa State Beach:
  831-763-7063

California State Parks,
  Santa Cruz District:
  831-429-2850

La Selva Beach also maintains a little city park back from the bluffs, Triangle Park, where Vista Drive enters Playa Boulevard. And the town prides itself on its family-oriented Fourth of July festival. Mayor Mike invites one and all to attend the festivities.

Manresa State Beach

Manresa State Beach is actually two parks in one. The main section of Manresa is the popular two-mile-long beach and surfing spot just off San Andreas Road, by the train trellis. Here you will find an enormous parking lot, bathrooms, and informative interpretive signs.

Stairway down to Manresa State Beach

The other section of the park, called the Manresa Uplands, is located just down the road from the main parking lot. Take Sand Dollar Drive off San Andreas Road and follow the signs. The uplands is an interesting spot. Not only is there a day use area with a large parking lot and some monster stairs down to the beach, but 64 campsites grace this spot as well. They aren't your typical campsites, though. These are no-car sites, and camping is allowed only in tents. You drive up, unload, and set up camp on a tall bluff covered with coastal sage scrub and a few eucalyptus trees. Then you must drive your car to a designated lot some 200 yards away (well hidden from the campsite) and walk back. No revving engines, no slamming doors, no generators—just the wind off the ocean and the distant sound of the waves. The beach is accessible from the campsites, and there are bathrooms and pay showers.

Just outside the uplands boundary is another beach access at the corner of Sand Dollar Drive and Sand Dollar Lane. This is a residential area, but the public can park and walk through a condominium complex to some stairs and the beach. Again, respect private driveways and local signs.

White-crowned Sparrow

The white-crowned sparrow (*Zonotrichia leucophrys*) is a year-round resident of the bay shoreline where coastal sage scrub dominates or the landscape is otherwise open and windblown. Its call of two thin whistling notes followed by a twittery trill is a typical, beautiful, and integral sound of the coast. White-crowns will often call while perched atop a coyote bush on the backside of dunes or from the upper branches of large coastal sage bushes growing on bluffs. The male's black and white striped crown is easily recognizable as the bird hops about on the ground looking for seeds and insects.

The white-crowned sparrow's song is commonly heard along the shore.

Monterey Bay Academy

Once you leave Manresa State Beach and move southeast toward Sunset State Beach you enter rolling hills devoted to agriculture (with a few housing developments scattered in). Halfway between Manresa and Sunset, on the ocean side of San Andreas Road, you'll see a complex of buildings spread out over the coastal bluff. This is the Monterey Bay Academy, a private school operated by the Seventh-Day Adventists. If you think some of the buildings look like barracks, you're right. Before the school opened here in 1948 this was Camp McQuaide, a National Guard facility established in 1938. During World War II it served as a base for various branches of the armed services.

GETTING AROUND

Seacliff State Beach is at the ocean terminus of State Park Drive, off of Highway 1. To get to the Forest of Nisene Marks from Seacliff, take State Park Drive inland to Soquel Drive; near the old part of Aptos, turn onto Aptos Creek Road. Look carefully for a small "State Park" sign on the other side of the railroad tracks.

Rio Del Mar Beach is at the ocean terminus of Rio Del Mar Boulevard off of Highway 1. Or take the pedestrian and bike pathway from Seacliff. Rio Del Mar State Beach is at the end of Beach Drive, which acts like a frontage road moving southeast next to some vacation homes. Hidden Beach Park can be found by turning onto Cliff Drive (or Townsend Drive) from Rio Del Mar Boulevard and continuing southeast through a residential area. Sumner Drive, also off of Rio Del Mar Boulevard, will bring you into Seascape. To move between Seascape and the string of sites off of San Andreas Road—La Selva Beach, Manresa State Beach, and eventually Sunset State Beach—take Seascape Boulevard inland by the Seascape Resort; continue through a residential area, then turn right on San Andreas Road.

Sunset State Beach to Moss Landing State Beach

Except for the pleasing diversion of downtown Watsonville, this portion of the shoreline is best described as beaches and fields. Most of the stretch between Sunset State Beach and Moss Landing State Beach is publicly owned, which means that it is open to everyone. Immediately inland from the beaches are acres of strawberries, flowers, artichokes, and other crops. These agricultural lands are vital to the local economy while serving as de facto open space that buffers the parks.

Sunset State Beach

Sunset State Beach takes in some three miles of unobstructed and spectacular shoreline. There are 90 campsites in the park (with pay showers), all upslope from the beach and nestled behind the tallest dunes along Monterey Bay. You'll actually find two sets of dunes here: a shorter set, just back from the beach, which are 20 to 30 feet high; then the towering stabilized system behind which the campgrounds are found.

From the well-marked dune trails leaving the campsites or the vista point where the paved road begins its descent toward the beach the views of Monterey Bay are unparalleled. Northward the shoreline wraps around in an easy arc toward Santa Cruz; southward, beyond the development at Pajaro Dunes, the smokestacks of the Moss Landing power plant soar skyward against a backdrop of rugged mountains tapering down to the Monterey Peninsula and the Pacific beyond.

To reach the beach from the campground, you can take one of the trails up and over the dunes. Or you can walk down the paved road, which leads to numerous parking spots in the large day use area. The beach parking site has numerous barbecue stands, tables, a large covered area with more tables, and bathrooms. There are also tables as well as beach access by the ranger's kiosk, back at the park entrance. An added feature by the entrance kiosk is the spectacular view to the northwest. Here the agricultural fields are cultivated right up to the edge of the parkland, creating open vistas and an intriguing transition from cultivated fields to natural vegetation.

Sunset State Beach

SHORELINE DOLPHIN WATCHING

Bottlenose dolphins can often be seen just beyond the breakers.

It is not uncommon to be gazing out at the bay from a bluff or strolling along the beach and suddenly see several bottlenose dolphins (*Tursiops truncatus*) only yards away, moving along at a leisurely pace just beyond the breaking waves. During the summer and autumn off the shore of Sunset State Beach it is possible to see large groups of these animals churning through the waters, feeding together as a group. It is not known if this species has always lived here, but in the early 1980s a large school was identified in the bay that appeared to be here year round, working the nearshore waters for food.

Bottlenose dolphins are beautiful animals, true mammals that suckle their young with rich milk. They are gray to black on top, white on their undersides, and very intelligent. With due respect to these wild dolphins of Monterey Bay, they are the same species as Flipper, the dolphin popularized on the long-running television show. They are also often used for research and for shows at aquatic parks.

Both dolphins and porpoises are members of the whale order, Cetacea. The names dolphin and porpoise are often confused, but in fact the two groups are quite distinct. To distinguish between porpoises and dolphins, look at their heads: porpoises have short stubby snouts, while dolphins' snouts are long, pointed, and somewhat flattened. Their teeth are different too—though you won't be getting close enough to have a good look.

More than 30 species of marine dolphins and six species of marine porpoises have been identified (plus there are five species of freshwater river dolphins). Of these, nine species are known to either live in or regularly visit the Monterey Bay National Marine Sanctuary: Pacific white-sided dolphin, northern right whale dolphin, Risso's dolphin, short-beaked common dolphin, long-beaked common dolphin, bottlenose dolphin, striped dolphin, Dall's porpoise, and harbor porpoise. Bottlenose, Pacific white-sided, and common dolphins and harbor porpoises frequent different sites in Monterey Bay.

Dark-eyed Junco

These quiet little birds aren't going to ruin a picnic or barbecue dinner; in fact, they'll help clean up afterward. Dark-eyed juncos (*Junco phaeonotus*) are part of the sparrow family and they live along the central coast throughout the year. They seem to be particularly abundant around campsites. They are easy to recognize, with their black heads and buff-colored backs. While they are feeding or quarreling among themselves, they'll often take a short hop in the air; when they do so the white feathers framing their tails are nicely displayed.

Most people take beaches for granted. After all, beaches are just there, waiting for us to walk down them, frolic over them, or lie down on their giving sands and rest. Beaches may appear to be dormant, static edges of the sea, but they are much, much more.

Think about it. Beaches are a dynamic transition zone between terra firma and the vast expanse of the ocean. They are both wet and dry. Beaches enable humans to come very close to a world they know very little about. Beaches are also very complicated. They change shape with the seasons and are home to an impressive array of animal life, serving, as a consequence, as a type of fast-food restaurant for a wide variety of shorebirds.

The world's beaches come in a variety of colors, from red and black to shimmering white. What a beach is composed of determines its color and shape. The beaches of Monterey Bay vary in their composition, but they are largely quartz, with traces of many other minerals. The sand here comes from cliff erosion, river and creek discharge, and weathered granite along the Monterey Peninsula shore.

The littoral zone—the strip of shore between high tide and low tide—is where waves, currents, and winds combine to form beaches and, in some places, dunes. Changes to beaches occur with each wave, as well as with the changing of the tides and the passing of the seasons. Any lover of the shore has noticed the difference in a favorite beach between midsummer and, say, Christmastime.

One author has described beaches as "long rivers of sand." It is an apt description because sand is constantly in motion. The summer look of a beach, known as the swell profile, is typically dominated by a wide and high berm (the terrace of sand built by waves—in other words, the beach) as small waves slowly build up the beach with material taken from offshore sandbars. In contrast, the winter look, or "storm profile," is characterized by a low beach as large waves erode the sand away and redeposit it in nearshore waters as sandbars.

Wave action not only shapes beaches, but it also determines the size of beach sand. On high-energy beaches with numerous and powerful waves, fine sand stays in sus-

"The three great elemental sounds in nature are the sound of rain, the sound of wind in a primeval wood, and the sound of outer ocean on a beach. I have heard them all, and of the three elemental voices, that of ocean is the most awesome, beautiful, and varied."

Henry Beston,
The Outermost House
(1928)

Opossum

Opossums (*Didelphis virginiana*) are North America's only marsupials. These house cat–sized animals occur across the eastern half of the country, up and down the Pacific coast, and in portions of the southwest. Opossums—commonly called "possums"—are renowned for playing dead when threatened by a predator, though this behavior is rarely seen. However, they can be spotted in the evenings as they shuffle about in search of food along the bay's bluffs, forests, and parklands. Opossums are omnivorous—they'll eat anything. After a vigorous night of wandering about, eating, and perhaps playing dead, these animals hide out in a favorite tree or den and sleep through the day.

Longshore Drift

Have you ever played in the waves at the beach? Did you notice that when you got out of the water you had

pension and is carried to deep water; only coarse sands and sometimes pebbles or boulders remain. High-energy beaches often have steeper slopes than low-energy beaches. An excellent example of this difference can be seen when you compare San Jose Creek Beach (a.k.a. Monastery Beach), south of Carmel, with the Carmel City Beach. San Jose Creek Beach, which receives the full brunt of the prevailing northwest swell off the Pacific, is a steep, coarse-sanded, high-energy beach. Carmel Beach, by contrast, receives some protection from the Pacific thanks to Pescadero Point. As a result, it is a gently sloping beach with fine sand.

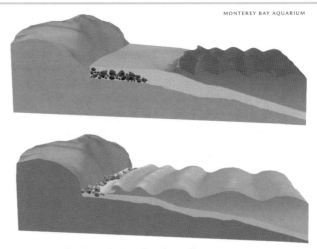

Summer (above) and winter beach profiles

Beaches typically encompass three distinct zones, or habitats. The high-tide zone stays the driest and in many ways is the harshest habitat for marine organisms. One of the most important sources of food here is kelp wrack (see page 265). The mid-tide zone, a bit farther down the beach, receives more inundation from tides than the upper zone. More animal species live in the mid-tide zone because they can maintain their moisture better and obtain food more easily. The low-tide zone extends into the water and is fully exposed to air only during extreme low tides. More species live here than in the other zones. Think about where you see the most shore-birds feeding: that is where small marine animals thrive.

moved and that you had to walk back up the beach to your towel?

Powered by consistent northwesterly winds, California's longshore drift—the movement of water, and with it debris (and swimmers), through the tidal zone—is almost always to the south. In Monterey Bay, sand originating above Año Nuevo curves around Santa Cruz and Soquel Points, bumps and grinds its way along the shore, takes on additional material from the San Lorenzo and Pajaro Rivers (and numerous smaller waterways), and gets deposited on beaches all along the way. This replenishment occurs as far south as Moss Landing and the mouth of the Monterey Canyon; at this spot, the sand cascades downslope into the canyon and is largely lost to the beaches and dunes beyond.

Beach Hoppers

Beach hoppers (*Megalorchestia* spp.) are typical beach residents in the high-tide zone. These little animals,

Beach hopper

sometimes called sand fleas, can crawl or hop and are commonly found in and under piles of kelp wrack. Hoppers are mostly nocturnal. They hide in their sand burrow during the day and emerge at night to move down the beach to feed. If you are digging for sand crabs and come up with something smaller that looks like a cross between a flea and a shrimp, it is probably a species of beach hopper.

Sand Crab

Sand crab

Sand crabs (*Emerita analoga*) play an important role in the mid-tide zone, and in the minds of young children everywhere. Anyone with a bucket and hand shovel can find these active little guys. Hold them in your hand with a bit of sand and they try to dig into your palm (it just tickles). Place them back on the sand and they'll dig in so fast they'll disappear as if by magic.

Sand crabs have to be fast to avoid their many aquatic and avian predators and to survive in their rough-and-tumble environment. To feed, sand crabs wait for a wave on the incoming tide, ride the wave up the beach, then dig in facing upslope. When the next wave passes over them they extend their hairy antennae into the water and wait for the water to roll back down the beach, catching small particles of food as it does. When the tide moves back out, the sand crab adjusts its location accordingly. Sand crabs body-surf up and down the beach all day long.

Pismo Clam

Pismo clam

A once superabundant low-tide dweller is the pismo clam (*Tivela stultorum*). Although they are most commonly associated with the Pismo Beach region to the south of Monterey—after which they are named—these brawny bivalves can be found here too, near the northern limits of their range. Clams are interesting in their own right, of course, but they're especially interesting to clammers—and the pismo clam is one of the largest and most sought-after clams along the California coast.

Although pismo clams have been recorded at a width of between seven and eight inches, most are only about five inches across. Even so, that's big for a clam (although there are a few even larger species). Pismos live in one to three feet of water and burrow down six inches into the sand. Their heavy shells and strong "foot" allow them to stay put in heavy seas. From their hiding place they extend a tube upward beyond the surface of the sand.

Sunset State Beach was one of the first beaches purchased by the state of California, in 1931. It has a long history of use—and overuse. Just 20 years ago Sunset's dunes were in sad shape. Years of trampling by visitors had destroyed native vegetation and created a series of deep paths criss-crossing the dunes. In many areas the sand had been blown away and soil exposed. Exotic European dune grass and iceplant had colonized large areas of the park. Today, after a concerted effort to remove exotic plants and revegetate the dunes with natives, they look better than ever. This is why it is critical to stay on the well-marked trails. (For information on how specialists and volunteers go about restoring dune systems, see page 176.)

Water is drawn in through the tube and passed over the clam's gills so it can extract food particles. The water is then expelled through a separate tube.

Pismo clams were once so abundant that they were harvested by the wagonload in southern California. The Department of Fish and Game once recorded an estimated 150,000 people removing some 75,000 pounds of pismo clams from Pismo Beach in a single weekend. By the early 1970s it was obvious that overharvesting was harming this clam's population; in addition, the resurgent sea otter population was adding a separate pressure on this species. Although the clam's population is today much lower than it was just a few decades ago, it remains stable.

Unless temporarily prohibited owing to shellfish contamination problems, digging for Pismo clams is permitted from September 1 through April 30 in Santa Cruz and Monterey Counties, and year round to the south. However, you must obtain a saltwater fishing license from the Department of Fish and Game, and only clams with shells measuring five inches in diameter or greater may be taken.

Other clam species you may uncover during shoreline walks are bent-nosed, geoduck (pronounced gooey-duck), gaper, soft-shell, Washington, razor, and common littleneck. To find out how to clam and about clamming rules and regulations, look for a copy of the California Sport Fishing Regulations wherever fishing licenses are sold (sporting goods stores and numerous convenience stores) or call the Department of Fish and Game's 24-hour message center (916-227-2244) to request a free copy.

Bird Bills

Although some mixture of shorebirds can always be found on the beaches of Monterey Bay, the greatest

MICROSCOPIC BEACH LIFE

There is a fascinating world in the sand. What do you think the beach hopper, sand crab, and scores of other small beach species are eating? The answer is a variety of plants and animals so tiny you need a microscope to see them. Collectively, this diversity of life that lives between grains of sand is called meiofauna (meaning literally "small animals" in a mix of Greek and Latin). Some move about, others are stationary; some live close to the surface, others deep in the sand; some like to stay moist, others need drier portions of the beach. Whatever their lifestyles, all meiofauna are important players in beach ecology.

Marbled godwits feeding on beach

abundance occurs during the fall and spring migration seasons. During this time, get out your binoculars and watch for a while. In particular, look at their bills: they'll tell you a lot.

Some shorebirds, such as willets and sanderlings, scamper up and down the beach following the waves; others, like godwits, wait higher up where the water just keeps the sand wet; still others, including whimbrels and snowy plovers, forage well above the high-tide mark. Because there is a gradation of microhabitats from shallow water to above the most recent high-tide mark, there is a variety of prey items living in and on the sand. A cross-section of the beach would reveal (heading downslope) kelp flies, beach hoppers, sand crabs, amphipods (small crustaceans), insects, polychaete worms, and clams. Different feeding locations thus allow the birds to partition the beach's resources without having to compete. Different sizes and shapes of bills only add to the ability to specialize.

Whimbrels and snowy plovers, for example, both prefer the higher reaches of the beach, but the two birds couldn't look more different. The whimbrel is tall and leggy with a large down-curved bill; the snowy plover is short, compact, and has a stubby bill. The whimbrel can probe deeper, while the plover explores the topmost layers of sand. Same location, but they find different food items.

Even birds with similar-looking bills, feeding over the same section of beach, may be doing so without competing. For example, knots and dunlins are both medium-sized sandpipers with medium-long bills. They look alike, and they feed in similar areas on the beach. Researchers have discovered, however, that they are eating two completely different food items: whereas knots feed on small mollusks, dunlins seek out polychaete worms. In this case, apparently, it's all a matter of taste.

Palm Beach State Park and Pajaro Dunes

This little park is a surprising find right in the middle of the Pajaro Dunes condominium complex. Here you can find fire rings, picnic tables, and bathrooms. A beautiful set of dunes separates the picnic area from the beach. Eucalyptus and cypress trees planted around the parking lot have grown right up onto these dunes; years of onshore winds have sculpted the trees into topiarylike hedgerows tapering away from the bay.

As early as the 1860s this area just north of the Pajaro River, by the Watsonville Slough, was a shipping port, called variously Pajaro Landing, Port Rogers, and Port Watsonville. Amazingly, steamship service operated between here (for the town of Watsonville) and San Francisco. During extremely low tides you can see some of the old pier pilings. In the 1880s a small hotel and seaside cottages were erected near here, together constituting a small resort, Camp Goodall. After a few decades a new owner

Pajaro Dunes

changed the name to Palm Beach. The port, the hotel, and the cottages have long since disappeared; however, the name Palm Beach remained.

In the mid-1960s another big change came to this area: the construction of a large condominium complex and convention center known as Pajaro Dunes. Since units can be rented for short- or longer-term stays, this complex is popular with vacationers and condominium owners alike. The expansive beach fronting the development, the nearby sand dunes, and the mouth of the Pajaro River make for a beautiful setting. It is also a strategic spot to stay while exploring the shoreline both north and south. If you hop in a car and drive north for about a half hour, you're in Santa Cruz; drive south the same amount of time and you can be cruising Monterey's Cannery Row. For information on rentals, call the Pajaro Dunes Property Management Company at 1-800-564-1771.

Chestnut-backed Chickadee

A common shoreline bird you'll find not on the beach but in the trees up the valley or on the bluff is the chestnut-backed chickadee (*Parus rufescens*). In fact, it does sport a chestnut-colored back and rump, and its scientific name means "red titmouse." It also has a distinctive black cap and bib, white cheeks, and a white belly. In addition to being descriptive, this bird's common name is onomatopoeic: the word "chickadee" comes from the sound the bird makes when it is feeding: "tseek-a-dee-dee." Another good example of an onomatopoeic name for a shorebird is the willet, whose call sounds somewhat like "pill-will-willet, pill-will-willet."

Chickadees seem to be constantly on the move through trees and tall bushes. They feed by gleaning small insects

WHAT'S THAT IN THE SKY?

While exploring this section of coast you may be astonished to look up and see a multicolored hang glider soaring quietly overhead. Don't worry, it hasn't catapulted itself from the towering bluffs out over the beach. Instead, hang gliders are towed behind ultralight planes from the nearby Watsonville Airport. When they reach a predetermined elevation over the nearshore, a lever is pulled and the hang glider is released from the ultralight. What a way to explore the shore! If you see some faster planes performing barrel rolls and fancy acrobatics over the bay, they too originate from the Watsonville Airport.

PAJARO

The Pajaro River has given its name to the valley, the coastal dunes, and a 19th-century seaside landing, but how did the river receive its name? The following excerpt from the diary of Miguel Costansó, a member of the 1769 Portolá expedition, explains it: "We pitched our camp on the bank of the river discovered by the scouts. . . . This was verdant and pleasant, covered with poplars, alders, and tall white oaks, live oaks, and another kind of tree we did not know. Here we saw a bird that the natives had killed and stuffed with grass; it appeared to be a royal eagle; it was eleven palms from tip to tip of its wings. On account of this find we called the river *el río del Pájaro* [Bird River]."

off of leaves, needles, and twigs, all the while chattering away at one another. You may also see them hanging upside down to reach a tempting morsel—a practice common with many birds in the titmouse and chickadee family. During the fall and winter, chickadees form mixed flocks with other species of small leaf-gleaners such as warblers and diminutive kinglets. So if you see a flock of chickadees coming your way, don't be surprised to catch a glimpse of yellow or red mixed in with the chestnut.

Pajaro River Bike Path

If you want a real challenge, and a beautiful one at that, grab your bike and explore the Pajaro River. You can bike the levee all the way from Watsonville to the sea, some eight miles one way. Although portions of the compacted-dirt trail are a bit rough at present, plans call for improving the levee and its various access points. You can consider this trail a work in progress. It is recommended that you use the buddy system when riding the full length of the levee.

Start your ride inland from downtown Watsonville at the corner of Halohan Road and Lake Avenue (Highway 152). Park here and look for the gated entrance to the trail along Corralitos Creek, on the southeast side of Lake. (There are also access points in town along residential streets like Bridge Road and by River Park, and further shoreward off Thurwatcher Road.) For the first half mile of the trail you move through a residential area mixed with apple orchards. The creek here still supports a nice growth of trees, which shoot up from the embankments. If you encounter any locked gates, simply walk your bike around them. The levee is entirely public.

The mouth of the Pajaro River

Soon you will ride into more open agricultural lands, with the Pajaro Valley spreading out before you. You can now follow the river with your eye all the way to the sea. Corralitos Creek turns into Salsipuedes Creek, which then flows into the Pajaro River just upstream from River Park.

As you approach the Highway 1 underpass at about the five-mile mark, notice how barren the river is in places. Just like the San Lorenzo River to the north, the Pajaro River has been channelized, rip-rapped, and deforested in an attempt to control its occasional flooding. Plans are afoot to replant the barren sections for the health of the river and—ironically, it would seem—to alleviate flooding. Most experts, however, now believe that riparian forests in fact ease flooding rather than making it worse. Also take note of the mud nests lining the underside of Highway 1. During the spring the air here is filled with the calls and antics of hundreds of cliff swallows.

Between the highway and Thurwatcher Road a nice section of streamside forest is a favorite spot for local bird-watchers. It is also the site of the Watsonville Wastewater Treatment Facility. Cross over Thurwatcher and you may be buzzed by airplanes—model airplanes, that is. Though not visible from Thurwatcher, a miniature airport maintained by local model airplane enthusiasts is located right next to the levee. Don't worry, the remote-control pilots are accustomed to bicyclists: they won't dive-bomb you for fun.

The remainder of the trail moves through pure agricultural lands. The river widens little by little as you approach the coast, and the streamside vegetation is thick. At the coast the Pajaro River is some 50 yards wide (though this varies seasonally). Shorebirds and land birds alike flock to this area to bathe, feed, and rest on bars of sand in the river and on the beach.

Watsonville Wastewater Treatment Facility

In with the bad water, out with the good. So it is at the Watsonville Wastewater Treatment Facility—and many other such facilities around the bay. This plant, which treats wastewater produced by some 50,000 residents, farms, light industrial companies, and small businesses, is located next to the Pajaro River, alongside the levee bike path. Purifying wastewater is important business, and the staff and technicians of these plants take their work very seriously. It's a good thing they do, for humans and wildlife alike.

Until relatively recently, many such facilities were allowed to dump their waste into rivers, bays, and the

WATSONVILLE

Watsonville is Santa Cruz County's second largest city and one of its oldest. The town was first mapped out and settled in the 1850s by Judge John Watson and some colleagues. Since then it has served as a critical transportation link for the region and, more importantly, as the center of a thriving agricultural industry across the fertile Pajaro Valley. The town of Pajaro is just over the county line—and across the Pajaro River—from Watsonville.

A visit to downtown Watsonville should include a stroll around the plaza and a stop by the William H. Volck Museum (corner of Beach and Lincoln Streets), where you can find out all about the town's history. The museum maintains a collection of everyday items from the 1880s to about 1920—dolls, games, clothing, household gadgets. It also provides a free brochure detailing a self-guided history walk through downtown. To find out museum hours, call 831-722-0305. For information about seasonal events in Watsonville and the valley, contact the Pajaro Valley Chamber of Commerce at 831-724-3900.

ocean with very little treatment. Also, discharge pipes were fairly close to shorelines, places where people swam and fished. Today the scene is much different, not only in Watsonville but throughout California. Here, state-of-the-art treatment processes remove an impressive amount of waste products and toxins before the effluent is discharged 7,350 feet offshore in about 70 feet of water.

This plant, like many such facilities today, produces biosolids by drying out solids removed in the treatment process. This material can then be composted and used as fertilizer for landscaping. Also, the methane produced by the treatment process is captured, stored, and used to power the facility. The facility offer tours for both small and large groups. Call ahead for reservations, at 831-728-6077.

Turkey Vulture

Perhaps the most visible shoreline scavenger—and some might say the ugliest—is the turkey vulture (*Cathartes aura*). Who would want to eat something dead and rotting, anyway? The vulture belongs to the family Cathartidae, from the Greek word meaning "to cleanse." Which is exactly what they do—and thank goodness. Without turkey vultures our environment would be a lot less healthy, not to mention a whole lot smellier.

Vultures are perfectly adapted to feed on coastal carrion. Their excellent eyesight and keen sense of smell enable vultures to find carcasses from far away. Their heads are featherless so when they finish a meal any infectious bacteria they encounter cannot hide under feathers and grow. Their digestive systems are industrial strength, full of strong acids and enzymes to kill any bacteria they swallow.

The turkey vulture is a relative of the California condor, an endangered species that, once common along the shores of Monterey Bay, is now being reintroduced in the Big Sur region to the south. In fact, many believe that the bird seen along the banks of the Pajaro River by the Portolá expedition was a stuffed condor.

Pajaro River Agricultural Loop

If you want to go for a bike ride or a short drive while checking out northern Monterey County's agricultural bounty, follow this route (in either direction). It's about four miles long, and you'll be treated to spectacular views of the coastal bluffs and the bay while passing through

acres of strawberries, lettuce, flowers, or whatever happens to be in season.

From the north, take Thurwatcher Road off Beach Road (near Pajaro Dunes) and cross the Pajaro River and county line. Thurwatcher becomes McGowan in Monterey County. Go right on Trafton to Bluff, then onto Jensen. Jensen dead-ends at Highway 1 by a large produce stand.

Zmudowski State Beach

This beach, which is named after Mary Zmudowski (don't pronounce the *z*), a Watsonville schoolteacher who donated a portion of the land, has a lot to offer. Certainly one of the most spectacular sights you'll be treated to is a parade of horses racing down the beach or splashing through the waves. It shouldn't be surprising that Zmudowski State Beach (as well as several others to the south) allows horses to romp on its shores. This stretch of coast between Watsonville and Monterey is more rural than urban, and people tend to have horses here. If you own a horse and would like to ride here, please note that riding is restricted to areas of wet sand. If you have any other horse-related questions, call State Parks' Monterey District Office, 831-649-2836.

Next to the possibility of seeing horses galloping down the beach, perhaps the most surprising thing about this beach is how you get there. Often, no doubt, first-time visitors convince themselves they've taken the wrong road and turn around. Why? Well, the two-mile road

Zmudowski State Beach

leads through agricultural fields—right through the *middle* of them—and as it does so it performs the asphalt equivalent of the mambo, rumba, and tango, all at once. There are so many zigs and zags to get to this beach the road is almost an amusement ride in itself.

Once you arrive, though, you will be treated to a wild section of Monterey Bay. The beautiful dunes here are in an advanced state of restoration. The work is not done yet, so mind the signs to keep to the trails, which are well marked. When you pop out onto the beach after crossing the dunes on the plank walkway, you are just as likely to see people fishing or clamming as sunning themselves. This is a wide-open spot with plenty of room for a full complement of beach activities.

This beach stretches all the way to the Pajaro River in the north. On fogless days you can see the condominium complex there. In the other direction (after crossing over Elkhorn Slough on the highway and working your way back to the beach at Moss Landing) you can walk all the way to the Salinas River and, if you're feeling ambitious, Monterey. Looking south, you may see the smokestacks of the Moss Landing power plant and the city of Monterey glistening in the distance.

Just beyond the parking lot along the road leading back to Highway 1, stop for a moment and do some bird-watching at the nearby McClusky Slough complex. Some of the lands here have been purchased by the Wildlife Conservation Board and will eventually be turned over to State Parks (you'll see a sign advertising McClusky Slough on Highway 1 at Springfield Road). These fresh-water sloughs are relics of the Pajaro River, which once curved southward from its present mouth and discharged together with the Salinas River by the Moss Landing Harbor. Amazing, but true.

Warning: Unfortunately, this remote parking area is subject to auto break-ins, and State Parks has posted signs to warn visitors. Be sure to carry all valuables with you.

WATERSHED WATCH—
RIVERS AND CREEKS

The Santa Cruz–
Monterey County sec-
tion of the Monterey
Bay National Marine Sanctuary is graced with the largest
rivers on the central coast: the
San Lorenzo, Pajaro, Salinas,
and Carmel. Numerous other
streams and smaller creeks
also spill into the bay. These
watercourses—and their
watersheds—not only make
the vast agricultural endeavors
in coastal Santa Cruz and
Monterey Counties possible,
but they also provide important habitats for a wide range
of plants and animals, both
on land and where they enter
the ocean. River mouths and
estuaries often feed into
marshlands, which support a
continuum of plant life, from
freshwater species such as tule
reeds to saltwater species such
as pickleweed.

Unfortunately, after some
150 years of intense use—and
abuse—by humans, most of
these waterways are today
severely reduced and de-
graded. Anyone who has
spent much time in California
quickly learns that water
issues are serious: there simply
isn't enough water to go
around. As a result, coastal
rivers and creeks have been
diverted for human use and
their streamside forests cut
down, first for wood and lumber, and more recently in the
name of flood control. The
animals that have been most
severely affected by this activity include salmon and steelhead, the Santa Cruz long-
toed salamander, red-legged
frog, California tiger salamander, San Francisco garter
snake, western pond turtle,
least tern, snowy plover, clap-
per rail, and numerous smaller
aquatic species.

Many of these waterways
naturally dry up or have a
reduced flow during the summer and fall months. Sometimes sandbars form at their
mouths and cut them off from
the ocean. Under normal cir-
cumstances, these natural bar-
ricades would be unplugged
with the coming of the first big
rains, when the rivers start to
flow again. But diversions have
been so intense that today the
sandbars often have to be
breached with tractors. The
rivers stay dry so long—or, at
best, maintain such a low flow
of freshwater—that saltwater
wedges are slowly creeping
into the aquifer, endangering
an industry that to some
degree caused the problem in
the first place because of its
dependence on freshwater:
namely, agriculture.

The Salinas River tells the
sad tale. One hundred and fifty
years ago the Salinas—which at
that point disgorged near
Moss Landing—supported a
dense riparian forest, a robust
fish population, and delivered
a healthy supply of organic
material to the bay. Today, the
forest is gone, the waters are
murky, and there is so little
water left by the time it reaches
the coast that the Salinas's
sandbar seems like a permanent fixture. (See page 164 for
more information on the Salinas River.)

The state of the region's
watersheds and waterways is
serious, and yet there is hope.
Not only do these habitats
retain a relatively rich biodi-
versity in spite of massive ecological changes, but restoration programs of varying
scope are being implemented
up and down the coast within
the boundary of the marine
sanctuary (see pp. 76–77
for information on the San
Lorenzo River, pp. 243–244
for the Carmel River).

Golden-crowned Sparrow

The plaintive three-note song of the golden-crowned
sparrow (*Zonotrichia atricapilla*) is a familiar sound along
the shores of Monterey Bay, particularly during winter
months. It is variously described as a version of "Oh-
dear-me" (descending, and delivered at a leisurely pace).
The adult golden-crown has a beautiful yellow-gold strip,
bordered by black, right down the middle of its head.

MARINE DEBRIS AND COASTAL CLEANUPS

During the winter and early spring this section of coast can be littered with an impressive array of driftwood and other flotsam and jetsam. By the height of the summer season, however, reliable tides—and a lack of storms—clean the beaches of most debris. Increasingly, however, plastic is a prominent component of this litter. Not only is it an eyesore, but it is deadly for marine species and costly to clean up. Young marine mammals and birds can easily get their heads stuck in plastic six-pack holders, which eventually strangle them. Open-ocean species, including sea turtles and the impressive ocean sunfish, may also eat floating plastic (and other garbage), mistaking it for jellyfish; the plastic either poisons them or obstructs their digestive systems, and they die. A few alarming facts:

- According to the state of California, 14 billion pounds of garbage is dumped into the sea every year. That's right, 14 *billion* pounds.

- In 1997 on California's Coastal Cleanup Day, now an annual event, 50,000 Californians picked up some 700,000 pounds of garbage—including tens of thousands of pounds of recyclable material. That's on a single day.

- Plastic garbage is the most commonly seen human-made object at sea.

- Common plastic objects, such as bottles and cups, together with blasting cap protectors and drill hole plugs used in the petroleum industry, have been found on Arctic beaches.

- Just under half of all marine mammal species are known to either eat plastic debris or get tangled in plastic netting; 36 percent of the world's seabird species are known to ingest plastic. Sea turtles around the world consistently eat floating plastic.

- Marine debris is expensive to clean up. In Santa Monica, California, one three-mile stretch of beach costs more than $1 million annually to clean; an average of 130 tons of garbage is collected and removed from that beach each month.

Impressed? Amazed? Depressed? Then get going. Why not bring a plastic garbage bag along on your next visit to the beach? No, don't throw it on the beach. Open it up and go for a walk. Every time you see a piece of garbage, pick it up. When the bag's full, take it to the nearest trash can and throw it away. It's a good way to get some exercise while performing a very important deed. If you'd like to participate in a local Coastal Cleanup Day, contact the California Coastal Commission at 831-427-4863, or visit their website at http://ceres.ca.gov/coastalcomm/web (where you can also learn more about marine debris).

Otherwise they are varying shades of brown with some white highlights. Like the white-crowned sparrow, this species is not especially conspicuous (unless singing). Individuals spend their time in small flocks working the bluffs for seeds and other tidbits.

Moss Landing State Beach

Standing on Moss Landing's northern jetty within this State Beach, you'll see a study in contrasts. Depending on the mood of the bay, the Pacific can stretch out before you like a cool blue sheet or boil and foam with startling energy.

THE MONTEREY CANYON

The Monterey Submarine Canyon

The Monterey Submarine Canyon is the single most amazing physical feature of the Monterey Bay National Marine Sanctuary— yet it is essentially invisible. Looking out over the waters of the bay, you may find it difficult to comprehend a canyon bigger than the Grand Canyon lying just at your feet. In fact, it's analogous to a classic V-shaped river valley in the adjacent coastal mountains. Narrow at its head, the canyon begins its descent a mere 100 yards offshore of Moss Landing. It plunges precipitously at first, to a depth of 4,300 feet, dissecting the continental shelf. It then broadens and levels out; where it exits the bay and opens up, the canyon is already 13 miles wide and approximately one mile deep. Sixty miles offshore, the Monterey Canyon has dived to a depth of 12,000 feet.

Geologists believe the Monterey Canyon was formed 30 or so million years ago near present-day Santa Barbara. Its first channel may have cut through a small coastal river valley, eventually growing into the southerly outlet for the entire Central Valley before California's Transverse Range formed. As it drained central California, the canyon expanded. Tons of gravel and sand scraped out side canyons, while faults and submarine avalanches split the continental shelf. Roughly 20 million years ago, with the formation of the San Andreas Fault, the canyon began its slow migration northward on the Pacific Plate.

Larger canyons and sea trenches slice through the ocean floor in other parts of the world—the deepest one is the 36,000-foot Mariana Trench in the North Pacific— but off the continental United States the Monterey Canyon system wins the prize. Its proximity to the shoreline is one feature that sets it especially apart. Because it is so close, it plays a vital role in the bay's ecology. The canyon, in fact, is responsible for Monterey Bay being one of the richest, most diverse habitats on the Pacific coast. Not only does it serve as an underwater passageway that draws open-ocean animals very close to shore, but along with the animals come cold, nutrient-rich waters from deep within the canyon. Marine mammals and pelagic birds more typical of locations far offshore can often be found well within Monterey Bay.

For those of us who aren't fortunate enough to view the canyon directly from a research vessel via an ROV (remotely operated vehicle) far down in its depths, real-time images of the canyon can be viewed at the Monterey Bay Aquarium almost every day (see pp. 212–213).

Northward from your rocky perch of rip-rap you can see the beach curve around some three miles to the Pajaro River and beyond. Southward, Moss Landing's boat-packed working harbor is the main feature, and the Monterey Bay Aquarium Research Institute's facility graces the near shoreline. There is also a marina, yacht club, and public launching facility on the north side of

MONTEREY BAY AQUARIUM

The beautiful anglerfish

One deep-sea creature, the anglerfish *(Linophryne spp.)*, typifies the popular image of life in the depths: it's truly bizarre looking. Not only that, but its natural history is also strange.

Female anglerfish of the species *L. coronata*, for example, carry their own bioluminescent lanterns out in front of them to attract prey. They also have long barbels that grow (and glow) under their chins. When a curious fish comes along, up jumps the lantern, and suddenly the poor fish is confronted with the long, curved, spiky teeth of this wily predator.

Even weirder is the reproductive strategy of this species. The male, it turns out, is a fraction of the female's size and very plain looking. To reproduce, he attaches himself to the female, and over time their bodies fuse together. In fact, the male is a parasite, gaining sustenance from the female's body.

Even though anglers live from 3,000 feet down, they start their life at the surface of the sea as eggs (which float to the top). After hatching and feeding for a while on plankton, the young anglerfish eventually sink back down into the deep sea and begin their unique lives.

CALIFORNIA LAND MANAGEMENT

You might notice that the staff in the kiosk at Moss Landing State Beach are wearing the uniform of California Land Management (CLM), not that of State Parks. That's because Moss Landing—along with Limekiln State Park farther south—is managed for the state by CLM, a private company that administers public park properties for a variety of government agencies. These two parks are considered "alternatively funded" pilot programs. According to CLM and the California State Parks Department, this type of arrangement may prove very beneficial to a park system that has had its fair share of financial worries in recent years.

the channel. Up above you loom the bay's most visible signs of industry: the 500-foot twin stacks of the Moss Landing power plant, which more often than not are shooting brilliant white steam hundreds of feet into the air. At the tips of the twin jetties on either side of the channel, stationary signals emit a deep repetitious ring to warn ships in inclement weather—a common and reassuring sound heard in small harbors up and down the coast. This maritime signal is joined by a low hum emanating from the neighboring power plant.

Inland, beyond the smokestacks, Elkhorn Slough meanders for several miles. Bayward, unseen to landlubbers, the Monterey Submarine Canyon drops down precipitously just offshore. While you're taking this all in, a gentle splash might catch your attention and you could find yourself 20 feet away from a belly-up sea otter paddling backward toward the bay after stuffing itself with clams in the slough.

The area around the harbors and the slough's mouth is interesting, but so is Moss Landing State Beach. Here you can ride horses on the beach or engage in some shoreline fishing and clamming. The park's dune system, restored and healthy after years of effort, is also worth a look. Interpretive signs explain the restoration process and describe some of the native plant species growing on the dunes. If you have a self-contained vehicle (van, truck with a camper shell, or recreational vehicle), you can camp here. Inquire at the entrance kiosk. To access the dune trails and the beach, look for one of several pullouts along the park's only road, Jetty Road.

Until fairly recently it was believed that the ocean floor must be a dark, cold, lifeless region. Scientists have since confirmed that, yes, it is dark and cold (except around hot-water seeps), but it is anything but lifeless. In fact, as humans continue to explore the deep sea with the help of submersible crafts and remote cameras, more and more plants and animals are being discovered. And considering that the deep sea comprises a huge percentage, by volume, of all the living space on Earth, it boggles the mind to think about all that is yet to be discovered.

Because the Monterey Canyon is so deep and so close to the shoreline, scientists from the region's research institutes and universities have had unique opportunities for studying deep-sea life. While the deep-sea habitat has many layers, all the animals in this

Periphylla: an animal of the deep sea

realm share one important feature: the ability to adapt. Some of their common names—lanternfish, shining tubeshoulder, vampire squid, California headlightfish, owl-fish—hint at the unique and fascinating methods they have evolved to survive in this severe environment. Giant clams and enormous worms, deep-sea crabs and squid, and other creatures that virtually defy description all share these dark, cold, deep waters, often surviving by means of chemical processes little understood by us humans.

Physophora siphonophore: another deep-sea denizen

They also thrive in an extremely high-pressure environment: in the deepest portion of the Monterey Canyon, the pressure is approximately 320 times greater than that on shore.

DAVID WROBEL / MONTEREY BAY AQUARIUM

DAVID WROBEL / MONTEREY BAY AQUARIUM

INFORMATION

Sunset State Beach and Palm Beach State Park: 831-763-7063

Pajaro Dunes Property Management: 1-800-564-1771

William H. Volck Museum and Pajaro Valley Historical Association: 831-722-0305

Pajaro Valley Chamber of Commerce: 831-724-3900

Watsonville Wastewater Treatment Facility: 831-728-6077

California Coastal Commission: 831-427-4863 Website: http://ceres.ca.gov/ coastacomm/web

Zmudowski State Beach and Moss Landing State Beach Rangers Office: 831-384-7695

California State Parks, Monterey District Office: 831-649-2836

Moss Landing Harbor District: 831-633-2461

Pelagic Shark Research Foundation website: http://www.pelagic.org

GREAT WHITE SHARK

MONTEREY BAY AQUARIUM

Great white shark

Great white sharks (*Carcharodon carcharias*) have a serious public relations problem thanks to Hollywood and humans' active imaginations. Certainly great whites have attacked people, but statistics show that we are far more likely to die in a car crash than from being bitten by a great white shark. In fact, Department of Fish and Game records tell us that from 1926 to mid-1989, only 63 attacks occurred along the entire California coast. And only eight of those were fatal.

Nonetheless, it is difficult not to use superlatives when discussing great whites. After all, they're like grizzly bears with fins. No kidding. They are fast, incredibly strong, and, yes, potentially lethal. That aside, they are also fascinating animals. And they're relatively abundant in the greater Monterey Bay.

Although great white sharks can grow up to 20 feet long and weigh close to 5,000 pounds, adult sharks probably average 12 to 16 feet long and about half that weight. They are the world's largest predatory fish (remember, killer whales are mammals). And although they are called great *white* sharks, their color can range from dark blue-gray to light gray on top, and white below.

Great white sharks are technically pelagic, or seagoing, fish. They share this open-ocean habitat with other pelagic shark species such as the basking, thresher, blue, mako, and salmon shark—just some of the 22 species of shark that are found in Monterey Bay. Nevertheless, great whites do come into nearshore waters to find their favorite food item, elephant seals (juvenile sharks eat fish until they reach about 1,000 pounds), and they have even been spotted in surf zones. When the shark sights an elephant seal from below, it accelerates and punches the seal with a knock-out blow while taking a large bite. It then circles and returns to feed.

Much of the great white shark's biology is unknown. It is thought that these animals migrate south to warmer waters to give birth, then move back up the coast, but nobody knows for certain (except, of course, the sharks themselves). Are they territorial? Do they always return to the same home range after migrating? We simply have no idea.

Until recently fishing for shark was unregulated, and fishing for great whites had become very popular. Because there was a concern that too many sharks were being removed from the population—both here and in other areas of the world—the state of California and the governments of South Africa and Australia recently granted limited protected status to the species. To find out more about shark biology and issues, visit the Monterey Bay Aquarium, or check out the Santa Cruz–based Pelagic Shark Research Foundation's website at http://www. pelagic.org.

Remember: although Moss Landing's jetties are favorite spots for fishing and exploration, this is an area of dangerous waves and treacherous waters. Because of complicated, strong currents, swimming is not recommended.

Barn Swallows

When you enter Moss Landing State Beach, the half-mile road leading to the jetty is sandwiched between the backside of the dune system and the waters of the north harbor. During spring and summer you can see dozens of swallows skimming over the waters and road snapping up insects. These are barn swallows (*Hirundo rustica*), friends of farmers and naturalists alike. Some swallow species are difficult to identify. Not so the adult barn swallow. Its deeply forked long tail, metallic blue-black topside, and tan to chestnut chest are very distinctive.

Barn swallows dine almost entirely on flying insects— one reason they are welcome guests around barns and farmhouses. They nest under the eaves of homes and in boathouses. These birds of wide open spaces are so agile that not only can they feed their young on the wing, but they can also mate in the air (true of other swallows and swifts as well). When not zipping back and forth catching insects, barn swallows can be seen gathered on telephone wires preening and resting.

GETTING AROUND

From Sunset State Beach to Moss Landing State Beach you can either travel the hug-the-coast backroads or simply take Highway 1. For the Highway 1 option, leave Sunset, get back on San Andreas Road, and work your way to the highway on either Buena Vista (to the north) or West Beach Road (south). To follow backroads, take San Andreas to West Beach Road and turn toward the ocean;

you'll dead-end at Palm Beach State Park. From there you can go inland to find the highway; if you want to continue on to Watsonville, simply proceed under the highway. Or (still at Palm Beach) turn inland on Beach, then take a right on Thurwatcher. This is the Pajaro River agricultural loop: Thurwatcher to McGowan to Trafton to Bluff to Jensen and back to Highway 1 (now a two-lane road).

Moving toward Moss Landing you'll pass Spring-

field Road (which dead-ends on private property). Struve Road is a loop road with two consecutive entrances off the highway. Both will take you to Zmudowski State Beach via Giberson Road. The turnoff for Moss Landing State Beach—Jetty Road—is another half-mile past Struve. At both Struve and Jetty Roads, use caution exiting from and merging back onto the highway.

4 Elkhorn Slough to Monterey State Beach

Perhaps no other stretch of shoreline along Monterey Bay blurs the line between land and ocean more than the region extending from Elkhorn Slough to the city of Monterey's northern edge. Certainly in the areas north and south of here, the rocky shore and abundant tidepools provide visitors with a feeling of closeness to the sea. But here, between the great extension of the bay that is Elkhorn Slough and the Monterey Dunes, some very special features give a completely different perspective on our relationship to the ocean.

At Moss Landing, for starters, the Monterey Submarine Canyon crawls up to the very edge of the continent and delivers the mysteries of the Pacific to your fingertips. The border between land and water is further blurred by murky tides that shuttle ocean-dwelling animals in and out of the slough, to rest, to feed, to bear their young. And then there are the Monterey Dunes, a magnificent relic landscape wrought from the bay, a leftover accretion of sand that is ever on the move.

Explore the slough, or walk the shoreline here, and you come in close touch with the ocean and the life it supports. It is all around you: in the form of a shark fin gliding through the quiet blue-green waters of the slough; in the calming, graceful lines of brown pelicans skimming the tops of snow-white cresting waves; in the salty essence of summer fog as it rolls in off the bay, dampening the sand, moistening your skin, and releasing the scents of the shoreline.

Elkhorn Slough to Salinas River State Beach

The region between Elkhorn Slough and the Salinas River State Beach once was a tangle of waterways and sloughs. A slough (pronounced "slew") is a type of wetland made up of a narrow, meandering marsh or mud-fringed waterway. It can be salty and brackish with an opening to the sea—like Elkhorn Slough—or it can be filled with freshwater and have no outlet to the ocean. Until 1908, in fact, the Salinas River ran north from its present location, passed through today's Elkhorn Slough, and entered the bay about one mile beyond Moss Landing, between Moss

◄ California brown pelican

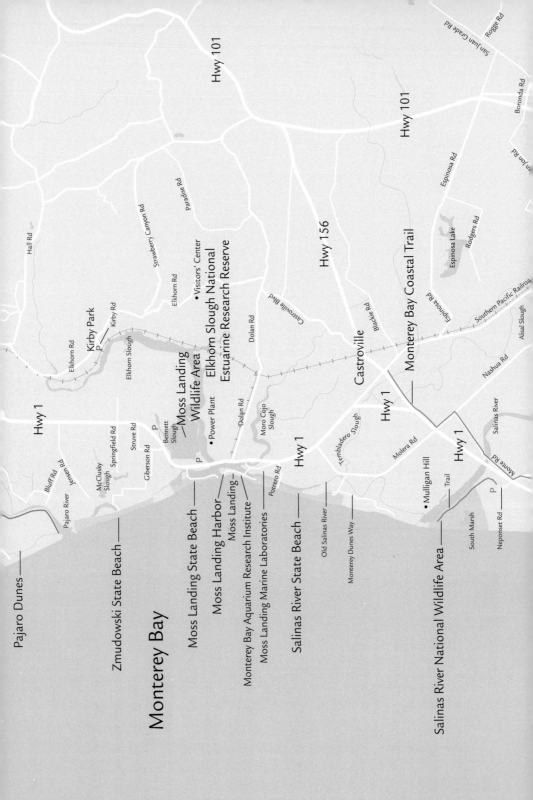

Pajaro Dunes

Zmudowski State Beach

Monterey Bay

Moss Landing State Beach

Moss Landing Harbor

Moss Landing

Monterey Bay Aquarium Research Institute

Moss Landing Marine Laboratories

Salinas River State Beach

Salinas River National Wildlife Area

Hall Rd

Hwy 101

Paradise Rd

Strawberry Canyon Rd

Elkhorn Rd

• Visitors' Center

Elkhorn Slough National
Estuarine Research Reserve

Hwy 101

San Juan Grade Rd

Rogge Rd

Boronda Rd

Espinosa Rd

Rodgers Rd

Espinosa Lake

San Juan Rd

Hwy 156

Castroville Blvd

Dolan Rd

Blackie Rd

Espinosa Rd

Southern Pacific Railroad

Monterey Bay Coastal Trail

Castroville

Alisal Slough

Nashua Rd

Salinas River

Monte Rd

Neponset Rd

South Marsh

Trail

• Mulligan Hill

Hwy 1

Molera Rd

Hwy 1

Tembladero Slough

Monterey Dunes Way

Old Salinas River

Hwy 1

Potrero Rd

Moro Cojo Slough

Dolan Rd

P

• Power Plant

Moss Landing
Wildlife Area

Bennett
Slough

P

Giberson Rd

Struve Rd

Springfield Rd

Bluff Rd

Jensen Rd

Pajaro River

McClusky
Slough

P

Kirby Rd

Kirby Park

P

Elkhorn Rd

Elkhorn Slough

Hwy 1

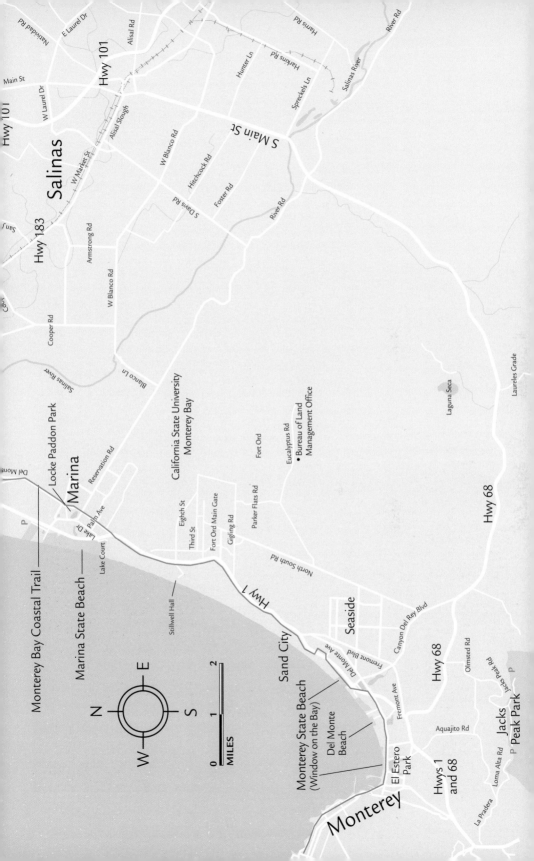

Landing and Zmudowski State Beaches. Because the Salinas has meandered across these coastal lands for thousands of years, the area is covered with prime agricultural soils and remnant waterways. Luckily for us, there are also numerous protected areas and parklands. This makes for fantastic wildlife viewing along with ample opportunities for recreation.

Elkhorn Slough: From Sharks to Oak Trees . . . and More

Two aspects of Elkhorn Slough are immediately impressive. The first is the fact that it still exists at all—most of California's coastal marshes and estuaries have been destroyed since 1850. The second is that you can drive right past it on the inland side, or right over its mouth along the coast, and not even know it's there.

In fact, Elkhorn Slough is the largest coastal wetland between San Francisco Bay and Morro Bay. And although it has been manipulated and abused in the past, it survives today as a vital link for numerous marine species and tens of thousands of migratory birds.

Here are some facts to get you started: The slough is seven miles long, taking in some 3,000 acres of inundated tidal lands and approximately 3,500 acres of preserved uplands. It is home to over 400 species of invertebrates (animals without backbones) and 80 species of fish, and 200 species of birds either live here or visit seasonally.

The magical entrance to Elkhorn Slough

I f you begin your sojourn on the backside of the slough, you have to visit the reserve's headquarters. In fact, this is the perfect place to start your visit no matter what your final destination is. The reserve—which was made possible through a cooperative effort by the state's Wildlife Conservation Board, California Department of Fish and Game, and the National Oceanic and Atmospheric Administration—maintains one of the nicest visitor centers on the central coast. Programs in and around the reserve are also helped out by the Elkhorn Slough Foundation (they have a small office here). The center's staff is very helpful, and you'll find plenty of free literature, informative exhibits, and a well-stocked natural history store. The center puts on a variety of educational programs, such as interpretive nature walks and slough-related workshops. Additionally, several thousand teachers have been trained here in estuarine education and tens of thousands of students have visited since educational programs began here in

Elkhorn Slough National Estuarine Research Reserve

1983. You can reach the reserve at 831-728-2822.

The 1,500-acre reserve also maintains some five miles of easy-walking trails. For a short walk from the visitor's center you can mosey downslope to the first observation platform (wheelchair accessible) or continue to the large barn where you can overlook the slough. Keep an eye open for the parallel ridges in South Marsh and try to figure them out. In the barn, which is all that remains of the old Elkhorn Dairy, you can find shelter on a drizzly day, use a bathroom, or search the rafters for barn owls. There are also impressive high-voltage towers high-stepping across the slough here, carrying electricity from the Moss Landing power plant.

To really feel like you're stepping back in time, and to

get a bit more exercise, hoof it on over to the old Empire Gun Club Site, across the railroad tracks (about two and a half miles round trip). It's an elevated piece of land right next to the main channel of the slough—keep an eye out for passing harbor seals. Reserve personnel and volunteers are undertaking some exciting restoration projects there.

Although the slough is a superb place to visit year round, the numbers of birds plummet during late spring and summer months when most nonresident species are nesting far to the north. Notable exceptions are the resident great blue herons and great egrets, which nest quite conspicuously in pine and eucalyptus trees here.

It is also the domain of six known endangered or threatened species.

A visit to the wildlife viewing sites near Highway 1 within the Moss Landing Wildlife Area gives you one view of the slough: a low-lying territory of daily tidal fluctuations rimmed with pickleweed. Visit Kirby Park or the Elkhorn Slough National Estuarine Research Reserve and you'll get a better feel for how the slough winds inland, encompassing both pickleweed-dominated tidal

The Elkhorn Slough Foundation is a non-profit organization that supports research, education, and conservation throughout the slough. Give them a call at 831-728-5939 if you'd like to find out more about their programs, check the status of slough projects, or find out how you can help protect and restore the slough; or check out their website at http://www.elkhornslough.org. They maintain an office next to the reserve's visitor center.

lands and acres of rolling oak woodlands. All of the flat and semiflat terrain not within protected lands has been cleared and converted to agriculture.

Organized slough events, such as walks and talks, are put on by the reserve (contact them at 831-728-2822) and the Elkhorn Slough Foundation (831-728-5939). You can also take a boat tour or rent a kayak out of Moss Landing—call Elkhorn Slough Safari Nature Boat Tours (831-633-5555) or the Kayak Connection (831-724-5692) for information.

Kirby Park Public Access

Just down the road from the reserve you can put in a small boat or kayak at the Kirby Park Public Access. At the north end of the parking lot you'll also find a nice trail right next to the slough (about one mile round trip), with interpretive signs. It slices through an almost continuous mat of pickleweed and a portion of it is elevated over a short side arm of the slough—a good spot to look

The brown pelican *(Pelecanus occidentalis)* is one of the slough's endangered species. That might be hard to believe, since 5,000 of these enormous birds have been counted in the former salt ponds on the north side of the slough, in late summer after their arrival from southern breeding areas. In fact, this is one of the brown pelican's most important roosting areas on the Pacific coast.

During the late 1950s and the 1960s, however, this pelican was devastated by the pesticide DDT. The breeding population on California's Anacapa Island alone plummeted from an estimated 5,000 pairs in the early 1960s

California brown pelican

to fewer than 100 pairs in 1968 (brown pelicans nest on islands off southern California and into Mexico). Although the pelican is still listed as endangered, it has made solid

moves toward recovery: there are now some 4,500 to 5,000 breeding pairs in southern California.

With a wingspan of well over six feet, this avian 747 is a comical-looking bird when roosting or while paddling on the water. In flight, though, brown pelicans are majestic, and when diving for fish from 30 feet above the water they look incredibly powerful. (But why don't they break their necks every time they plunge beneath the surface?) When they arrive in Monterey Bay in midsummer from their southern nesting grounds, most adult birds are dusk colored with white or yellowish heads. Juveniles are all dusky or brown. Interestingly, they once nested at Point Lobos; perhaps they will again one day soon.

Humans have been attracted to Elkhorn Slough for thousands of years. Evidence shows that coastal Indians thrived along this waterway for generations. The natural resources were plentiful, the climate mild, and the site centrally located for excursions up and down the coast and inland.

18th century Spanish explorers and missionaries put an end to the Indian's life here. They also introduced cattle and horses to the environment. Ecological changes followed quickly as big game (elk and grizzly bear) disappeared from the area and domestic livestock took over, altering the native vegetation forever.

Additional changes to the slough and its surrounding uplands continued in the mid-1800s as American settlers diked off portions of the slough and farming began in and around the body of water. By the 1870s, 100-ton steamships were plying the slough's waters all the way up to Hudson's Landing, and the railroad was soon to follow.

However, the single most radical change to the slough occurred in 1947, when Moss Landing Harbor was opened.

Prior to that event, tidal action in the slough was sporadic and very confined—these were quiet, still waters, and with a higher proportion of freshwater. With increased tidal action, species composition in the slough changed, and erosion of the channel and mudflats increased dramatically. By the 1970s people concerned with the future of the slough began efforts to protect it. Today there is still much work to be done to ensure the integrity of the slough, but there is no doubting that most of Elkhorn Slough—as we know it today—is safe from further harm.

ILLUSTRATION COURTESY OF OUR LADY OF REFUGE PARISH, CASTROVILLE, CALIFORNIA

A 19th century view of Elkhorn Slough's entrance, and south to the Monterey Peninsula

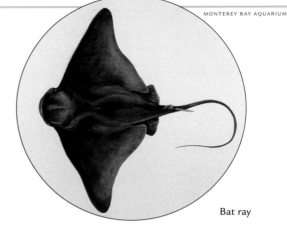

MONTEREY BAY AQUARIUM

Bat ray

The bat ray *(Myliobatus californica)* is a year-round resident in Elkhorn Slough. These blackish-brown relatives of sharks can grow up to six feet across and weigh up to 200 pounds. It's an impressive sight when an adult bat ray glides by in the slough's murky waters looking for a dinner of bottom-dwelling animals. They use their large fleshy wings to stir up the mud and reveal a meal. Bat rays have odd-looking plates in their mouths which they use to crush mollusks of all kinds. Oyster farmers here, as well as in San Francisco Bay, loathed them.

Female bat rays give birth to little live rays—up to six at once—in the slough. Within a few days they are swimming about freely and their stinging spine, located just behind the tiny dorsal fin at the base of the whiplike tail, is ready for action. Bat ray stings are venomous, capable of inflicting very painful lesions, and should be treated immediately.

Also seen in the slough on occasion are round stingrays *(Urolophus halleri)*. They arrive in the fall and winter from the sand flats just offshore.

for marine animals and fish during high tide. The trail ends at a small brush-covered knoll (watch out for poison oak). This trail was made possible by the Elkhorn Slough Foundation, the Coastal Conservancy, the local community, and the Nature Conservancy (owners of a 400-acre preserve north of Kirby Park).

Moss Landing Wildlife Area

Part and parcel of the slough's protected lands is the 800-acre Moss Landing Wildlife Area, managed by the Department of Fish and Game. A good-sized piece of this area once supported a thriving salt extraction business on the northern bank of the slough. Today, the former salt ponds have reverted to wildlife habitat, which can attract thousands of brown pelicans and countless other shorebirds and waterfowl.

Presently there are two access points to view wildlife and stretch your legs: North Entrance and South Entrance. The North Entrance is directly off Highway 1, right where the road curves sharply after passing Struve Road (coming from the north). Look for a wooden sign announcing the wildlife area; it's next to a dirt road that leads past an agricultural field to a dirt parking lot. From the parking lot, about four miles of trails wind through the former salt ponds and along the north shore of the slough. During wet weather the short dirt road and parking lot can get very muddy.

The South Entrance is located directly across from the Moss Landing Yacht Harbor and the public boat ramp, and immediately north of the highway bridge over the slough. This is public property, so don't be fooled by the trucks and machinery (slated for removal after 2000). From the parking lot here you can follow the levees along the northern edge of the slough. To find out more about the wildlife area, call the Department of Fish and Game at 831-649-2870.

Hudson's Landing

It's hard to imagine today, but almost 150 years ago Elkhorn Slough was an important transportation link for the young town of Watsonville and the fertile Pajaro Valley. At the very head of the slough—only four miles south of Watsonville—a dock was built in the 1860s. It soon became known as Hudson's Landing, in recognition of the landing's first agent, Mark A. Hudson, who worked there from 1868 until 1910. He oversaw the shipment of goods from Pajaro Valley. Produce was loaded onto flat-bottomed boats—and eventually large steamships—and transferred down to Moss Landing. From there, goods were loaded onto larger ships en route to San Francisco.

If you ever take a ride on Amtrak's Coast Starlight, keep your eyes open when you cross the slough. If you look close, you can still see the foundation of Hudson's Landing sticking up from the mudflats and pickleweed—the silent reminder of a time long gone.

Western Sandpiper

More than a dozen species of sandpipers flock to Elkhorn Slough annually, but one species outshines them all when it comes to number: the western sandpiper (*Calidris mauri*). A mere six inches from head to tail and weighing next to nothing, the western is believed to account for some 75 percent of the slough's bird population during the migration season.

Western sandpipers

SANCTUARY NOTE
SLOUGH SHARKS

Leopard shark

Sharks are one of the oldest animals on earth: they've been around some 400 million years. And unlike most fish, the world's 360 or so shark species (and some 400 species of rays and skates) have skeletons made of cartilage instead of bone. That's the stuff in the bridge of your nose. Their tough skin is composed of thousands of denticles, or tiny scales, which all point backward. Next time you're swimming with a great white shark (just kidding!), run your hand from its head toward its tail—smooth. Run your hand the other way—rough like sandpaper.

Here are three species of sharks you can see with regularity in Elkhorn Slough and close to shore throughout the marine sanctuary. Researchers believe 22 species of sharks can be found in Monterey Bay, and even more in the sanctuary as a whole.

■ **Leopard shark**
(Triakis semifasciata)
Leopard sharks are easily recognized by their distinctive color pattern: tan or gray bodies with bold dark spots and bars across their backs. Males can grow up to five feet long, and females to six feet. This shark species is known for being gregarious—that is, it occasionally forms large schools that roam the nearshore waters or hover about the kelp forests, especially during the winter months. Although some shark young are born live, the female leopard produces eggs, which then hatch in the water. Up to 40 young sharks, or pups, can be produced by a single female. This shark is an opportunistic diner—it eats any prey item it can catch, including other sharks.

■ **Brown smoothhound**
(Mustelus henlei)
and
Gray smoothhound
(M. californicus)
Both the brown and gray smoothhound shark can be seen in Elkhorn Slough from winter through late spring. It's uncertain why they enter the estuary, since they don't breed here, but by summer they're sure to have returned to their foraging grounds just beyond the breaking waves offshore. Both species cruise the bottom looking for crabs, small fish, and shrimp.

The two species are very similar looking. However, the brown smoothhound is actually a dark reddish brown or dark brown, while the gray smoothhound is a tannish gray color.

Brown smoothhound shark

Thousands of these sandpipers arrive each autumn from breeding grounds in the Russian and Alaskan tundra. Many continue on south to winter in Central America, but others stay here to rest and feed throughout the winter and spring before returning north. These diminutive peeps (as many small sandpipers are called) are true precision flyers. At the slightest sign of danger or disturbance, great flocks lift off together from the mudflats to perform flawless in-flight maneuvers. They quickly resettle and resume their frantic search for food. Western sandpipers and their kin present a rather awesome quandary for avian researchers: How can a bird so small migrate some 1,200 miles in 24 hours? They have been known to do just that when returning to their tundra nesting sites.

Terns

Perhaps the most graceful fliers in the slough, and along the Monterey Bay shoreline generally, are terns. They hover on finely tapered white wings over still waters, or just beyond the waves, then crash-dive into the water after a fish dinner. Here are the most common terns you will see and hear overhead:

Caspian tern *(Sterna caspia)*

The husky Caspian tern is the largest North American tern, measuring almost two feet from head to tail—about the size of a California gull. The adult has a brilliant orange bill, a jet black cap (which fades in winter), and black legs and feet. The body is light gray above and white below; the tail is slightly forked. It is a common bird around the bay, but its num-

Caspian terns

bers diminish during the winter. Like all terns, the Caspian dives head first for its dinner of fish. Its raucous calls, "kowk" and "ca-arr," are very distinctive. Once heard, this bird is hard to forget. In fact, you can often hear a Caspian before you see one.

■ Forster's tern *(S. forsteri)*

Forster's tern is Monterey Bay's most common tern, seen here from approximately March through October. As they fly over the nearshore in groups, they are in constant verbal contact, uttering a high-pitched, coarse "kyarr, kyarr" or "keeik-keeik." These 14-inch birds look somewhat like a smaller version of the Caspian tern, except that the Forster's bill is thinner and orange-red (with a distinct black tip), its legs and feet are orange-red, and its tail is deeply forked. Forster's terns dive for fish, but they also eat insects. After their shallow plunge into the water, typically just beyond the breaking waves, they resume flight, then often give a quick shake as if to dry off a bit. They are colonial nesters in fresh and saltwater marshes.

Forster's terns are often seen feeding just beyond the surfline.

Elegant terns

There are many types of wetlands through-out the state of California—salt marshes, freshwater and brackish marshes, shallow lagoons, sloughs, tidal mudflats, and fens (peat-forming areas). Unfortunately, most of them are gone. Historically, wet-land areas have been easy targets for drying out or filling in; this was done in order to farm their fertile soils or to construct buildings or housing in strategic or attractive settings.

Only recently have we realized the critical role these benign landscapes play, for both wildlife and humans. They serve as vital feeding, nesting, and resting sites for migratory birds. Many marine fish (including many popular sport and economic species) use coastal wetlands as nurseries for their young. Wetlands also act as buffers against storm waters, while serving as natural purifiers of wastewater. And last—but not of least importance—wetlands are beautiful. Any-one who has visited a thriving wetland at sunrise or sunset, or walked its edges during spring or fall migration, comes away both amazed and inspired.

■ Elegant tern *(S. elegans)*

A summer and fall visitor to the region is the elegant tern. Looking much like a cross between the Forster's and the Caspian terns, the elegant is slightly smaller than the Caspian; it has a long, thin orange bill; a black cap, legs, and feet; and its tail is forked almost as deeply as the Forster's. When the elegant tern is at rest, a small tuft of feathers can be spotted on the backside of its head. Its call is a sharp "kea-rick."

Mudflats

If ever there was a misunderstood and little-loved part of wetlands, it has to be mudflats. At low tide vast stretches of mud are exposed in Elkhorn Slough between the water channels and the bands of pickleweed slightly upslope. There is no arguing that mudflats can emit strong odors at times, and they are virtually impossible to extract yourself from if for some reason you decide to take a stroll through the mud (not a good idea), but they are also incredibly rich environments. Just ask any shorebird.

Thousands of organisms live in a handful of mudflat gunk, and they have all devised ingenious ways to survive in their unique environment. Everything from microscopic phytoplankton, zooplankton, diatoms, and bacteria to worms, snails, shrimp, mussels, clams, and crabs thrive in mudflats. Most mudflat species are burrowers, so inspect the surface carefully. Fat innkeeper worms and ghost shrimp leave visible signs of their homes: shrimp form mounds—like miniature volcanoes; worms produce short mud tubes rising above the slippery surface. Numerous clam species also produce a variety of openings at the surface for their siphons. Mud crabs hide in cracks and crevices where mudflats are uneven or where the mud oozes around a solid object like a rock or a clump of pickleweed.

Because of this abundance of life, you'll be able to scope a fantastic variety of shorebird species probing and pecking for food at low tide in mudflats. When the waters return, so do the rays, sharks, and numerous fish species, while topside, diving ducks and cormorants move in to feed across the inundated flats.

Pickleweed and Dodder

Common pickleweed (*Salicornia virginica*) is by far the most dominant plant species in Elkhorn Slough, making up some 90 percent of the plant cover in areas influenced by the tide. The remaining portions of shoreline are occupied by salt-tolerant species such as salt grass, alkali heath, and jaumea. The chubby, segmented little branches of pickleweed are also common on inlet shores throughout the entire marine sanctuary.

Pickleweed and dodder

Unlike most other marsh plants, pickleweed does not have salt-excreting glands. Instead, pickleweed concentrates salt in its end segments (its genus name means "salt horn" in Latin). In the fall the salt-packed tips of the branches turn red, dry up, and drop off. Goodbye salt. This makes for some spectacular fall colors in coastal marshlands. Break a green stem open and touch it to your tongue, and you'll taste salty juices; in fact, people once gathered spring pickleweed and ate it like asparagus. Interestingly, not many animals eat pickleweed, and scientists believe its major contribution to the ecosystem kicks in after it dies and decomposes. It is also important habitat. A variety of species—insects, crabs, birds, and several types of mice—find shelter in pickleweed.

During summer months acres of pickleweed and other marsh plants are masked by an orange webbing, as if some monster marsh spider has been at work. That webbing is a parasitic plant called dodder (*Cuscuta salina*). Dodder roots on the pickleweed, then slowly extracts moisture and nutrients. This same species of dodder can also be found in interior desert regions—an indication of how precious freshwater really is in a slough or salt marsh, and how, ironically, marsh habitats share some ecological characteristics with desert regions.

Herons and Egrets

Herons and egrets are very beautiful birds. Because of their height and coloration, they tend to stick out in horizontal marsh habitats and so are easy to spot. For this reason, and because of their interesting feeding behaviors, they are also fun to watch. Even kids can see these birds easily. Along some parts of the shoreline, herons and egrets have become somewhat accustomed to people, so you can approach fairly close.

■ Great blue heron *(Ardea herodias)*

Great blue herons strut about marshlands and sloughs like avian enforcers. These four-foot-tall birds are slate blue and stately. If you are a mouse or a fish, however,

their approach is cause for alarm—they have a voracious appetite and will eat just about anything. Like all egrets and herons, the great blue can also be spotted in open fields and grasslands stalking voles and mice at a leisurely pace. Although great blues will defend feeding sites from other great blues and egrets, when it comes to the breeding and nesting season, it is common to see herons and egrets nesting side by side atop tall trees. During this time of year the great blue puffs out its chest feathers and its coloration

Great blue heron

intensifies. Locally, great blue herons nest in pine trees close to Elkhorn Slough starting in early spring; you can see them especially well along the South Marsh Loop Trail, on the far side of the small pond.

■ Great egret *(Casmerodius albus)*

Great egret

Great egrets truly are great, even regal. Standing over three feet tall, they are all white with large yellow bills and yellow legs. Adults grow long plumes on the backs of their necks during breeding season, which they flip about with apparent abandon. They, too, nest in large numbers within the slough area. A slow, methodical hunter, this bird stands perfectly still, like a statue, in shallow water until it sees a fish pass by. A quick jab, and a fish is soon in its bill.

■ Snowy egret *(Egretta thula)*

Snowy egrets are two-thirds the size of their tall cousin
the great egret, but they make up for their size with
showy feathers and quick actions. Snowy egrets have
slender black bills, black legs, and bright yellow feet
below black legs—the bird with golden slippers. Snowies
look like young rock stars in training with their wispy
head feathers and almost hyper body movements. They
saunter about their stage of shallow water stirring up
food with their brilliant feet, and repeatedly jab at the
water. Their long graceful head feathers were the targets
of plume hunters at the turn of the century, an activity
that decimated their populations until it was banned.
They are most easily viewed in the winter time.

Snowy egret

Moss Landing Power Plant

The twin stacks of Moss Landing power plant—or
Mighty Moss, as some locals call it—can be seen far out
at sea. On land, you certainly can't miss them. In fact,
they are visible from
shoreline vantage points
both north and south. It
might seem strange that
PG&E chose this partic-
ular location for a power
plant back in 1952. It is
strange until you realize
that in order to keep
their enormous turbine-
turning boilers cool the
plant requires up to 1.3
billion gallons of cold
water every day. A good
source of cold water, of
course, is the ocean.
After the water is used
to cool the boilers, it's
returned to the bay.

Mighty Moss power plant overlooking Moss Landing Harbor

This plant operates 24 hours a day, seven days a week.
At full capacity it burns an estimated 18 million cubic
feet of natural gas every hour. When natural gas supplies
are low, the plant is also equipped to burn low-sulfur
fuel oil. The landmark towers were built up 500 feet to
create a current of air that aids in the burning of the gas
and oil. The plant was recently sold by PG&E to another
power company.

The harbor town of Moss Landing

Moss Landing

Stroll down Moss Landing Road for a couple of blocks (it doesn't go much farther) and you'll realize that marine stores and antique shops must go together. At least, they do in Moss Landing. Several antique shops can be found on the main drag, next to eating establishments and marine supply stores. Of special interest is the town's friendly United States Post Office. The employees couldn't be nicer, and the walls are adorned with an impressive collection of historic photographs of the region (on long-term loan from the antique dealer across the street). Stop to study the photographs and read about local history and the area's cast of characters. Make sure to inspect the old aerial photographs and landscape shots. You won't believe how much the local landscape has changed.

From Moss Landing Road, cross over the old Salinas River channel on the one-lane Sandholdt Bridge (named after a former mayor of Monterey, Dr. John Sandholdt). The bridge brings you to what the locals call "The Island." Actually, it's the harbor's south jetty, home to more marine-related businesses, old canneries (closed in the 1940s), an assortment of eclectic structures, and two of the major centers for marine research on Monterey Bay: Moss Landing Marine Laboratories and the Monterey Bay Aquarium Research Institute. (Although Moss

MARINE RESEARCH AND MONTEREY BAY

Monterey Bay Aquarium Research Institute's *Western Flyer*

The Moss Landing–based Monterey Bay Aquarium Research Institute (MBARI) and the Moss Landing Marine Laboratories are just two of 22 marine research facilities on Monterey Bay. The marine laboratories serve a consortium of six state universities, while MBARI is a private non-profit outfit. Other institutions, public as well as private, have chosen to locate on Monterey Bay because of its rich history of marine study and because of the living laboratory the bay and the larger marine sanctuary provide. The recently established California State University Monterey Bay is continuing this fine tradition on the former grounds of Fort Ord.

You would be hard put to find another spot in the world with such diversity—from the riches of Elkhorn Slough to the extensive dunes to the open ocean, and down into one of the world's deepest marine canyons—and all of it protected. It is an ecological continuum ripe for exploration and study. Not only will the flourishing marine research facilities around the bay be discovering new wonders for years to come, but their work will also help maintain the ecological integrity of the region. The benefit to residents and visitors alike is immense.

If you'd like to find out more about marine research in Monterey Bay, access the websites for MBARI (http://www.mbari.org) or Moss Landing Marine Lab (http://color.mlml.calstate.edu/www/mlml.htm). For even more information you can go to a general linking site called "Oceanography around Monterey Bay" at http://www.oc.nps.navy.mil/local.html. You can also get in touch with the National Marine Sanctuary, at 831-647-4201; or go to its website at http://www.mbnms.nos.noaa.gov.

Landing Marine Lab used to have its main facilities on the jetty, the 1989 Loma Prieta earthquake caused extensive damage to the institution and its facilities have been scattered in various locations since then. The new main office is off Moss Landing Road—on the mainland near the town's water tower—and a new research station is in the process of being built at that site.) You can drive to the northern tip of this jetty, park, and explore the beach or go fishing. (Watch out for broken glass here—the parking area is also a favorite pullout for late night revelers.) There is also a beach access between the two research buildings on the west side of the jetty; look for the Coastal Conservancy's public access sign: two bare feet venturing toward a wave. Or, where Sandholdt Bridge touches down on the south jetty, you can go left instead of right and drive to Salinas River State Beach.

As long as people have been able to walk the shores of the world's oceans or set to sea in boats, they have hunted marine mammals. With time, improved skill, and better equipment we became so proficient at hunting marine mammals that at least one species is now extinct—the Steller's sea cow, in the late 18th century—and many more have been pushed to the brink of extinction. Because of this reality, in 1972 the Marine Mammal Protection Act was made into law. With a few minor exceptions, it is now illegal to harass or hunt marine mammals in U.S. waters. Today, thanks in part to this act, many once-threatened species, such as the gray whale and the sea otter, have made a comeback. Even so, they still have a long way to go before approaching a healthy semblance of their historic population levels.

The newly restored dune on your immediate right was the site for the former Moss Landing Marine Laboratories before the earthquake.

Moss Landing is named after Captain Charles Moss, an East Coast native who came to this quiet section of coast in the mid–19th century with his family. With the help of Cato Vierra, a Portuguese whaler from the Azores, Captain Moss built the first wharf on this stretch of the bay. Whaling stations soon sprang up here, and tall-masted ships were anchoring just offshore while steamships offered service to San Francisco. Since then Moss Landing has witnessed the coming and going of many marine-related enterprises.

Major changes started in 1946 when the Army Corps of Engineers began their construction of what we now know as Moss Landing Harbor. By the end of 1947 they had breached the dunes and dug out a portion of the former Salinas River channel. Today, the harbor is touted as one of the safest places for boats along the central coast. The T-shaped port is split into the North Harbor (by Moss Landing State Beach) and South Harbor (by the town of Moss Landing). The North Harbor, which maintains 100 recreational slips, is home to the Moss Landing Yacht Club and a handful of other water-related businesses (you can rent kayaks here). The South Harbor is a real working harbor, a fact immediately obvious to anyone who stops and watches.

With some 500 slips here filled with commercial fishing boats of all shapes and sizes, Moss Landing is home to one of the largest commercial fishing fleets in the state. Local fisherman haul in northern anchovy, Pacific herring, albacore, tuna, squid, crabs, salmon, and a lot more besides. A large parking area (and bathrooms) on the inland side of the South Harbor is also home to the Moss Landing Harbor District. There are no real recreational facilities here because this is the parking lot for the people working on the boats. Nonetheless, take a minute and try to figure out what type of fish an individual boat catches by looking at its shape and the equipment on its deck. Don't be afraid to ask. Fishermen are a friendly bunch of people, and they love talking about their boats and their profession. While you are watching or talking, cock an ear and listen for the different languages floating on the salty air—these professionals hail from all around the world.

If you would like to find out more about Moss Landing and its annual summer Antique Fair, call the Moss Landing Chamber of Commerce at 831-633-4501. The Harbor District will also provide you with boating and recreational information; you can reach them at 831-633-2461.

Whaling Stations

Whaling took place along the entire Monterey Bay shoreline from the late 1700s, when whaling ships began coming here from New England, well into this century. Early on, processing was done on board the ships; the first land-based station hereabouts was established in 1854 by Captain John P. Davenport in Monterey with a crew of Azorean Portuguese whalers (the captain founded Davenport Landing in the late 1860s). Other stations were established at Pigeon Point (north of Año Nuevo), Santa Cruz, Moss Landing, Carmel Bay, and in Big Sur.

Old whaling station at Moss Landing

Although Indians in the Pacific Northwest once hunted whales principally for meat, Monterey's pioneer whalers were interested only in rendering oil from the animals' blubber. Eventually, gray whale baleen (a comblike structure on the roof of the mouth used to strain food) was collected and used as a strong, flexible material in woman's corsets, skirt hoops, umbrellas, brushes, and much more.

When kerosene was created in the 1880s whale oil prices plummeted and the industry fell on hard times. The last whale to be taken by shore-based whalers in Monterey Bay was a humpback, in 1905. And it was none too soon for the whales, whose populations were by then severely depleted. The pursuit of these great animals had been relentless. The mainstays of the industry, humpback and gray whales (though other whales were killed if the opportunity arose), were being taken along the entire Pacific coast and up into Arctic waters as well, and gray whales had been imperiled even more after their calving grounds were discovered in Baja California in 1855.

The reprieve was short, however, for soon a new wave of whalers was back at work. They were using modern equipment to catch the animals farther out at sea, then processing them on shore in Moss Landing. They killed and processed 700 humpbacks during this period between 1919 and 1925, harvesting them mainly for whale oil, which was used industrially for a lubricant, and baleen.

"It is impossible to describe either the number of whales with which we were surrounded, or their familiarity. They spouted every half minute within half a pistol shot of our frigates, and caused a most annoying stench."

Jean-François de La Pérouse, anchored in Monterey Bay (1786)

Many 19th-century Monterey Bay beaches were covered with whale bones.

ILLUSTRATION COURTESY OF LEON TROUSETT, AMON CARTER MUSEUM, FORT WORTH, TEXAS

Gray whales are the most common whales off these shores (see page 49), though there are other species out there as well, including humpbacks, blues, and minkes. Less common, but also seen from time to time, are orcas, fin, sei, pilot, and Baird's beaked whales. On a calm day and at the right time of year—when the bay and the greater Pacific Ocean look like a tightly drawn blue sheet—a puff of vapor rising off the water, isolated whitecaps, or the splash of a tail pointing skyward can indicate the presence of whales.

Simply put, whales are among the largest animals on earth. Blue whales, in fact, are the largest animal: they can tip the scales at 100 tons and

stretch out over 100 feet. These warm-blooded mammals bear their young alive, and baby whales suckle milk from their mothers. Scientists divide whales into two basic groups, or suborders: baleen whales (Mysticeti, meaning mustachioed whale in Greek-Latin) and toothed whales (Odontoceti, meaning they've got teeth). Baleen whales—such as grays, humpbacks, and blues—have large filters in their mouths to remove food from seawater; they also have two blowholes. Toothed whales—such as sperm whales and orcas—catch their prey with their teeth, and they have a single blowhole.

■ **Humpback whale**
(Megaptera novaeangliae)
Humpback whales are large baleen whales common to these waters. Although the local population was once

Humpback whale at mid-breach

hunted to near extinction, they've recovered enough that shoreline watchers can occasionally spot them out in the bay and up and down the coast, particularly in the fall, but most humpback sightings take place from whale watching boats offshore. They feed mostly on euphausiids—small shrimplike krill.

Humpbacks are popularly known for their complicated songs and for their extremely long pectoral (side) fins. Still

The writing was on the wall, though. Elsewhere the U.S. whaling industry collapsed shortly before World War I, when petroleum came on the scene and spring steel gradually replaced baleen. The last active whaling station in this country was at Point San Pablo, in San Francisco Bay; it was shut down in 1971 when the United States banned whaling.

Today, the legacy of whaling can be found all around the bay: from the now-barren coves north of Santa Cruz that once supported beach-based whaling stations to Moss Landing, with its rich whaling history, Monterey's Old Whaling House, and such Monterey Peninsula and Big Sur place-names as Whalery Hill, Whalers Cove (and the Whalers Cabin), and Whalers Knoll.

Salinas River State Beach

Salinas River State Beach stretches between Moss Landing and the mouth of the Salinas River, just over three miles to the south. It consists of several hundred acres of beau-

photographs of humpbacks swimming make it look as though they are flying through the ocean. These are stocky whales that can grow to more than 50 feet long. To the top-side observer they can look very dark, and they have a very small dorsal, or back, fin. Humpbacks are also famous for their acrobatics. They can be seen breaching far out of the water and doing a little twist in the air before crashing back into the sea.

■ Blue whale
(Balaenoptera musculus)

Blue whales are true blue-blood whales—they are the kings. They commonly grow to 85 feet long, but can reach lengths of more than 100 feet, and their weight has been recorded at over 150 tons. Unlike the chunky humpbacks, blues are long (*very* long) and streamlined; like humpbacks,

they have small dorsal fins. This animal, the largest on earth, is a baleen whale. That's right: the blue whale attains its gargantuan proportions by straining tons of tiny euphausiids from the water.

It is believed that several thousand blue whales frequent the waters off California. In the fall, when krill can concentrate in the nearshore waters, blue whales are commonly observed off the Farallon Islands to the north, in Monterey Bay, and even around the Monterey Peninsula.

■ Minke whale
(Balaenoptera acutorostrata)

Minke whales, another baleen whale, measure around 35 feet as adults, a bit smaller than the gray whale. Even though its size might confuse shoreline watchers into thinking they are observing a gray whale, several features will

help you distinguish between the two. Grays have broad backs covered by small ridges or bumps and no dorsal fin; also, they are typically seen in groups. Minke whales have slender bodies, a pointed, almost triangular head, and a ridge running down the back; they also have a dorsal fin. In the Monterey Bay region, moreover, minkes are usually seen alone.

Although the minke is found worldwide, because it is relatively small it was never pursued by whalers. However, after the International Whaling Commission declared a moratorium on whaling starting in 1986, at least two countries began catching minkes in the name of research and because they are very plentiful. Overall, though, the world's minke population appears to be stable.

tiful beaches and impressive dunes—some say they are the best-preserved dunes on the entire bay. The slough that runs behind the dunes for the entire length of the beach is the old channel of the Salinas River. This is a favorite spot for people who really want to stretch out during a long shoreline walk. Surf fishing and horseback riding (on wet sand and on the well-marked interdune trail only) are also popular pastimes here.

There are three different entrances to the beach. The first is right in Moss Landing. Cross Sandholdt Bridge, turn left immediately, and you'll see a parking lot. The other two entrances are beyond Moss Landing off Highway 1 to the south. These are the lots you'll use if you're trailering a horse in for a ride on the beach. For the middle access, turn right on Potrero

Boardwalk across dunes, Salinas River State Beach

From Watsonville you can catch a Monterey-Salinas Transit (MST) bus and travel all the way to Monterey (and, during summer months, beyond to Big Sur). Many of their buses have bicycle racks. You can also get off in Salinas and catch an Amtrak train. Call MST for schedule information: 831-899-2555.

Road, just past the cemetery; you'll cross the old Salinas River and end up in a large parking lot behind the dunes. To find the southern access point, continue on Highway 1 to Molera Road; turn right, then right again on Monterey Dunes Way. You'll see the parking lot set in against the backside of these well-vegetated dunes (continue on and you dead-end at the Monterey Dunes Colony).

No matter which access spot you choose, brace yourself for stunning views of the bay and miles of shoreline to explore. There is a trail system between the middle and south access points. Please stay on the marked trail because State Parks is trying to eliminate the network of older connector trails and allow dune vegetation to recuperate.

Castroville, "Artichoke Center of the World"

Many of the agricultural fields surrounding Monterey Bay are dedicated to a very distinct crop: the amazing artichoke (*Cynara scolymus*). Most Californians are familiar with its globe-shaped set of leaves, but first-time visitors from America's heartland or the East Coast are often perplexed and amused when presented with a freshly cooked artichoke to eat.

It is believed that the artichoke was introduced to California right here in Monterey County by Italian farmers in 1922. From that point on there was no looking back: this unique vegetable has thrived in the region's moist maritime climate ever since. Today's artichoke fields cover upward of 6,000 acres—a far cry from the original 150-acre crop—and the annual harvest is valued at some $37 million. One hundred percent of the U.S. commercial crop of artichokes is grown in California, and 75 percent of that in Monterey County. In fact, the artichoke is Monterey County's official vegetable.

Whether you prefer your artichoke steaming hot or cold, with melted butter (and a pressing of garlic) or a dollop of mayonnaise, or simply as an ornamental in your garden (they have beautiful flowers), artichokes are superb all the way around. For general information, contact the California Artichoke Advisory Board at 831-633-4411. They'll mail you some tried-and-true artichoke recipes from people who know how to treat an artichoke right. If you specifically request it, they'll also include their "Official Artichoke IQ Test"—an offbeat way to impress your friends and neighbors.

It can be argued that the humble artichoke put the town of Castroville on the map. The second oldest town in Monterey County, it was founded in 1863 by Juan

Artichokes growing near the shoreline

From whales to countless phyto- and zooplankton (small, free-floating marine plants and animals), the waters of Monterey Bay and the marine sanctuary are a veritable soup of animals that feed on each other and, in turn, serve as food for a wide spectrum of other marine life.

Here are two of the most important types of zooplankton—critical links in the great marine eating game:

■ Euphausiids

Euphausiids are better known as "krill," small free-swimming crustaceans favored by many fish, marine mammals, and birds. Although some species can grow to approximately an inch long, most are much smaller. Euphausiids have many different lifestyles and habits, but most of them share a particular behavior that is quite fascinating. During the daytime, the majority of euphausiids hover far below the surface of the ocean, probably to avoid predators. When night begins to fall they rise to the surface to feed on phytoplankton and microscopic zooplankton under the cover of darkness. This daily vertical migration is as predictable as . . . well, as the setting and rising of the sun.

It is not known why, but euphausiids form huge clouds underwater. As a result, one area of the bay may be thick with euphausiids, while another is all but devoid. Euphausiids also experience seasonal population fluctuations. Normally, when upwelling decreases during the winter months, so do phytoplankton populations—and so, then, do euphausiids, which depend largely on phytoplankton for food. El Niño events (which usher in warm waters and suppress upwelling) also usually cause a decrease in euphausiid population.

Even though their distribution is somewhat patchy and their numbers fluctuate, researchers believe that they constitute a significant portion of the oceans' biomass. Their numbers are so great in antarctic waters that some countries have even started harvesting the krill for human consumption.

Euphausia krill

Copepod

■ Copepods

Like euphausiids, copepods are small crustaceans, averaging about a third of an inch in length. Also like euphausiids, they're found in huge numbers in the seas; in fact, marine biologists believe copepods are even more numerous than euphausiids. Perhaps this is because copepods live just about everywhere, from the deepest ocean trenches to the highest mountain peaks (not all live in the ocean). Being so tiny, copepods are favorite food items for larval fish and other small marine animals.

Copepods have adapted numerous survival mechanisms. Some are parasitic and carnivorous, while others live strictly on phytoplankton. Like other crustaceans (crabs and lobsters as well as euphausiids) and arthropods (insects and spiders), copepods have what's called an exoskeleton, or a hard outer covering. They have tiny jointed appendages and their body is compartmentalized into segments. To move about in the water they use their appendages to swim in short jerky moves.

NAMES ON THE LAND

MULLIGAN

Until Mighty Moss power plant came on the scene in the 1950s, little old Mulligan Hill was one of the most prominent physical features along this stretch of Monterey Bay. This sandy hill rises only some 60 feet above the bay's waters, but on a clear day it can be seen from the ocean, far out beyond the bay. For this reason it appears on many early maps of the region. Its contemporary name comes from an early 19th-century Irish settler, John Mulligan (though no one knows if he lived there or just named it).

In October 1769, the Gaspar de Portolá party explored the Salinas River, where they camped for several days. Some of the men followed the river downstream and probably stood on this sandy hill to look out over the bay—which, alas, they failed to realize was the famous Monterey harbor described by an earlier expedition.

Bautista Castro in the southwest corner of his father's vast holdings, Rancho Bolsa Nueva y Moro Cojo. (His house still stands on the corner of Merritt and Rico Streets.) The town has led a sleepy existence as a coastal agricultural town ever since its founding. Drive through downtown Castroville today and stop at the corner of Merritt and Preston, near the large sign proclaiming Castroville as the "Artichoke Center of the World." Get out and wander around, or if you're hungry, stop in at one of the restaurants downtown. If you want to see Castroville at its best, the town's annual Artichoke Festival, held each September, is a great excuse to visit and pick up some fresh artichokes. Contact the Castroville Chamber of Commerce at 831-633-6545 for more information.

Monterey Dunes Colony

In the midst of the Salinas River State Beach is the Monterey Dunes Colony, a 120–beach house development. It is at the end of Monterey Dunes Way, just beyond the southern parking lot for the state beach (no public access through the front gate). Originally designed to be twice as large, this development was in the plans just as the California Coastal Act was passed in 1976. The newly established Coastal Commission scaled it down to its present size. Today, all of the beach houses have spectacular views of the bay. For information about rentals here, call the Monterey Dunes Colony at 831-633-4883.

Molera Road

This side route off Highway 1, about one mile south of Moss Landing, is well worth exploring, either to access

INFORMATION

Elkhorn Slough National
Estuarine Research Reserve:
831-728-2822

Elkhorn Slough Foundation:
831-728-5939

Elkhorn Slough Safari Nature
Boat Tours: 831-633-5555

Kayak Connection, Moss
Landing: 831-724-5692

Moss Landing Harbor
District, including Kirby
Park Public Access:
831-633-2461

Moss Landing Wildlife Area,
Department of Fish and
Game: 831-649-2870

Moss Landing Chamber of
Commerce: 831-633-4501

Monterey Bay Aquarium
Research Institute website:
http://www.mbari.org

Moss Landing Marine
Laboratory: 831-633-3304
Website: http://color.mlml.
calstate.edu/www

Monterey Bay National
Marine Sanctuary:
831-647-4201
Website: http://www.
mbnms.nos.noaa.gov

Castroville Chamber of
Commerce: 831-633-6545

California Artichoke Advisory
Board: 831-633-4411

Salinas River State Beach:
831-384-7695

California State Parks,
Monterey District Office:
831-649-2836

Monterey Dunes Colony:
831-633-4883

Monterey County Department
of Transportation:
831-755-8961

Monterey-Salinas Transit:
831-899-2555
Website: http://www.mst.org

Amtrak: 1-800-872-7245

the state beach or simply to go for a drive. Most notably, it passes through acres and acres of artichoke fields. During the active times of planting or harvesting the fields are crawling with workers and equipment of all types. The road brings you right back to Highway 1. As you swing around toward the highway you can spy a distinct mound of land next to the mouth of the Salinas River. That's Mulligan Hill, which, until the coming of the power plant, used to be one of the most prominent features around.

The Monterey
Dunes Colony and
artichoke fields

STACEY H. GEIKEN

There are several places to visit at Elkhorn Slough. Kirby Park Public Access and the National Estuarine Research Reserve are both immediately off of Elkhorn Road. Both are well signed. You can reach Elkhorn Road from downtown Watsonville, via Main and Porter Streets, or cut in from Highway 1 on Salinas Road, then head south on Elkhorn Road. Closer to Moss Landing, Dolan Road (just after the power plant) leads directly to Elkhorn Road.

To find the Moss Landing Wildlife Area, the Department of Fish and Game suggests accessing the north entrance while going north on Highway 1: southbound, it is simply too dangerous to stop in this busy road waiting for a chance to turn left. If you are heading south, turn off at Struve Road toward the bay, follow it back to Highway 1, then turn left onto the highway. The wildlife area entrance is just up ahead on your right. Although the south entrance is also easier to access while northbound, you can turn in while driving south, or cross over from the Moss Landing Yacht Harbor. Follow the short dirt road past a machine shop and look for the interpretive signs at the trailhead, near the old salt ponds. This looks like a private road, but it is all public. The machine shop buildings will be removed sometime after 2000.

The town of Moss Landing, Sandholdt Bridge, South Harbor, and the Salinas River State Beach northern parking lot can all be accessed via Moss Landing Road, about a quarter-mile south of the Elkhorn Slough bridge as you head south on Highway 1. There is a prominent sign advertising the town of Moss Landing. The Potrero Road entrance to Salinas River State Beach is at the southern tip of Moss Landing Road, precisely where the latter merges back onto Highway 1 (by a corner convenience store). Molera Road is approximately 1 mile beyond Potrero Road off Highway 1. The southern entrance to the state beach and access to the Monterey Dunes Colony are off Molera Road on Monterey Dunes Way. To reach Castroville, look for a left-turn lane on Highway 1 past Molera; that will take you directly into town. To get to the Monterey Peninsula, stay to the right on Highway 1.

Salinas River National Wildlife Refuge to Monterey State Beach

The transition from a largely rural and agricultural shoreline to a more urban setting takes place soon after you leave the Salinas River National Wildlife Refuge en route to the Monterey Peninsula. The towns of Marina, Sand City, and Seaside spread out behind the Monterey dunes, with the former lands of Fort Ord, a fascinating mix of parkland, development, and a new state university, sandwiched in between. Salinas is due east. There are towns and a fairly large population here, and yet you'll also find miles of beach and the impressive Monterey dune system, once described by a local naturalist as some of the most abused and yet best preserved dunes along the Pacific coast. Today, the abused portions have been largely mended, and what is open to the public is indeed a sight to behold. However, there is still private property in these dunes, and several development plans on the drawing boards. Remember, if you see "Private Property" signs, they are real and you should refrain from trespassing.

Salinas River National Wildlife Refuge

This wildlife refuge, managed by the U.S. Fish and Wildlife Service (USFWS), isn't much to look at from the road, but it's worth the effort. To get there, turn off on Neponset Road (the former site of a Southern Pacific Railroad station), drive through an agricultural field to the parking lot (very muddy after rains), and venture forth. You might see some "Private Property" signs along the sides of this dirt road, but they refer to the adjacent cultivated fields; the refuge itself is public. Once you start moving along the river—and definitely when you reach the shore—you'll realize why this place is worth seeking out. It takes about 20 minutes to reach the beach from the parking lot.

The wildlife refuge is lovely any time of year. During fall and spring migration the mouth of the river is packed with water birds. Spring also ushers in a riot of color as wildflowers bloom throughout the grassland and the dune vegetation comes alive with blues, reds, and yellows. Summer months bring nesting in the grassy areas and on several narrow islands in the languid river. Wintertime is cool and quiet, but a perfect time to study overwintering water birds and explore the beach in solitude.

To the south of the river's mouth is a brackish body of water called South Marsh. Though separated from the bay by a low ridge of dunes, it does receive fresh doses of seawater during storms and exceptionally high tides. The marsh is a great place to watch for avocets, black-necked stilts, and other shorebirds. It is ringed by pickleweed and salt grass.

The refuge's grasslands and the surrounding agricultural fields provide a rich hunting ground for several avian predators. In the early morning or on the edge of evening, keep an eye open for the low-flying short-eared owl. During the day watch for the teetering wings of the northern harrier as it works the fields down low, or look up to spot white-tailed kites searching for mice from on high. There is never a dull moment in the refuge.

Salinas River National Wildlife Refuge, foreground, and the Salinas River. Note the river's old channel, by Mulligan Hill, meandering toward Moss Landing.

STACEY H. GEIKEN

Hunting is allowed here seasonally, and only along specific reaches of the river. Call the USFWS at 510-792-0222 for more information about the refuge and to find out about hunting times.

Salinas River

The Salinas is known to river watchers for several reasons. For one thing, it is long, stretching out some 170 miles from its origins in San Luis Obispo County. It is also one of the only south-to-north-tending rivers in the United States. And finally, much of its waters flow underground—in fact, some have called it the Upside Down River.

The Salinas River is still an important part of Monterey Bay's ecology, but it is a mere trickle of its former self. The main reason is that the river's water is in high demand, for agriculture as well as drinking water. Between 1940 and 1965 three major reservoirs were constructed in the headwaters of the Salinas, dramatically cutting its flow. Extensive groundwater pumping has likewise drastically reduced the region's aquifer, in turn affecting the river.

The lower 50 miles of the Salinas River are extremely flat, with a gentle flow. In recent history the Salinas dog-legged over five miles to the north, paralleling the beach on the backside of the dunes, and discharged north of the Monterey Canyon above Moss Landing. By 1910 this north-tending channel was abandoned when the river broke through the dunes at the mouth's present location and reclaimed what researchers believe was a previously used outlet to the sea. With the help of artificial dikes on its north shore, the river has remained there ever since, though during exceptional storms it can still overflow into its north-tending channel. The lack of a forceful current at its mouth means that the river is less able to breach the sandbar and carry sand and sediment into nearshore waters. Nowadays that happens naturally only during heavy-rainfall winters; otherwise county workers appear with heavy machinery and dig a channel through the sand after the year's first rains (as at the Carmel River as well).

The Salinas's former channel and many of the waterways that once fed into it—Moro Cojo Slough, Tembladero Slough, and Alisal Slough—are still important to the local ecology (when they have water in them). The Salinas's former channel is filled with aquatic plants and a healthy cross-section of insects. This rich environment provides a productive habitat for many resident fish, as well as visiting fish that use the channel as a nursery for their ocean-bound young.

American Avocets and Black-necked Stilts

Two very graceful wading shorebirds, the American avocet and black-necked stilt, can be found around Monterey Bay year round, but particularly in places like Elkhorn Slough, the mouth of the Salinas River, and at South Marsh in the Salinas River wildlife refuge. From a distance these two birds appear rather similar: lots of leg and slim bodies with long bills. This makes sense because they belong to the same family of birds, the Recurvirostridae (Latin for "curved beak"). Upon closer inspection, though, they have noticeable and beautiful differences. Both species nest locally.

■ American avocet *(Recurvirostra americana)*

Whether you get to see avocets in summer or winter, they are always stunning. In summer their heads and necks turn reddish-tan; in the winter they don a set of gray feathers. Year round their wings are covered with a bold black and white pattern, much like the underwings of willets. Their legs are a distinctive bluish-gray color.

Perhaps the strangest things about the avocet is its bill. Both the male and female have bills that turn upward, as if they had been forcibly bent. This bill is used in a very special way. Avocets sweep the shallow waters of estuaries and mudflats with their bills in a sideways motion, stirring up aquatic insects and other goodies. It is a spectacle to behold. These ballerina-like birds have elaborate courtship displays and are also known to be keen defenders of their nests.

American avocets feeding at low tide

Black-necked stilt

■ **Black-necked stilt** *(Himantopus mexicanus)*

Compared to their relative the avocet, black-necked stilts seem a bit nervous. Their diminutive body sits atop long red legs. Adults sport distinguishing black and white plumage (black on top, white underneath and up the neck). Their black bills are straight and very pointed. They put these sharp bills to good use probing in water a few inches deep for their favorite food: small insects and crustaceans. Because they seem to take to the wing often, you'll have many opportunities to hear their distinctive call, a rapid, buzzy "keer-keer-keer." Although they breed locally, these handsome, formally attired birds can also be found throughout the Americas down to Argentina.

Monterey Dunes

California's world-renowned coastline is graced with a scattering of major sand dune systems—for example, at Eureka, the Point Reyes Peninsula, Pismo Beach, and a handful of other locales. The southern edge of Monterey Bay, however, boasts a sand dune landscape that few others in the state can rival: the Monterey dunes.

Stretching southward from the Salinas River to Monterey's harbor, the Monterey dunes, actually an amalgam of different-aged dunes with a complex geologic history, are the sole remnants of a once-extensive sand dune system. During the past 800,000 years, at least seven major episodes of glaciation in the northern latitudes, followed

The Monterey Dunes

Sand dunes of varying size are found along almost a quarter of California's coastline. The creation of these dunes requires a great deal of sand, wind, and landward space not far above sea level. Wave action piles the sand on the beach, and the wind takes it from there.

In fact, dunes can be likened to waves of sand, formed, like sea waves, by the action of the wind and moving in the same direction. A young dune begins as wind-blown sand that settles around an object on the surface of the upper beach—a pile of kelp wrack or drift-wood, for example. Gradually, a gentle slope forms on the windward (seaward) foreslope, while the inland, lee side, slopes steeply. Young dunes move, or migrate, in the direction of the wind, often becoming larger and taller as they develop.

Once the dune is established above the high water mark it's likely to be colonized by grasses and other flowering plants. By interrupting the surface wind patterns, these pioneer species cause more sand to be deposited on the dune. As the dune grows and migrates inland, conditions become favorable for greater varieties and numbers of plants. Mature sand dune systems, in fact, are not just a single, homogeneous habitat; rather, they harbor a mosaic of habitats that are best identified by differences in vegetation.

On top of an interesting geologic history—three distinct dune types can be found along California's coast, extending back thousands of years and all layered together—dunes are also shaped in identifiable patterns. From the ocean heading inland, dunes are typically divided into four basic zones: foredunes (active dunes), middunes (stabilized dunes), rear dunes, and a transition zone (where artichokes are often grown).

by warming periods, have caused changes in sea level that in turn send the shoreline moving back and forth on the continental shelf. During periods of low sea level, when the shoreline was several miles to the west, onshore winds powered by strong Pleistocene storms scooped up tons of debris from the dry floor of Monterey Bay and cast it into rippling fields of dunes that crawled inland toward the Salinas Valley, Aromas, and San Juan Bautista. The region's sandy, well-draining agricultural lands, which today nourish prize-winning strawberries, artichokes, lettuce, and other produce, are actually former dune fields. The old dunes were topped with fine silts and clays—fragments of the surrounding mountains that were carried down toward the sea.

As the last vast ice sheets melted between 15,000 and 6,000 years ago, the Pacific inched its way up to its present elevation, and tiny chunks of weathered minerals were reclaimed by incoming waves. The dunes remaining above the water line eventually stabilized, held in place by the roots of countless small plants and shrubs. Along the eyebrow of the renewed bay, however, a more recent and much smaller dune field—those that we see today—took shape on top of the ancient dunes rimming the shore.

Anna's hummingbird (*Calypte anna*) is a true local: it's the only hummer that lives along the coast year round (most other species fly south to warmer climes). In order to overwinter, the Anna has adapted by becoming slightly larger than most other hummers—though it still weighs in at only several ounces and stretches out to a mere four inches. No matter what the month, these little dynamos can be seen zipping from flower to flower or gleaning small insects from plants.

Annas have solid green backs, and the males sport brilliant deep-red throats. These two markings, along with their slightly larger size, can help you identify them in the field when other species are present. During late winter and spring, when males gear up for the mating season, another set of distinctive behaviors will help you know who you're looking at. Male Annas perform their courting flight by rising slowly straight up in the sky, all the while producing a continuous raspy call. They pause briefly, then dive at break-neck speed toward the female (who is watching the show perched on a branch). Just before impact the male pulls up, flashes his throat colors, and pops out a loud "cheeeek" sound.

The male of another common summer resident, the Allen's hummingbird, also dives, but he produces more of a "zeeeee" noise. After his dive, he swings back and forth in front of the female, calling some more. Male Allens have rufous plumage on parts of their backs and all over the tops of their tails.

The best introduction to the Monterey dunes is a slow and gradual one, beginning at the Salinas River National Wildlife Refuge. It is here, southward from the calm waters of the river, that both the marvelous beauty and severe degradation of the dunes can best be seen, and all within a few short miles. The hour-long walk from the refuge to Marina State Beach brings you past a cross-section of dune types, conditions, and uses that typify the entire system. Also in these few miles you will encounter the full compliment of plants and animals native to the Monterey dunes. Here, shoreline explorers can learn why sand dunes are one of the world's most fragile ecosystems.

South of the river's mouth, a gathering of minidunes makes up the coastal edge of the wildlife refuge. This unassuming sandscape is a gentle entrée to the much larger dunes rising to the south, and an excellent scaled-down showcase for dune-building processes and the ways in which plants adapt to an ever-moving habitat.

At the southern end of these minidunes, the crescent-shaped face of an older, better-stabilized dune system rises in a clean, steep curve—a curve carved by the past meanderings of the Salinas River. Covered with lush stands of dune plants, including beach sagewort, sand verbena, beach lupine, and California poppy, these rolling sand hills rise to between 50 and 100 feet high. Known as the Martin Dunes, this 320-acre northern tip of the Monterey dune system preserves a small slice of some of coastal California's most spectacular dune habitat. Please note that these dunes are privately held, and signs will tell you so. You can enjoy them by observing them from the beach, which is always public below the high tide mark.

Just beyond the beauty of the Martin Dunes another story is told in the sandy property of several sand-mining companies. Here the vegetation has been broken up by years of mining and vehicle use. Such abuse promotes sand blowouts—enormous wind-created divots that are popped out of poorly vegetated or denuded dunes. A quick inspection by the shoreline stroller will reveal more bare sand than vegetation along this stretch; unnaturally sharp contours replace the soft dips and rises of less-disturbed dunes. These dunes are also private property, but again, the beach is open to all. Just south of these lands, Marina State Beach's once-tattered dunes are making a slow but impressive comeback.

From the Salinas River southward, the entire Monterey dune system has been harmed to varying degrees over the past century. However, even on the most damaged sections of dunes small clumps of native plants and a wide range of common, threatened, and endangered species survive in protected pockets. With proper care and management, these natural remnants—biological satellites of sorts—can serve as the centers from which restoration can take place.

SALINAS

Any town that boasts of being the center of "The World's Lettuce Bowl" has to be interesting, and healthy for you as well. Salinas is both. Incorporated in 1874, this once-small town has grown to be Monterey County's largest; it is also the county seat. The town's Spanish name literally means "salt ponds"—though just how the area got this name is open to debate. Nevertheless, it has endured.

Salinas is a great place to visit as a side trip from the coast. You'll find countless restaurants and city parks, and the town is home to many interesting seasonal events. The Steinbeck Festival and the Salinas Rodeo, held each summer, are perhaps the best known. But Salinas seems to be busy with celebrations year round.

Of course, this is the birthplace of John Steinbeck (1902–1968), and the town and the valley both figure prominently in much of his writing. Two of his books are centered here—*East of Eden* and *The Red Pony*—and several short stories. In addition to the annual Steinbeck Festival, you can also visit the new National Steinbeck Center, the Steinbeck House, and the John Steinbeck Library (there is also a John Steinbeck School and Steinbeck Park). At the Steinbeck House, in fact, you can have a meal: the author's childhood home has been converted into a restaurant.

For information about seasonal events in Salinas and the various Steinbeck-related sites, call the Salinas Chamber of Commerce at 831-424-7611 or access their website at http://www.salinaschamber.com.

NEARSHORE
BIRD PRIMER

I dentifying the shorebirds and seabirds of Monterey Bay and the marine sanctuary is a daunting task. Not only is there a fantastic variation of species in different habitats (pelagic, inshore, beach, brackish water, freshwater), but seasonally the species come and go.

However, no matter where you are looking, or in what season, you are bound to have success. This is because Monterey Bay ranks among the richest feeding grounds in the world—whether the birds are far out in the middle of the bay, just beyond the breakers, or working the shoreline, there is a rich supply of food for them.

Market squid, anchovy, juvenile rockfish, sardines, surfperch, and smelt are just some of the prey items of birds in the bay and beyond. Closer to shore, many diving birds can be seen searching for small fishes, crustaceans, and small mollusks. The beach, meanwhile, offers a variety of insects and sand-dwelling animals. Inland waters, too, satisfy the appetites of many birds that don't feel compelled to stick to saltwater.

Scope the nearshore waters or coastal inlets with binoculars, or perhaps venture out on a boat, and you'll soon begin to recognize some familiar faces. Here are a handful of common nearshore water birds that spend most of the year, if not all year, in

and around the greater Monterey Bay. (You'll find descriptions of other species, including marbled murrelets, sooty shearwaters, gulls, and cormorants, scattered through the book.)

Western grebe

■ Western grebe
(Aechmophorus occidentalis)

The western grebe is North America's largest grebe. With its dazzling black and white plumage, swanlike neck, long greenish-yellow bill, and red eyes, this grebe is stunning indeed. Its large, powerful legs help it swim underwater in pursuit of fish. The western grebe can be seen throughout the marine sanctuary during all seasons except summer, when it moves inland to nesting grounds around lakes.

■ Common loon
(Gavia immer)

The loon is a real low-rider. Typically, all that you see of a loon in the water are its head, neck, and back. This is the loon with the call you've heard countless times in nature movies symbolizing the mystery of the wild—though you won't hear it here very often: it vocalizes most in its breeding sites, at northern lakes and ponds.

Around here, you'll usually see these wintertime visitors in their nonbreeding plumage:

Common loon

uniform dark gray on top and white below, with dark eyes. If you see a low-riding, red-eyed bird in striking black and white plumage, though, consider yourself lucky: that's a breeding loon. Regardless of their attire, these loons are graceful birds with formidable bills, good for eating small fish and even some crustaceans.

An amusing and easily seen trait of the loon is its habit of swimming along with its head underwater looking for fish. When they spot one, they disappear in a split second: the underwater chase has begun.

The Pacific loon (G. pacifica) is seen here as well, and in its nonbreeding plumage can be mistaken for the common loon; the common loon's bill is much larger, though.

■ Ruddy duck
(Oxyura jamaicensis)

The ruddy duck is a small, chubby bird. Male ruddies have cinnamon bodies, white cheek patches, and a beautiful baby-blue bill in breeding season, and their tail feathers may point stiffly skyward. In fact, ruddy ducks belongs to a group called the "stiff-tailed ducks." The brown female is rather drab in comparison, and her cheeks have less white. During nonbreeding times, the male, too, becomes brown, though he keeps those white cheeks. This duck's small stature and short wings

Ruddy duck

Surf scoter

give it a "buzzy" flight pattern.

The ruddy duck is a common year-round resident of the slough and other inland waters, where it finds ample roots, insects, and seeds in all seasons. When he's trying to attract a mate, the male will float across the water calling so vigorously and bobbing his head so intently that his entire body bounces around in the water.

■ American coot
(Fulica americana)

There is no doubting that coots are successful as a species—you can find them just about anywhere. They are commonly seen on and around lawns next to water, where they waddle about like dark overfed chickens, unconcerned by the proximity of humans. When they take flight they run across the water for considerable distances before lift-off. Even though they might not seem like a wildlife species, they are. And they are really very attractive, with their white bills, red eyes, plump dark bodies, and large, lobed yellow-green feet.

■ Surf scoter
(Melanitta perspicillata)

The surf scoter has the dubious distinction of being called the skunk-head coot or

skunk duck, thanks to the male's black plumage and two white head patches. However, this bird of the waves and open bay is far removed from both skunks and coots. The male scoter has a wonderfully colorful bill: orange, yellow, white, and black. Female surf scoters are dusky brown and lack the wild bill. Although scoters are tundra nesters, they can be found in Monterey Bay year round.

During the winter months, scoters can be seen in large flocks, called rafts, on the open water. When they fly off, they form a single line and stay close to the water. When feeding (often in pairs or small groups), they bob just beyond the breaking waves, repeatedly diving to grub around for mollusks with their large bills. The white-winged scoter (M. fusca), though not as common in Monterey Bay and beyond, occasionally shows up in large numbers during the winter months. Unlike surf scoters, they have white patches under their wings, and instead of white on the back and front of the head, male white-winged scoters have a dash of white under each eye.

■ Mallard (Anas platyrhynchos)

Look at a range map for the mallard duck and you'll see

this species is spread across all of North America. These birds are also common to Elkhorn Slough and other freshwater bodies close to the coast. A true generalist, the mallard eats just about anything. And like the coot and Canada goose, the mallard flourishes around humans and human-made bodies of water (they've even been known to land in people's swimming pools).

Male mallards are the well-known green-headed, yellow-billed ducks of city lakes, ponds, and farms. Females are mottled brown with a whitish tail. Mallards feed by dabbling—that is, straining mucky water through their comblike bills to remove food. They can also be seen bottoms up, searching the muddy bottom for marsh grasses and small aquatic animals to eat. Mallards often cross with other duck species, so don't be surprised if you come across some interesting ducks that look like mallards but have slightly different coloring.

■ Northern shoveler
(Anas clypeata)

At first glance a northern shoveler looks somewhat like a mallard . . . until you see the bill. The shoveler's bill is large and wide, not unlike a large spoon. Basically, these ducks are master dabblers, swimming along and filtering food from the murky waters of sloughs and inlets. The shoveler rarely dives, though you might see it imitating an avocet by swinging its bill from side to side to aid in the filtering process.

Summer-season fog (along the central coast, typically present May through August) is a fairly rare phenomenon across the globe, associated with the world's Mediterranean climate regions—areas that experience mild wet winters, long dry summers, cold upwelling coastal waters, and onshore winds. In addition to the central coast of California, central Chile, southwestern Australia, and the southern tip South Africa have similar climates and fog seasons. (Not the Mediterranean, though, because it alone does not have cold-water upwelling, which is a significant ingredient in fog production.)

The fog that pours across Monterey Bay on hot summer days can be best seen if you take a bluffside walk: get a bit of elevation off the shore and a clear view out over the water and you'll be able to watch it form, ease across the water, work up side canyons on land, and change moods almost instantaneously.

When moist marine air moves toward the coast it passes over the cold upwelling waters offshore by the continental shelf and condenses into fog. It is being pushed onshore by the northwesterlies, but it is also pulled inland by hot interior temperatures and surface low-pressure systems. Nature abhors a vacuum, as they say, and fog is there to fill it when necessary. Fog not only cools the atmosphere and the land, but it can also pro-

Fog forming over Monterey Bay

MONTEREY BAY AQUARIUM

duce measurable quantities of precipitation below coastal trees and shrubs in the form of fog drip.

Fog has many shapes, depending on climatic conditions. It can blast into the bay as a solid wall hundreds of feet tall, creating a regional white-out in a few hours. Or it might hug the water just 30 feet off the surface, flick at Point Santa Cruz and Point Pinos, retreat, then inch its way toward Moss Landing and into the Salinas Valley. It can also slide along high overhead with a slick flat bottom, as if slipping along a glass ceiling hundreds of feet above the bay.

Marina State Beach

Marina State Beach is a gorgeous spot to learn about dunes and their inhabitants, take hang gliding lessons, or simply set out for a leisurely stroll. However, swimming is not recommended because of the steep beach and strong currents.

For those who prefer to experience the shoreline from behind the wheel of a car (an option not generally recommended in this book), this is the spot for you. Not only is the main parking lot immediately off Highway 1 on Reservation Road, but each parking space enjoys an unobstructed view of the bay (unless you park behind an RV). You can even spot dolphins and whales from here—without unbuckling.

For less mobile people, in fact, this is a lovely place to park and watch the bay and the waves. Bottlenose dolphins can be viewed moving through the waves, shorebirds fly by, and fog rolls in and out. A small concession stand, next to the hang gliding pad and the Western Hang Glider School, sells food and drinks, and there are several picnic tables edging the parking lot.

Beyond the wonders of the asphalt pad, the shoreline explorer can spend an entire day in the park and still not see everything. Several visits are recommended. Marina State Beach is an excellent example of a dune area where formerly uncontrolled access destroyed and altered large sections of dunes but where today management techniques have reversed the destruction while actually improving recreational and educational opportunities for visitors. Asilomar State Beach on the Monterey Peninsula is another prime success story along these lines.

"The beautiful curved line of the bay seems like an immense semicircle, thirty-five miles across, but every part of the arc distinct. Monterey is obscured by fog, but the mountains rise above it in the clear air. Fog forms at the head of the bay and rolls up the great Salinas Valley as far as we can see, but we are far above it and looking on the top of it—it seems like a great arm of the sea, or a mighty river, stretching away to the distant horizon."

William H. Brewer,
Up and Down
California (1861)

Hang glider at Marina State Beach

NONNATIVE DUNE PLANTS

Exotic, or nonnative, plants are bad for many reasons, but perhaps the most important are (1) they are difficult to eradicate; and (2) they can dominate entire sections of dunes by killing off, then excluding, native species. This in turn impacts wildlife species that depend on native plants for food and shelter.

Iceplant

The following selection of nonnative plant species are on most biologists' list of the "Ten Most Unwanted" dune plants. (Because European dune grass [*Ammophila arenaria*] is so dominant at Franklin Point to the north, that species is profiled in the section on the Año Nuevo Reserve; see page 22.)

Two species of sea rocket, *Cakile edentula* and *C. maritima,* are found in almost all dunes along the central coast. Of these, *C. maritima* is especially widespread in the greater Monterey Bay area. It looks like a low-lying version of wild mustard, with rose-colored flowers. Both species of sea rocket are in the mustard family (Brassicaceae), as their thin, succulent leaves and fat little seedheads might suggest.

Chilean iceplant *(Carpobrotus chilensis)* and South African iceplant *(C. edulis)* are distinct species, but to most people they are simply ice-

plant (in fact, even their common names vary). Although they look somewhat similar, the Chilean iceplant has pink-purple flowers, while the South African species produces yellowish flowers. To confuse the matter further, they routinely hybridize in coastal areas, producing a mixture of shapes and colors. South African iceplant is far more aggressive and widespread— it can grow up to eight feet annually. Hundreds of species of iceplants and their relatives have been cultivated in Californian gardens, and dozens of species are used as ground cover throughout the state. From these domesticated areas they escape into parks and other coastal sites.

Of the iceplant species that cover urban gardens with their plump, thick skinned leaves, several are native to

South Africa. Some botanists once regarded iceplant as native to California, or it may have immigrated from Chilean shores centuries ago in the ballast of Spanish galleons. The debate continues to this day.

Regardless of its true origin, iceplant is painstakingly pulled up by state park employees and volunteers, or sprayed with a mild herbicide. In some sections of the Monterey dunes, especially throughout the land that will be Fort Ord Dunes State Park, it will take a herculean effort to remove the feisty pest. But plans are afoot to do just that. Most of this new park's dunes are completely covered by the multicolored iceplant, which makes them veritable deserts for native animals and plant species.

Just south of the parking lot a dunetop wooden walk-way guides you through a set of beautifully restored dunes. Nice interpretive signs help you begin to understand the complicated life of a sand dune, pointing out some of the plants and animals that live there. This is home to such rare native plants as the Monterey paint-brush, dune gilia, Monterey spine flower, and Menzies's wallflower. In early spring every swale and ridge is high-lighted by the pale lavender and white of lupines, the orange yellow of poppies, and fiery paintbrush reds. Gray foxes make their homes here, as do jack rabbits, mice, raccoons, and skunks. A rich variety of resident and migrant land birds also rely on the dunes for shelter and food.

At the northern terminus of Dunes Road (off Reservation Road just outside the park) there is another public access point for the dunes and the beach. (You pass an old sand mining operation on your left and hotels and an RV park on your right en route to this trailhead.) An old, informal path through this section of dunes—which once were mined extensively—has now been improved and formalized by the Coastal Conservancy and the Monterey Peninsula Regional Park District. Walking this trail will give you an appreciation for just how large these dunes really are: the beach doesn't even come into view for half a mile or so. Although this path is nice any time of year, the spring wildflowers make for an especially enjoyable experience.

Yet another access point for the state beach is south-ward, at the corner of Lake Drive and Lake Court in the town of Marina. You will see a set of wooden-slat steps leading over an older stabilized dune to the beach. *Note:* Hang gliders must register at the main parking lot before using this area.

Human Impacts on Dunes

There is no doubting the importance of the dune ecosys-tem to resident species of plants and animals. Yet the dunes are also extremely fragile and must be treated with care.

By simply running down the face of a vegetated dune, we humans do long-term damage: plants are uprooted, burrowing animals trampled, and erosion can be initi-ated. A single joy ride in an off-road vehicle can harm dunes for decades. In dunes, the entire habitat can up and blow away if the plants are removed.

Besides the actions of individual humans, an even

The art of dune restoration has been refined over recent years in the Monterey area, particularly at Marina and Asilomar State Beaches. Basically, there are two methods for revegetating dunes. The first method is less expensive but labor intensive as volunteers, inmates, and court-referred laborers work side by side with state or regional park employees to hand-pick native plant seeds. Some of the seeds are then stored, while the remainder are either planted in special nurseries or sown directly into prepared dunes. Planting is timed to rely on winter rains for irrigation.

The second, more expensive method relies on contracted help and machines. This "high tech" method uses bulldozers to shape dunes (instead of manipulation by hand and shovel) and "hydromulching," the spraying of a mixture of native dune plant seeds and a "mulch fixative" directly onto the dunes. A drip system is then installed to provide water during the crucial first two years of growth.

The top priority for restoration is sections of dunes with healthy native plant growth that are being threatened by nonnative plants like European dune grass and iceplant. Once the nonnatives are removed, the existing native plants—which are surprisingly resilient if left on their own— flourish. The next priority is unstable sand areas that need to be reshaped, then planted. Last in line are dune areas completely overgrown with iceplant (like much of the Fort Ord dunes). Removing iceplant takes a lot of work, whether accomplished by hand or mechanically. After all this, or sometimes in parallel, park personnel and volunteers reroute trails and shut down others. They've also built boardwalks across many portions of public dunes to minimize impact while maximizing education and access.

Once dunes have been cleared of nonnative plants, replanted, or stabilized in one way or another, native plants such as sand verbena and beach sagewort move in quickly. This is critical, because these pioneer species help create an environment where other dune plants and animals can thrive.

bigger force in the Monterey dunes has been sand mining, a business active in this area since 1906. Until recently, two companies maintained four operations in the Monterey dunes. Today, only one remains active, north of Marina State Beach. Two types of sand mining have been practiced here. One removes sand from the middune zone; another, former method actually dragged the surf zone with enormous land-based scoops attached to cables. The Monterey dunes are among the few areas in the United States where surf-zone mining has been allowed in recent history. Most other coastal municipalities maintain aggressive programs to conserve what sand remains on their shores, even going so far as to actively replenish their dune and beach resources.

Erosion rates along the bayside of the Monterey dunes are alarming. Although statistics vary from study to study, it is believed that from the Salinas River to Monterey's Municipal Wharf, approximately 400,000 cubic yards were lost each year up until the late 1980s, when the surf-zone mining ceased. Along the shoreline of the former Fort Ord alone, that translates to an annual erosion rate of about seven feet—that is, each year the coastline

LIFE ON THE MOVE: DUNE PLANTS

Beach primrose

Many of the plants found in sand dunes grow nowhere else. They have become adapted to a harsh environment: blowing sand and salt spray, low nutrient levels, seasonal drought, and extreme temperature variations. In many ways, sand dunes are like miniature coastal deserts. One of the adaptations that makes life possible under these conditions is small, thick leaves, often light green or gray in color. The thick leaves help prevent water loss; the light color absorbs less heat than would a darker color. Also, many plants have a low profile to avoid being blasted by blowing sand. Some, like sand verbena, store water in large roots or in succulent leaves. Many grow quickly, produce seeds early in the spring, and then become nearly dormant or die. These seeds may be distributed over long distances, washing out to sea and landing on distant beaches. Or they may lie dormant during the summer drought and germinate only when winter rains have washed most of the salt out

of the sandy soil, as is the case with poppies. Yet other seeds are distributed with the aid of the shore's consistent winds or by birds and mice.

Dune-colonizing plants like the common yellow sand verbena must grow quickly and establish themselves or they will be blown away or covered with sand. They must also flower and produce seed quickly, tolerate salt, and survive on small amounts of nutrients.

The more stabilized middle of dunes supports less mobile species, which secure the sand beneath them. These areas are home to beach sagewort, beach primrose, buckwheats, mock heather, silky beach pea, and the coastal subspecies of the California poppy. These plants are somewhat less tolerant of salt and blowing sand and require higher nutrient levels than the pioneer plants of younger dunes.

The mature rear dunes usually support a combination of the plants mentioned above, plus yellow bush lupine. In some areas, terrestrial plants invade the mature dunes from the landward side (the transition zone); these include Monterey pines, live oak, and manzanita. Coyote bush is also common on mature dunes and in the transition zone.

Because dunes are so fragile, and when disturbed stay in that condition for long periods of time, it shouldn't be surprising that many of the region's endangered plants are dune species. Menzies's wallflower, Seaside bird's beak, beach layia, Yadon's wallflower, Tidestrom's lupine, dune gilia, and the Monterey spine flower all find sanctuary on untrodden dune areas.

receded inland some seven feet. In the Marina area, three to four feet disappeared yearly.

Anyone who doubts these figures has only to look at Stillwell Hall in the newly established Fort Ord Dunes State Park (scheduled to open after 2000). When first constructed in the 1940s, it was hundreds of feet from the shoreline. Today Stillwell Hall stands precipitously on the edge of sand cliffs, but efforts are being made to stem the

Directly next to Marina State Beach's parking lot you'll see some industrial buildings (behind the hang glider area). This is the desalinization plant of the Marina Coast Water District. Like many of the freshwater aquifers around the bay, the aquifer from which the district once pumped its drinking water, the Salinas Valley groundwater basin, has been invaded by saltwater. This invasion, called seawater intrusion, is due to the simple fact that more groundwater is being removed from the aquifer than can be replaced by rainfall.

The two topmost aquifers of the basin have already been tainted by saltwater, so the district has to go down some 2,000 feet to find freshwater. And yet they know that even this lens of good water will soon be invaded. To help alleviate some of its problems, and to plan for the future, the district established a desalinization plant here in 1996. Today it supplies about 12 percent of the district's needs.

The saltwater is extracted through a well dug into the sand. The sand-filtered saltwater is then treated, mechanically filtered, and pushed through a reverse-osmosis membrane under high pressure. This removes the salt. The extracted material—called brine in the industry—is then injected into another well and allowed to mix with the top layer of groundwater and slowly return to the bay. The freshwater obtained from this process receives post-treatment, then is added to the system.

erosion and open the building to the public. The hall might even be moved inland several hundred feet.

How much of this erosion was caused by sand mining? How much is natural? No one really knows. One thing that is sure is that surf-zone sand mining resulted in erosion far greater than might be expected, in that it not only removed sand from the environment but also interrupted the nearshore flow of sand. It is hoped that erosion rates are slowing now that surf-zone mining has ceased, but only time will tell.

Fortunately, although middune sand mining continues, it's less of an industry than before, so less sand is being extracted today than in earlier years. Also on the positive front, in the past decade dune restoration has been perfected in the Monterey region; this means that the dunes are finally being cared for with the skill and patience these ancient landforms deserve.

Animals of the Dunes

Walk through the dunes at noon, and scarcely an animal is to be seen. Walk in the early morning, and the telltale tracks of several species will be evident on the sand. A variety of beetles, and deer mice, hide under bushes or lie in burrows beneath the sand by day, but emerge at night in search of a meal. The black legless lizard is not so easy to find. Sequestered in its specialized world under leaf litter, this small lizard lives a sedentary life in the dunes.

Burrowing owls, jackrabbits, and cottontail rabbits occupy burrows in the rear dune area. Several snakes—among them the western diamondback rattlesnake—probe those burrows in search of prey. Butterflies, including the celebrated Smith's blue butterfly, feed and lay their eggs on the plants while pollinating many of them as they move about.

Seeds and insects attract birds, including the house finch, American goldfinch, and white-crowned sparrow. The imperiled western snowy plover nests along some sections of the Pacific coast in the beach zone and fore-dunes, though according to the U.S. Fish and Wildlife Service, only a handful of plover nesting sites remain on Monterey Bay's sandy shores (see page 41).

Here are some of the common, and not-so-common, native species of the dunes:

■ Deer mice *(Peromyscus maniculatus)*

Although deer mice are most active at night, it is possible to spot them zipping from bush to bush as you scout the dunes during daylight hours. Just look for a dark brown to reddish brown ball of fur about four inches long. Early morning visits will often reveal their diminutive prints in the moistened sand. Their prints are about half an inch long, and in places with more soil than sand, you can actually discern their toes.

It is easy to joke about how fecund rabbits and mice are, but it really is true. Deer mice, for example, can begin reproducing at the age of six weeks. Females carry their young for a mere four weeks, then are ready to pro-duce another litter. It is no wonder that they are a favorite prey item of foxes, hawks, owls, and even great blue herons: they're bite sized, and there are lots of them.

Resting gray fox

■ Gray fox *(Urocyon cinereoargenteus)*

Gray foxes are beautiful animals with sil-very gray coats and bright outlines of reddish brown and white on their chests, along their bellies, and on the undersides of their long tails. Weighing around ten pounds, they might look like a small dog or large house cat. Not surprisingly, gray foxes frequent dune areas looking for mice, but they also eat birds, berries of all kinds, insects, and even mushrooms. Their scat is often packed with the seeds of native shrubs (especially manzanita).

Gray foxes possess one skill that isn't needed in the dunes: they regularly climb trees looking for prey or fruit. Anyone with an orchard on the outskirts of a town can probably verify this. These foxes are mostly active at night, but early mornings and early evenings are also good times to find them quietly hunting on the backside of the dunes or nearby fields. In the evenings they often call to each other with a series of barks that sound like someone with a raspy sore throat.

■ Black legless lizard *(Anniella pulchra nigra)*

The black legless lizard is a very unusual lizard because it looks and behaves like a cross between a snake and a centipede. It really has no legs. This pencil-sized reptile is shiny black above and light below and spends most of its day burrowed in the sand or under the leaf litter of larger dune bushes. To adapt to their subterranean lifestyle these lizards have small eyes, no ear openings, and their heads are shaped like miniature shovels. In the early evening and at night these lizards emerge to slither after insects and spiders. The silvery legless lizard (*A. pulchra pulchra*) occupies similar habitats along the central coast. Both are considered "species of special concern" by the California Department of Fish and Game.

■ Smith's blue butterfly *(Euphilotes enoptes smithi)*

One of the dunes' most celebrated residents is the Smith's blue butterfly, one of the first insects to be federally listed as endangered in 1976. Found only in coastal Monterey, Santa Cruz, and San Mateo Counties, it became endangered because much of its habitat was being destroyed or harmed. Where present, these petite

LOCKE-PADDON PARK

When leaving Marina State Beach you can continue on Reservation Road under Highway 1 (bear to the right at the stop light) and visit another great park: Locke-Paddon Park. Just look for the extremely tall communication towers on your left. There is a smaller pond with observation platforms back at the stop light, but no trails. Locke-Paddon is a 17-acre park maintained by the City of Marina on the site of what was once an extensive fresh-water wetland area—a rare habitat around Monterey Bay.

The park was developed with the help of the State Coastal Conservancy and the Monterey Peninsula Regional Park District. There is a nice picnic area here, walking paths, interpretive signs, and bathrooms. During migration season the waters of the park can be packed with waterfowl. The park is named after the founder of Marina, William Locke-Paddon, who purchased lands here in 1912. The town was officially incorporated in 1975.

one-inch butterflies are always in close proximity to their two host plants, seacliff buckwheat and coast buckwheat. Females have brown wings, while the male sports bright blue.

These buckwheat species are so important to the Smith's blue that the butterfly couldn't live without them. The insects use these plants for every aspect of their lives. Adults typically emerge from their cocoons in June, and they only live about a week. But while they are alive they use the buckwheats as platforms from which to find mates and reproduce. Eggs are laid on the buckwheat flowers, and the larvae feed on the plants for several months before spinning a cocoon. It is a one-stop shopping arrangement for the butterfly. Present efforts to save this species are concentrating on habitat preservation and maintaining healthy stands of their host buckwheats.

Fort Ord: From Military Stronghold to State Park . . . and More

In one form or another (and under differing names) Fort Ord has been part of the Monterey Bay region since 1917, when the U.S. government purchased 15,000 acres here. The fort was named for Major General Edward Otho Cresap Ord, a Civil War general. Prior to that war, however, General Ord was in charge of the Monterey garrison for several years starting in 1847.

Since 1917 the fort grew to some 28,000 acres and became increasingly important as a military training and staging site on the Pacific coast. In 1993 the fort closed as part of the military's downsizing, and people were quick to realize that enormous tracts of prime real estate—including about four miles of dunes and beachfront—would soon be up for grabs. Approximately 800 acres will remain under military control.

The University of California, Santa Cruz, has opened its Monterey Bay Science and Technology Center here, and a new university, California State University, Monterey Bay, opened its doors in 1996. Many of the neighboring cities, and the county of Monterey, have also petitioned for lands.

Of the fort's former land holdings, about 65 percent will be permanently protected. The Bureau of Land Management (BLM) is overseeing some 8,000 acres that are open to the public and another 7,000 that remain off-limits owing to the presence of live ammunition. On the segment open to the public there are 50 miles of trails for mountain biking, horseback riding, and hiking, most of which are best accessed from the Salinas end of Highway 68.

Y ou may notice signs warning of unexploded ordnance during your visit. That's because acres upon acres of this area was used for target practice by military personnel or by ships just offshore (local residents didn't have to wait for the Fourth of July to hear bombs whistling overhead). The military has programs to identify and clear dangerous materials —including an ongoing toxic cleanup—but there are still live explosives here.

All dangerous areas are off-limits. Nevertheless, please read all signs and warnings. Don't touch unfamiliar objects, especially if they are metal. If you find something questionable, contact a BLM employee or other officials before you leave.

On the west side of Highway 1, almost 900 acres have been designated a new state park: Fort Ord Dunes State Park. It is the second largest state park along the greater Monterey Bay shoreline, after Wilder Ranch State Park. Although final plans for the park are still evolving, camping will definitely be allowed, eventually. Major restoration efforts on the dunes will be a key part of this park's management for years to come. This will be a big task, since the park takes in four spectacular miles of dunes and beachfront.

The conversion of this fort has been very important for education, the local economy, and land preservation. Because these lands have been off-limits for decades, vast tracts of coastal habitat remain relatively undisturbed. The BLM estimates there are 35 species of rare plants and animals within the former fort's boundaries. Inland, where the BLM manages the trails, the area also contains some of the best examples of maritime chaparral anywhere along the central coast. It is a remarkable landscape noted for its stands of oak trees and fascinating vernal pools.

For more information about the public lands of the former Fort Ord, contact the BLM office at 831-394-8314. They will be happy to send you trail information and directions to access points. For information about the status of Fort Ord Dunes State Park, call the State Park offices in Monterey, 831-649-2836.

Some Fort Ord Wildlife

Just back from the shoreline between Marina to the north and Seaside and Sand City to the south is some of the wildest land around the bay. It is a fabulous place to go bird-watching and to seek out wildlife. Here is a sampling of species you might find just inland from the shore.

■ Spotted towhee *(Pipilo erythrophthalmus)*

The spotted towhee is one of the best-kept secrets of coastal chaparral areas. One of our most attractive resident birds, the male has a jet black back splashed with white, chestnut or rufous sides, and white undersides (it was once called the rufous-sided towhee). Females are brownish, but they too are attractive. To top it all off, they both have brilliant red eyes. These birds tend to be reclusive and prefer dense chaparral—you won't see them singing from the top of a telephone pole at midday.

Spotted towhees do sing, however—or rather, they vocalize with a buzzy call while perched atop bushes during early morning and early evening. If you startle them they dive into the bushes, but if you stand quietly they continue calling. During the day they can be seen flying low to the ground between bushes, much like brown towhees, their inconspicuous cousins.

Because they feed on the ground, typically under dense brush, you often hear these towhees before you can see them. Listen for a "scritch-scritch" as they scratch with both feet at once—back and forth, back and forth—in the duff below bushes. They are looking for quick meals of insects and grubs.

■ Bobcat *(Lynx rufus)*

Bobcats are at once secretive and surprisingly nonchalant about humans. On the back trails of the former fort you can see their prints and scat on the soft sandy dirt. It is

Bobcat

Appropriately named, Sand City was home to a booming sand mining business for years, though today all mining has ceased. This city of sand is a mere 350 acres, but it was incorporated in 1960 and has been thriving ever since.

Interestingly, prior to 1996 open space and parks were not permitted land uses in Sand City, in spite of the fact that some 30 percent of the land here was held in public ownership by the Monterey Peninsula Regional Park District and State Parks. Reason ultimately prevailed, however, and now almost 80 percent of the dunes within Sand City's city limits are scheduled for a variety of public uses—and luckily so, since some of the dunes here are home to pockets of native vegetation that will be critical for future restoration efforts. A new portion of the Monterey Bay Coastal Trail moves through Sand City west of Highway 1, with a short detour under the highway (on Playa Avenue to Metz Road), then back over the highway (on Tioga Avenue).

not uncommon to see a solitary cat bounding away when you come around a turn or crest a small hill, though on rare occasions you may come around a corner and find yourself looking straight into the eyes of one. Usually they'll run away; sometimes they linger for a good look then walk slowly into the underbrush—they are about as predictable as their cousin, the house cat. Extremely adaptable animals, bobcats live in all counties in California except San Francisco County.

Bobcats are larger than your basic domestic cat but much smaller than a mountain lion, averaging around 20 pounds. Their name may come from their cut-off-looking, or bobbed, tail. When you spot one sitting, walking, or running, one of the first things you'll notice—besides its ear tufts and beautiful spotted coat—is that it has large powerful hind legs and relatively short front legs. Those oversized back legs allow the bobcat to run quickly and leap on prey with great force. Its front paws, equipped with long claws, hook into prey until it can grab hold with its mouth. The list of its prey items includes rodents of all sorts, birds, reptiles, and even an insect here and there.

■ American kestrel (Falco sparverius)

The kestrel, also known by some as the sparrow hawk (its former name), is a handsome little falcon that lives around the shoreline and inland areas year round. Regardless of what you like to call these ten-inch powerhouses, they are a joy to watch, and the males add a brilliant splash of color to any landscape. Both the male and female have distinctive double black stripes on their white faces. The females are mottled russet brown on back with a white chest. The male, however, is the true dandy. In addition to the russet back, the males have gray-blue feathers covering the wings and the tops of their heads. A russet spot is located in the center top of their head. When hovering you can see their dashing white and black underwings.

Kestrels are often seen perched on telephone wires or on the tops of bushes. Look closely and you might see that they are grasping a mouse, a small reptile, or a big insect in their talons. These birds eat a wide variety of food. They can also be seen hovering over grassy fields and road median strips in search of prey. Their distinctive shrill call—"kitty-kitty-kitty"—can be heard during the mating season, when they are chasing away perceived threats such as larger hawks, or while dive-bombing domestic cats.

Monterey Bay Coastal Trail

The 29-mile Monterey Bay Coastal Trail meanders along the bay's southern shoreline between the cities of Castroville and Carmel. It is a work in progress, a cooperative effort between the Monterey Peninsula Regional Park District, the California Coastal Conservancy, several other agencies, and numerous city governments, and new sections are constantly being added. When completed, you will be able to ride all the way from Castroville to Carmel Bay (and Point Lobos) on this specially designated pathway.

Monterey State Beach, Humboldt Street access

Whether you are walking, jogging, biking, or roller blading, you will be treated to incomparable vistas along this trail, and you'll be pleased at the sheer quantity of public access points to the shore. Gulls and terns will be your topside companions, and the constant beat of the surf will either drive you on or lure you to the water's edge for a bit of relaxation.

Between the towns of Castroville and Seaside, the pathway is a Class I trail (separated from road), with only a few minor breaks where it is necessary to cross intersections. From downtown Castroville the trail can be located on the east side of Highway 156, moving south toward Highway 1 and the city of Marina. At Nashua Road the trail jogs east to the Monte Road en route to Marina. In Marina it runs alongside Locke-Paddon Park, where you can pause for some casual bird-watching or read the interpretive signs and learn about the ongoing wetlands restoration project there. Shoreward is Marina State Beach, where a sinuous 2,000-foot-long boardwalk leads you through an impressive dune restoration project. Where barren dunes or monotonous mats of iceplant once greeted visitors, today one finds lush stands of native beach sagewort, beach sand verbena, beach lupine, California poppy, and Monterey paintbrush. Early spring here can present the visitor with an impressive show of flowers, and all seasons are perfect for expansive views of the bay and access to miles of beach.

As the trail leaves Marina and continues south it fronts the newly established Fort Ord Dunes State Park. The faded bunkers, small arms firing ranges, and Stillwell Hall are vivid reminders of this region's military history. Stillwell Hall was once a thriving and exquisite officers' club. It has also proved to be something of a yardstick for coastal erosion: when first built in the 1940s it was hundreds of feet from the shoreline; today, it teeters on the edge of unstable cliffs. The new park plan calls for restoring the majority of the four-mile stretch of coastal dunes —a monumental, exciting undertaking.

Continuing south, the path enters Sand City, where a new section of Class I trail takes the rider from where Fremont Boulevard crosses under the highway and continues along the backside of the dunes, west of Highway 1, until Playa Avenue. The trail moves back under the highway on Playa to Metz Road, turns south and continues to Tioga Avenue, then crosses back over the highway toward the bay. Along this portion of the trail there is undeveloped beach access at the terminus of both Tioga Avenue and Bay Street (past the wastewater pumping plant). There are some private inholdings here, so please respect any No Trespassing signs you might encounter.

Leaving Sand City, the trail scoots by a wonderful dune restoration project at a unit of Monterey State Beach, popularly called Seaside Beach (this state beach is presently distributed in three sections between here and Monterey's Municipal Beach). This is one of the most popular beach access points on the southern sweep of bay. Nearly every weekend there is a riot of kites flying overhead, sun bathers are sprawled across the sand, and beachcombers bend-and-pick, bend-and-pick along the shore like a slow-motion flock of oversized sandpipers. In the fall, patient observers can witness thousands of sooty shearwaters streaming by just offshore in a collective feeding frenzy. Later in the season gray whales spout offshore and raise their massive tails in gargantuan high-5s before diving.

The trail winds its way past Roberts Lake in the city of Seaside, then lines out toward downtown Monterey past the Naval Postgraduate School. Some southern sections of the trail will be designated as Class II (where the trail is on the road's shoulder, separated from cars by road striping) and Class III (where the trail shares the road with cars) until the entire project is completed. (The portion of the trail on the Monterey Peninsula is described on pp. 194–196.)

Monterey State Beach: Humboldt Street Access

Monterey State Beach is presently divided into three sections. One access point is at the terminus of Humboldt Street, next to a very visible beachfront hotel, to the immediate west of Highway 1. It is popularly called Seaside Beach. There is limited parking here for a weekend

INFORMATION

Salinas River National Wildlife Refuge: 510-792-0222

Salinas Chamber of Commerce: 831-424-7611

National Steinbeck Center: 831-753-6411

John Steinbeck Library: 831-758-7311

The Steinbeck House: 831-424-2735

Marina State Beach, Fort Ord Dunes State Beach, Monterey State Beach Rangers Office: 831-384-7695

California State Parks, Monterey District Office: 831-649-2836

Western Hang Glider School, Marina: 831-384-2622

Marina Dunes RV Park: 831-384-6914

Marina Coast Water District Desalinization Plant: 831-384-6131

Marina Chamber of Commerce: 831-384-9155

Bureau of Land Management/Fort Ord: 831-394-8314

California State University Monterey Bay: 831-582-3330

crowd. If it is full, drive past the hotel on Sand Dunes Drive (toward the Monterey Peninsula), where you'll find another parking lot.

At the Humboldt Street access point a nice dune restoration project is in full swing with colorful interpretive signs. A couple of picnic tables and some bathrooms round out the facilities. But the beach is the real attraction here. On any given day if the sun is out and the wind is up even slightly, there are kites in the air. Come on a windy weekend, and the sky will be crammed with colorful kites of all sizes. Beneath them you'll find people dozing on the sand or dodging about playing football or tossing frisbees.

Venture out on the beach here and, if the fog is behaving, you'll have a picture-perfect view of Monterey's waterfront on your left. On your right, you can see the bluffs of the Monterey dunes lining out to the north, with Stillwell Hall teetering on its perch about four miles down the beach.

Roberts Lake

If you are looking for some casual—and easy—birdwatching, this is the spot. There is a resident flock of friendly ducks here, and if you scope the waters or the lakeside vegetation of tules you may spot seasonal visitors migrating along the Pacific Flyway. In and around the tules keep an eye open for pied-billed grebes and green-backed herons. There is usually a large flock of Canada geese here also. If birds don't tickle your fancy, then the lake's occasional amateur model boat races might.

From Roberts Lake you can venture inland along Canyon Del Rey Boulevard to several other parks: Laguna Grande Park, Work Memorial Park, Del Rey Park, Frog Pond Nature Preserve, and, if you keep on going down Highway 68, Laguna Seca Recreation Area. Roberts Lake and Laguna Grande were once connected as a single brackish lagoon with tidal action from the bay. But diking, development, and roads have divided them and cut off the tidal action. Nonetheless, they remain today as small but important habitat sites.

To find the Salinas River National Wildlife Refuge, take the Neponset Road exit off Highway 1, due south of the junction of 1 and Molera Road. After you exit, turn immediately to the right and follow the dirt road straight to the refuge parking lot, about half a mile. The road crossing back over the highway is Del Monte Boulevard. The town of Salinas can be reached by following Highway 183 out of Castroville some six miles, heading inland (southeast).

Marina State Beach is immediately off Highway 1 at the shoreline terminus of Reservation Road, approximately 2 miles south of Neponset Road. The Marina Coast Water District Desalinization Plant is to the right of the park's parking lot. The other coastal access trailhead is past the hotel and RV park at the terminus of Dunes Drive, off Reservation Road. The southern access point for Marina State Beach is at the corner of Lake Drive and Lake Court, in the town of Marina. Take Reservation Road inland, past Locke-Paddon Park, to Del Monte. Turn right (south) on Del Monte and proceed to Palm Avenue (look for the pedestrian bridge arching over Del Monte). At Palm, turn shoreward to Lake Drive, turn left (south) on Lake Drive, and move under Highway 1. You'll see the set of steep wooden slat steps leading over dunes to the beach.

Locke-Paddon Park runs alongside Reservation Road, just inland from Highway 1. To access the public lands of Fort Ord, you have many options. The best bet is to take the California State University Monterey Bay turnoff from Highway 1, approximately 3.5 miles south of Reservation Road. Cross over the highway; make a right onto North-South Road and proceed to Eucalyptus Road; turn left onto Eucalyptus and continue for about 2 miles, until you see the signs for the Bureau of Land Management office, on your right. Stop for trail information there. You can explore some trails just north of the BLM office, off Parker Flats Road. There are also trailheads inland, off Reservation Road and off Highway 68.

Sand City and Monterey State Beach are to the south, right next to Highway 1. For an interesting detour through Sand City and Seaside, take the second Del Monte Boulevard exit, also signed for Fremont Boulevard. Cross under the freeway and veer to the right onto Del Monte; continue south to the intersection with Canyon Del Rey Boulevard (Highway 218). Roberts Lake is directly in front of you. If you continue straight (south) through the intersection you will eventually hit downtown Monterey. To get to Monterey State Beach, however, turn right at this intersection; the road becomes Humboldt Street, then passes back under the freeway and dead-ends at the parking lots for Monterey State Beach and the large beachfront hotel.

If you prefer not to take this detour, simply continue on Highway 1 and take the Seaside–Del Rey Oaks turnoff; turn right to find the beach parking lots, or left to find Roberts Lake. If you pull a rightward U-turn at the foot of the exit ramp, you will find yourself on Sand Dunes Drive, which has beach access points at Bay Street and Tioga Avenue. The Monterey Bay Coastal Trail can be accessed at almost any point along its length.

The Monterey Peninsula: Del Monte Beach to San Jose Creek State Beach

The Monterey Peninsula together with Carmel is a region unto itself. It is as if by some geologic sleight of hand this magical slice of coast was transported to its present location and stitched to the mainland with threads of pine and cypress.

Historically, these lands have played a key role in the lives of coastal Indians, European explorers, early Spanish and Mexican settlers, and the first citizens of the new state of California. Biologically, scores of unique plants and animals claim this territory as their home. Scientifically, the first marine station on the Pacific coast was established on this ragged thumb of land. Culturally, Monterey, Pacific Grove, and Carmel have taught the world the finer points of California coastal living, of cuisine, music, art, and literature. Pebble Beach alone is an icon for upscale living and world-class golf.

Certainly, this region has grown up a bit in the last few decades, if reluctantly. It is possible now to be stuck in commuter traffic while visiting here, and the variety of problems and challenges that face urban areas across the United States are not unknown to local residents. And yet, even at the height of the tourist season, it is possible to stroll along sections of the shore here and feel like you've been transported back in time. As a cool fog eases in from the Pacific, taking the edge off a hot day, you might almost expect to see the 1940s sardine fleet come chugging into port riding low in the water, or catch Ed Ricketts up to his knees in the tidepools, or glimpse Robinson Jeffers strolling down Carmel Beach as his mind soared far above his salty feet.

Work your way just a few blocks in from the shoreline—toward the heart of the peninsula or up the hill from Carmel Beach—and you can experience not only quiet and serene neighborhoods, but also scores of historic sites, museums, galleries, restaurants, and shops. The Monterey Peninsula and Carmel are the types of places that make people stop in their tracks, look about, breathe deeply, and confess out loud, "Yes, I could live here."

◄ Fanshell Beach

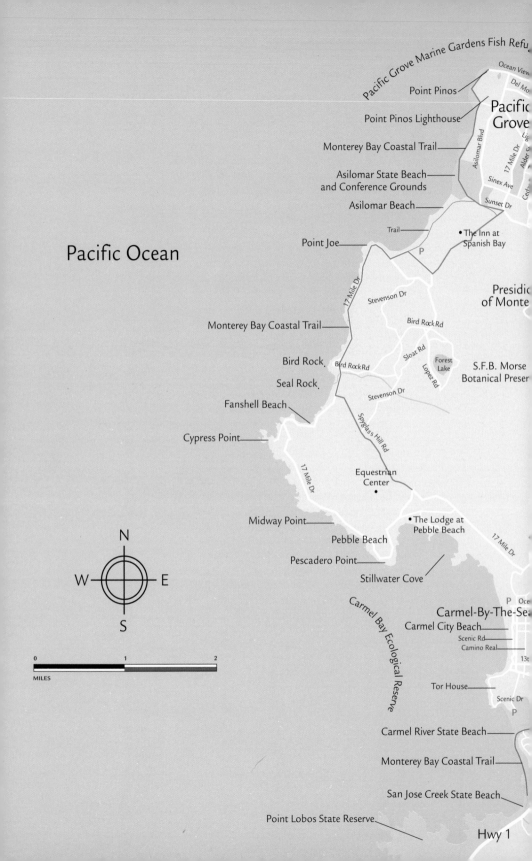

Pacific Grove Marine Gardens Fish Refu...

Ocean View

Del Mo...

Point Pinos

Pacific
Grove

Point Pinos Lighthouse

Li...

Asilomar Blvd

17 Mile Dr

Alder...

Monterey Bay Coastal Trail

Cedar...

Asilomar State Beach
and Conference Grounds

Sinex Ave

Asilomar Beach

Sunset Dr

Trail

• The Inn at
Spanish Bay

Point Joe

P

Pacific Ocean

Presidio
of Monte...

Stevenson Dr

Bird Rock Rd

Monterey Bay Coastal Trail

Sloat Rd

Forest
Lake

S.F.B. Morse
Botanical Preser...

Bird Rock

Bird Rock Rd

Lopez Rd

Seal Rock

Stevenson Dr

Fanshell Beach

Spyglass Hill Rd

Cypress Point

17 Mile Dr

Equestrian
Center

•

Midway Point

• The Lodge at
Pebble Beach

17 Mile Dr

Pebble Beach

Pescadero Point

P   Oce...

Stillwater Cove

Carmel-By-The-Se...

N
W   E
S

Carmel Bay Ecological Reserve

Carmel City Beach

Scenic Rd

Camino Real

13t...

0   1   2

Tor House

MILES

Scenic Dr

P

Carmel River State Beach

Monterey Bay Coastal Trail

San Jose Creek State Beach

Point Lobos State Reserve

Hwy 1

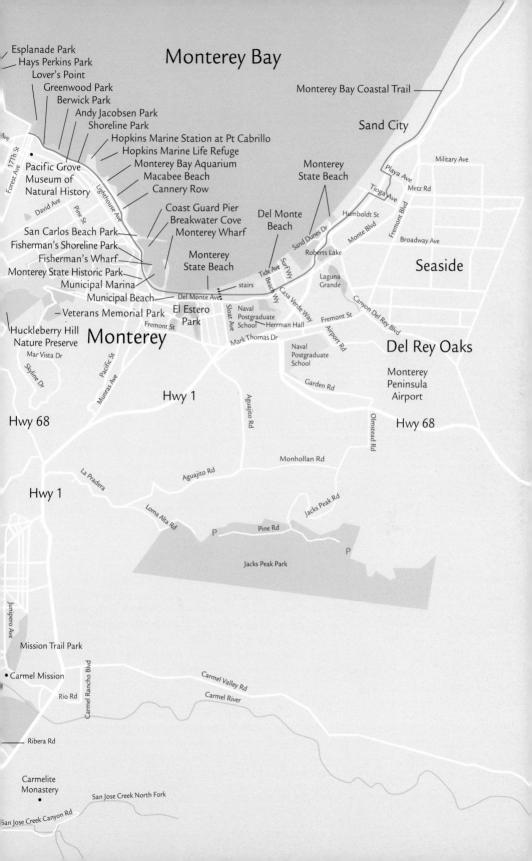

Monterey Harbor on a
summer's day

Del Monte Beach to Asilomar Beach

This stretch of shoreline is perhaps the best-known and
most-visited section of the greater Monterey Bay. It begins
at a little-known city beach, skirts downtown Monterey
and its world-famous bayside attractions, and ends at a
beach where the sand is so white it defies description.
This segment of the coast also boasts a shoreline trail
along its entire length, as well as some of the wildest,
most spectacular waters anywhere.

Monterey Bay Coastal Trail

At Roberts Lake you leave Seaside and enter Monterey's
city limits on a spectacular Class I stretch of the Monterey Bay Coastal Trail. It parallels Del Monte Boulevard
along a three-mile section of the former Southern Pacific
Railroad—the old Del Monte Express line. You pass the
turnoff to Del Monte Beach and soon move through a
corridor framed by towering eucalyptus trees. In the
midst of these trees, about 100 yards south of a small
parking lot (across from a main entrance into the Naval
Postgraduate School), is a turnout equipped with bike
racks. You can stop here and walk up and over the
dunes—restored by the navy in the 1990s—on a wooden
staircase. Although the beach here is still a work in
progress, it is a nice place to venture to, being somewhat
off the beaten path.

Continuing on toward Monterey's wharves, you come upon the most southerly segment of Monterey State Beach, called Window on the Bay Beach. It is next door to Monterey's Municipal Beach and Wharf. Between the wharf area and the Monterey Bay Aquarium (a distance of about one and a half miles) you will find more than a dozen parks, public areas, and historic sites, not to mention an abundance of stores and restaurants.

The buzz of activity in and around Custom House Plaza, by Fisherman's Wharf, is reminiscent of the 1800s, when the Custom House was the center of public life in Old Monterey. As the trail bends along the curve of the shoreline, sandy beaches are replaced by a rocky shore; here is where Edward Ricketts could often be found, poking around in his beloved tidepools. Next to the Coast Guard Pier you'll find San Carlos Beach, a breathtaking (or perhaps breath-restoring) stop as well as a popular scuba-diving location.

Continue along the old rail line past historic Cannery Row and you reach the Monterey Bay Aquarium—about three miles from Roberts Lake. This portion of the trail, which runs along the backside of Cannery Row, is perhaps the most developed section. It has two wide lanes and stop signs, and the entire route is landscaped and lined with benches and small turnouts. Stop off at the aquarium to view the intimate crannies and vast expanses of Monterey Bay and the Pacific Ocean. Be sure to give yourself plenty of time: there's a lot to see.

If you can pull yourself away from the aquarium, continue down the path toward Pacific Grove. Here the trail hugs the rocky blufftop and you can look northeast across the bay toward Santa Cruz and take in views of the coastal mountains. Just a few blocks inland from Lovers Point is the Pacific Grove Museum of Natural History, at the corner of Central and Forest Avenues. There are many bench stops along the trail here, and the beach at Lovers Point is very popular. Once at the point you can rent a kayak and tour the coastline, play some volleyball, go surfing, scuba dive and snorkel, or have a picnic.

The trail continues through Pacific Grove on Ocean View Boulevard as a Class III pathway. A smaller foot trail (no bikes) makes its way along the bluffs here as well. When you reach the corner of Ocean View and Asilomar Avenue you have traveled some five miles since leaving Roberts Lake. The trail—now on Sunset Drive and redesignated Class II—rounds Point Pinos and the Point Pinos Lighthouse and soon arrives at Asilomar State Beach, a favorite of visitors to the Asilomar Conference Center. Just south of the rocky bluffs you can't miss Asilomar Beach (known on maps as North Moss Beach).

On the Monterey Peninsula many of the Monterey-Salinas Transit (MST) buses have bike racks. The MST also operates a waterfront shuttle service called the WAVE (Waterfront Area Visitors Express) from Memorial Day to Labor Day. For the truly adventurous, you can catch a bus (number 22) from downtown Monterey (intersection of Munras, Pearl, and Tyler) and go as far south as Pfeiffer Big Sur State Park and Nepenthe from late May to late August. It takes about one and a half hours. For bus numbers and schedules, contact the MST at 831-899-2555 or check out their website at http://www.mst.org.

At the Window on the Bay section of Monterey State Beach (across from El Estero Park) you will find picnic tables and volleyball nets. A large lawn fronting the road is a perfect spot to rest or to let the kids run around. You can walk from this beach directly toward Monterey's Municipal Wharf via Monterey's Municipal Beach. There is no break from one beach to the next, just a lot of nice sand.

You can also switch gears here—and your mode of transportation—by renting a kayak from Monterey Bay Kayaks immediately next to the beach (you can't miss their sign and yard full of boats). The waves along this section of bay are usually very gentle and the waters calm—perfect for putting in your kayak en route to the kelp forests just offshore. Cruise the shoreline looking for rock-pounding sea otters and boisterous sea lions, or head out into open waters to catch glimpses of dolphins or gray whales. Or simply rest your paddle and watch patiently—you'll be amazed at the life above you, around you, and below you.

Continuing up Sunset Drive, the trail arrives at the Pacific Grove Gate of Seventeen Mile Drive—approximately eight miles from Roberts Lake.

Del Monte Beach

This public beach might go unnoticed by the visitor who is concentrating on reaching the peninsula itself. Tucked in between the Humboldt Street access to Monterey State Beach to the north and the Naval Postgraduate School to the south, Del Monte Beach was rather nondescript until recently. The dunes were covered with nonnative plants and a bit worse for wear. However, a recent cooperative project has helped breathe life back into this sandy stretch. Today the dunes support a healthy cross-section of native plants, and instead of a maze of destructive footpaths, a sturdy wooden walkway leads into the area.

To find Del Monte Beach, turn off of Del Monte Avenue onto Casa Verde and move uphill onto Surf Way en route to the beach. Comfortable benches are scattered about, and parking is available in front of the houses on Tide Avenue or in the small parking lot at the terminus of Beach Way. The dunes here are a real joy, and the beach is only steps away from the parking areas. From this beach you can walk on sand all the way to downtown Monterey, or turn 180 degrees and set out for the Salinas River Wildlife Refuge and even Moss Landing.

El Estero

El Estero, across the street from Window on the Bay Beach, is a horseshoe-shaped body of water surrounded by a 45-acre park. The park is outfitted with everything you can imagine: Dennis the Menace Playground (no kidding—it's designed by local resident Hank Ketchum), a par course, picnic sites, a baseball park, and other facilities. You can even rent a paddleboat (the kind you power with your legs) and cruise around in El Estero. If you are crossing Del Monte Avenue to reach the park, keep your eyes open and use the crosswalks—traffic can be very busy here.

As you stand on the Monterey Bay Coastal Trail and look across to El Estero, it might strike you as odd that this bit of water isn't connected to the bay. After all, there is only a road and some sand separating the two. In fact, El Estero was originally what its Spanish name describes: an estuary. In the 1870s the Monterey & Salinas Railroad came along and built their tracks where today's roadway and Coastal Trail are located. When they built up the railroad bed, they cut El Estero off from the bay.

The Monterey Peninsula Visitors and Convention Bureau maintains a satellite office in the old French consulate building with free literature and advice. Find it at the intersection of Camino El Estero and Franklin Street.

The Wharves

Between the foot of Figueroa Street and the start of Cannery Row—a distance of less than one mile—three wharves jut out from the shoreline near downtown Monterey: the Municipal Wharf, Fisherman's Wharf, and the Coast Guard Pier. All three are open to the public. In fact, it might take you an entire morning or afternoon to explore them all—there is a lot to see, experience, and taste on this short section of coast.

Monterey's Municipal Wharf

■ Municipal Wharf

The Municipal Wharf—also known as Wharf No. 2—was built in 1925, at the height of the sardine boom, as a working wharf for the area's fishing fleet and to accommodate large boats. Today you can grab a bite to eat here or try your luck with your own hook and line (on the east side of the pier). Or you can just stretch your legs on this 1,750-foot wharf and watch the fishermen working on their boats or unloading a catch at the end of the pier.

Fisherman's Wharf viewed from
Fisherman's Shoreline Park

Ample metered parking is available between the wharf
and Del Monte Avenue.

The Monterey Marina, tucked in between this wharf
and Fisherman's Wharf, contains some 425 berths. En
route to Fisherman's Wharf via the Coastal Trail, keep
your eyes open for the side trail leading to downtown.
It is well signed.

■ Fisherman's Wharf

Monterey's first wharf was built on this site in 1846,
immediately shoreward from the Custom House. Over
the years it was reworked and extended. In the 1870s the
Pacific Coast Steamship Company rebuilt the wharf so its
boats could conduct business here. These steamships fer-
ried supplies to merchants up and down the coast; stops
included Moss Landing and Hudson's Landing to the
immediate north. In Monterey and Moss Landing they
would fill their storage compartments with lumber,
canned fish, and occasionally dried squid produced by
local Chinese fishermen. Up at Hudson's Landing Pajaro
Valley produce would be added to the cargo.

Monterey's wharf soon became home to a thriving fishing fleet. After the turn of the century the city of Monterey assumed management of the wharf, by then known
popularly as Fisherman's Wharf. This old collection of
pilings and eclectic buildings has undergone many additional face-lifts and renovations since steamships plied
these waters. At the height of the fishing industry here,
the bay and wharf were crowded with hundreds of working boats. In addition to the famous sardine, these hard-
working people hauled in salmon, albacore, mackerel,
anchovies, rockfish, lingcod, squid, and other treasures
from the Pacific.

Today most of the commercial fishing is done from the
Municipal Wharf, but Fisherman's Wharf is still home to
party-fishing boats and whale-watching tour boats. There

is also a public dock here, halfway between Fisherman's Wharf and the Municipal Wharf. Most people, of course, come to this area to browse through the various shops, grab a bite of seafood, take in some theater, learn about local history, or simply people-watch. It is a perfect place for all those activities, and a lot more.

■ Coast Guard Pier

Near Cannery Row and Foam Street, veer to your right by Breakwater Cove and walk out on the Coast Guard Pier. The breakwater at the end of this 200-yard-long jetty, built in the 1930s on top of an older structure, is almost always festooned with a bawling bunch of sea lions. This spot is popular for people wanting a leisurely walk and great vistas. Local divers also put in near here, at San Carlos Beach. When the tide is low in Breakwater Cove, check out the nearshore rocks. They are often topped with a sleepy harbor seal or two. For a better look, work your way to the backside of the cove and watch from the Coastal Trail.

Coast Guard Pier and California sea lions. Sea kayaking is a favorite pastime for both residents and visitors to the peninsula.

Monterey State Historic Park

This little corner of Monterey Bay seems to have more history packed into it than the rest of Monterey County and most of Santa Cruz County combined. Although Juan Rodriguez Cabrillo sailed by the peninsula in 1542, he didn't land here. That honor belongs to Sebastián Vizcaíno, who sailed into the bay in 1602. He gave Point Pinos its name and set anchor in what we know today as Breakwater Cove, claiming the land for Spain. Vizcaíno and his men later camped near the Carmel River for several weeks before continuing on their way.

In 1770 Father Junípero Serra landed in this same spot and met Captain Gaspar de Portolá and Father Juan Crespí, who had arrived by land shortly before. Historians believe that it was here, under the same oak tree where Vizcaíno and Father Antonio de la Ascensión celebrated mass 168 years earlier, that Mission San Carlos Borromeo de Monterey and the Presidio of Monterey were founded. After Serra's landing, Monterey was

Custom House Plaza, the heart of historic Monterey

named capital of both Alta and Baja California. The mission was soon moved to Carmel to be closer to freshwater and better soils.

In 1821 Mexico gained independence from Spain, and Monterey became the Mexican capital of California. Just over 20 years later, in 1846, the Custom House was taken over by American commodore John Drake Sloat, who was followed by John C. Frémont and his men. When California became a U.S. state, Monterey was named the capital. In September 1849 the first constitutional convention met in Colton Hall to establish a government for the new state. After the discovery of gold attention turned to San Francisco, and soon the capital was moved to Benicia on the Carquinez Strait, and eventually to Sacramento.

The Monterey State Historic Park comprises a dozen historic buildings scattered throughout the city. You can begin to explore it directly in front of Fisherman's Wharf. It is difficult to imagine today, but when most of these buildings were erected in the early to mid–19th century you could stand on a high point and see every one of them, with open lands extending in between.

You might want to consider a visit during the Christmas season, for the annual Christmas in the Adobes tour. Volunteers dress up in period clothes, and glowing luminaria lead you from house to house where you can sip cider and munch on cookies.

For information about the Monterey State Historic Park, including hours of the buildings (some of which are quite limited), locations of historic gardens, and a schedule of special events, call 831-649-7118, or stop by the visitor center in the Stanton Center or at the Cooper-Molera Adobe; you can also get information at

http://www.mbay.net/~mshp. Below are some of the historic sites closest to the shore.

■ Custom House

This beautifully restored adobe—California's first officially designated historic landmark—is the oldest public building on the Pacific coast, and it is the only building still standing in the state that was built by the government of Mexico. As the name suggests, it served as the Mexican customs office between 1822 and 1846. It originally stood directly on the shore, and all cargo ships entering California were supposed to stop here for inspection and to pay taxes. (Interestingly, recent archeological work has confirmed that the Custom House was built next to a site where an older Spanish structure—recorded on several 18th-century maps—stood for many years.)

After the United States took possession of the western territories, the Custom House went through several changes. The federal government closed the building in the late 1860s, and at one point it was a private residence. In the late 19th century the area on the bay side of the house was filled for a railroad extension to Pacific Grove. Saved from obscurity and demolition, the building was restored around the turn of the century and has been well maintained ever since. Inside you'll find dry goods, tools, scales, and furnishings, much as they were when the Custom House was in full operation.

■ Pacific House

Pacific House, which faces Custom House Plaza, was built in 1847 and was home to many different businesses and government interests during the 19th century.

FIRST BRICK HOUSE

This nicely restored home on Oliver Street was erected in 1847 by the Dickinson family using bricks made right here in Monterey. It is the first house built with bricks in California. Next door, on Decatur Street, is the Old Whaling Station, also built in 1847. Like many of the historic buildings in this park, the Old Whaling Station has seen various uses since it housed Portuguese whalers in the 1850s.

J ust off Pacific Street by
the Presidio's entrance is
a very large cross marking
the approximate site where
Sebastián Vizcaíno and Padre
Junípero Serra made their historic landings. The oak tree
under which they both held
mass, 168 years apart, no
longer stands, but a section
of its trunk is preserved at the
San Carlos Cathedral.

A t the corner of Pacific
and Scott Streets is
California's First
Theater, built in 1846. Originally opened as a boarding
house and saloon, it was also
let out to local soldiers who
wanted to put on plays for
their own amusement. Al-
though the plays eventually
stopped being produced,
they are back today in the
form of classic melodramas.
The building has also been
furnished with items from the
days of the '49ers, and it is
open to the public. For information about the plays and
visiting hours, inquire at the
historic park.

Perhaps the most interesting period was when it was home to Monterey County's courtroom, jury room, clerk office—and a tavern. Today it is home to a new visitor center and the museums have recently been renovated. Downstairs, exhibits tell of the area's early history as the capital of Spanish and Mexican California. Upstairs you'll find the Museum of the American Indian. The building's old corral is now a pleasant garden—a great place to rest up before continuing your historical trek. It might be a quiet spot today, but in its heyday, this was the site for Sunday bear and bull fights.

Presidio of Monterey

Although not part of the state historic park, the Presidio of Monterey, founded in 1770, is plenty historic. Not only is it one of the oldest military posts in the United States, but with the closure of the San Francisco Presidio in 1994 it became the only active Presidio in the country. The presidios never played an actual defensive or offensive role under Spanish or Mexican rule; in fact, they were often falling apart, and the military men had to contend with little or no supplies.

During the American period a short-lived fort, Fort Mervine, was built on the site of the Presidio overlooking the bay. The U.S. Army slowly built up the facilities around the turn of the century, and today it is occupied by the Defense Language Institute. There are many historic sites and monuments within the grounds—including a Rumsien Indian site—and some fantastic views. The public is welcome. Contact the Presidio for information about their self-guided tour, at 831-242-5184.

■ Boston Store

The Joseph Boston Store was built in 1845, one of many properties owned by Thomas Larkin, an early businessman in Monterey and U.S. consul during the period of Mexican rule. It is located at the corner of Scott and Oliver Streets. Also known as the Casa del Oro, the building has seen many uses over the years, but it is now back to being a general store, operated by the Historic Garden League, with proceeds going to improve the historic gardens of Monterey.

Maritime Museum of Monterey

The Maritime Museum of Monterey, located on the Custom House Plaza in the Stanton Center, is not itself historic, but it *contains* history. The museum, which houses a sizable archive, is dedicated to Monterey's rich maritime history and to maritime research. The museum's exhibits include model ships, an enormous lighthouse lens, and ship paraphernalia. Call ahead (831-375-2553) for hours and information about special programs. State Historic Park information can also be found within the Stanton Center.

Downtown Diversions and Free Information

Immediately inland from the shoreline portion of the Monterey State Historic Park you can search out additional celebrated buildings (most, but not all, part of the park) while exploring the shops and restaurants of downtown Monterey. There are also several small downtown parks where you can rest.

Also, make sure to stop by the Monterey Peninsula Visitors and Convention Bureau and Monterey Peninsula Chamber of Commerce at 380 Alvarado Street (between Franklin Street and Del Monte Avenue), or give them a call (bureau, 831-649-1770; chamber, 831-648-5360). The staff of both organizations are friendly and they have plenty of free information.

Casa Soberanes

■ Casa Soberanes

Located at 336 Pacific Street, Casa Soberanes is a fine example of an early adobe from the Mexican period. A residence constructed in the 1840s, it was the home of the Soberanes family from 1860 to 1922.

■ Casa Serrano

In the 1840s this nicely restored adobe was both a home and a small school. Its address is 412 Pacific Street.

■ Casa Estrada

This three-story structure, on Tyler Street between Bonifacio Place and Pearl Street, was built in 1823. It has housed several businesses, including a hotel and a bank.

This museum's permanent and temporary exhibits feature American and Asian art, works reflecting international themes, photography, and works by local artists. It has two branches: one across the street from Colton Hall, next to the Civic Center; the other, known as the La Mirada Adobe, on Via Mirada behind El Estero Park. Call the museum (831-372-7591) for hours and information on current exhibits.

■ Larkin House

Thomas O. Larkin, American businessman and U.S. consul to Alta California, built this two-story adobe in the 1830s on the corner of Jefferson and Calle Principal. In addition to serving as his residence, the Larkin House doubled as the consulate. The house, with its generous eaves and large porch, had a decidedly American flavor in the Monterey of Mexican rule, and defined an architectural style that came to be known as the Monterey Colonial Style or simply the Monterey Style. This style quickly spread throughout California, the most elaborate example being General Mariano Vallejo's adobe home and compound near today's city of Petaluma.

■ Casa Amesti

This 1825 adobe at 516 Polk Street incorporates some American influences into a generally Mexican style. This building belongs to the National Historic Trust.

Historic buildings abound throughout the entire Monterey Peninsula, and over in Carmel as well. If you see what appears to be an old edifice, stop and take a look; you are likely to find a placard stating the name of the original occupants and the year the building was erected.

■ Cooper-Molera Adobe

At the corner of Polk and Munras, this large homestead on 2.5 acres was the residence of John Rogers Cooper, a New England sea captain, and his wife, Encarnación Vallejo. Mrs. Cooper's brother was General Mariano Vallejo, California's first Mexican military commander from 1836 to 1846 and later one of early California's most prominent citizens. The complex, constructed in the 1830s, takes in many buildings, including two houses and two barns; there is also a museum store and a visitor center. Information about the State Historic Park can be found here as well.

■ Colton Hall

This New England–style building at 559 Pacific (between Madison and Jefferson) was constructed between 1847 and 1849, in California's infancy. The town hall was on the second floor, and Monterey's first public school was

downstairs. This is where the new state's first constitution was debated and written in the fall of 1849.

■ Stevenson House

Robert Louis Stevenson, author of *Kidnapped* and *Treasure Island,* spent time in Monterey in 1879; in fact, some believe Long John Silver's island is based in part on locations Stevenson visited around the peninsula and in Point Lobos. Stevenson lived in this house at 530 Houston Street briefly in 1879. Originally constructed in the 1840s or earlier, this house was saved from near ruin, restored, and given to the state of California. Today several rooms are devoted to period furnishings and Stevenson memorabilia.

San Carlos Cathedral

San Carlos Cathedral has the appropriate address of 550 Church Street. The site was consecrated in 1770, the current church was completed in 1794 (several temporary structures preceded this sandstone building), and it has been in continuous use ever since. The cathedral, also known as the Royal Presidio Chapel, is Monterey's oldest building. In 1961 it was designated a National Historic Landmark by the U.S. Department of the Interior. The trunk of the oak tree under which both Vizcaíno and Serra reportedly held mass (in 1602 and 1770, respectively) is housed here. A self-guided tour pamphlet is available at the church.

FIRST FRENCH CONSULATE

El Estero Park is home to this 1830s adobe, which served as the French consulate to California starting in 1845. Originally built on Fremont Street, it was moved to El Estero by the Monterey History and Art Association in the 1930s. It's now occupied by the Monterey Peninsula Visitors and Convention Bureau.

Peninsula Camping

The only spot to camp on the Monterey Peninsula is Veteran's Memorial Park, where you'll find 40 first-come, first-served sites. The cost is $15 a night. There are tables, barbecue pits, bathrooms, and showers but no hook-ups for recreational vehicles. A few group sites can be reserved by calling 831-646-3865. From downtown Monterey, take Pearl Street to Jefferson Street and work your way uphill. Jefferson leads directly to the park.

Fisherman's Shoreline Park

After exploring Monterey's historic downtown you can easily return to the shoreline at Fisherman's Shoreline Park. This narrow five-acre greenspace wraps around Breakwater Cove en route to Cannery Row. It is nicely landscaped and outfitted with numerous benches and pullouts. A pleasant section of the Coastal Trail runs through the middle of it—a good place to look for harbor seals on the nearshore rocks. At the park's Fisherman's Wharf side, be sure to stop and admire the statue of Santa Rosalia, patron saint of Monterey's Italian fishermen.

Cannery Row

This bustling eight-block stretch of waterfront was popularly known as Cannery Row long before John Steinbeck immortalized it in his 1945 book of the same name. There is no doubting, however, that Steinbeck's depiction of the Row in that famous novel brought this spicy, smelly mix of sardine canneries, tin shacks, smokestacks, storefronts, and rattling railroad cars to life in people's imaginations. To make things official, the city renamed the street in 1953 (it had been known as Ocean View Avenue). A bronze bust of Steinbeck faces Cannery Row in the parking lot above McAbee Beach (between Prescott and Hoffman Avenues).

Not only does the name predate Steinbeck, but the fishing industry had also long been in place before

Colorful Cannery Row

BRUCE ARISS, ARTIST, MONTEREY BAY AQUARIUM

Pacific sardine

the sardine canneries began to boom. Chinese fishermen—the true pioneers of the region's fishing industry—were living and working along this shoreline as early as the 1850s (see page 214).

The sardine fishery was in existence by the turn of the century, but it really exploded in the 1920s. During Cannery Row's heyday—from the 1920s through the 1940s—some 19 canneries and 20 reduction plants were processing an estimated 250,000 tons of sardines annually.

Pacific sardines (*Sardinops sagax*) were canned as an inexpensive yet nutritious food item, and in the reduction plants they were ground up for their oil and for processing as fertilizer. Most of the canneries were right on the shoreline, with direct access to the boats. Related buildings were across the street, next to the railroad for easy shipping. Several aerial crossovers connected the buildings above the street; these were used for sending cans back and forth on conveyor belts. Several of these crossovers still exist.

By 1950 the fishery had collapsed. It was always thought the collapse was due simply to overfishing. Today, although experts still believe that overfishing was the principal cause of the sardine's precipitous decline, made possible in part by technological innovations, they also contend that a long-term cyclical shrinkage of the fish's population may have added to the problem.

Sardines do still live in the bay in large numbers (though not approaching previous levels), and following a fishing moratorium imposed from 1967 to 1986, the fishery has regained vigor. In 1996, for example, sardines led the list of commercial species by weight, with a take of over 8,500 tons. Most of these fish are frozen and sold overseas.

Today, instead of factory workers crowding the street during shifts and the ripe smell of processed sardines hanging in the air, Cannery Row is packed with tourists and the air is spiced with seafood, candy, and hot coffee. Most of the factories and warehouses are gone, though some have been refurbished to house everything from hotels to art galleries, restaurants, and variety stores. You can also visit the Monterey County Vintners and Growers Association tasting room at 700 Cannery Row, just a few doors down from the Monterey Bay Aquarium, for a fine selection of local wines. There is even a wax museum and an antique carousel. And, the old Hovden Cannery at the

"Cannery Row in Monterey in California is a poem, a stink, a grating noise, a quality of light, a tone, a habit, a nostalgia, a dream."

John Steinbeck,
Cannery Row (1945)

end of the Row is now home to the beautiful Monterey Bay Aquarium.

If you are interested in the history of Cannery Row—if you want to stand in front of Edward Ricketts's Pacific Biological Laboratories or stroll through a former bordello—take a walking tour. To locate a tour company, just ask at the Cannery Row Visitor Center, located on the Coastal Trail between Prescott and Hoffman in the railroad car. You can also call the Cannery Row Foundation, 831-372-8512, for a recorded message regarding Cannery Row events.

San Carlos Beach Park and McAbee Beach

Two small beaches can be found a few blocks apart along Cannery Row. San Carlos Beach Park is at the foot of Reeside Avenue, a short stroll away from the Coast Guard Pier. This small beach is a perfect place for some easy shoreline rock hopping; when you want to rest, you can go back upslope and find a bench or stretch out on the well-manicured lawn. There are excellent interpretive exhibits here, as well as a memorial to David Packard, co-founder of Hewlett-Packard and a moving force behind the Monterey Bay Aquarium and MBARI. Standing on this small slice of open shoreline, you will marvel at the beauty of the peninsula. On a warm summer day, after the morning fog recedes leaving behind crystalline air and squeaky-clean vistas, no occupied shoreline in the world is more beautiful than this.

San Carlos Beach Park, a favorite of both beachcombers and scuba divers

McAbee Beach is tucked away between McClellan and Prescott directly off Cannery Row. It once served as a Portuguese shore-whaling station and then as a small sunbathers' resort developed by John McAbee in the late 19th century. It is reportedly one of the warmer spots along the peninsula's northeast shore. After a 1906 fire destroyed the Chinese fishing village between today's

DEL MONTE BEACH TO SAN JOSE CREEK STATE BEACH

Monterey Bay Aquarium and Hopkins Marine Station, the village was relocated to this beach for a while. Today, the beach is a favorite entry point for divers and a perfect spot to sit on a rock and enjoy the watery view.

Monterey Bay National Marine Sanctuary

The Monterey Bay National Marine Sanctuary, established in 1992, is one of 12 sanctuaries, found from Florida to Hawaii. Embracing one-fifth of California's coast, from Marin County south to Cambria in San Luis Obispo County, and extending an average of 30 miles offshore, it encompasses 5,300 square miles—an area much larger than either Yosemite or Yellowstone National Park. In fact, it is the nation's largest marine sanctuary.

The Monterey sanctuary encompasses not only one of the world's deepest marine canyons, but also the nation's

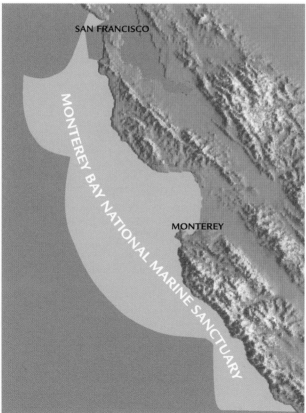

The Monterey Bay National Marine Sanctuary

MONTEREY BAY AQUARIUM

Squid

Even though salmon is only sixth on the list of Monterey Bay's commercial species by weight, that pink-fleshed fish consistently brings in the most money for the industry. Surprisingly, sardines are once again the bay's number-one harvest, at least by weight. During the late 1990s, the sardine harvest for Santa Cruz, Moss Landing, and Monterey combined hovered around 8,500 tons a year. That's nothing compared to the historic high of 250,000 tons taken by the Monterey fleet alone, but still, it's nothing to sneeze at. Below is a who's who of the bay's four other most important commercial species—rated by tons caught per season, not by economic value (salmon always wins that contest). Look for these familiar (and not so familiar) characters in a store or restaurant near you.

- **Squid** *(Loligo opalescens)*
This amazing-looking cephalopod, commonly known as the market squid, is very abundant in Monterey Bay. From mantle to tentacle tip, the adult is around one foot long. scuba divers often see squid and their tubular white eggs sacks just offshore around the kelp beds. Monterey is an important spawning area for the squid; every fall under cover of darkness countless individuals rise to the surface of the water to mate, descend again to lay their eggs, then die.

You may have encountered this creature in the frozen food section or in a restaurant, where it's known more fancily as calamari. In some parts of the country the market squid isn't taken seriously as a commercial species, but here in Monterey Bay it has been a prized catch since the 1850s, when Chinese fishermen took to the bay at night with torches hanging from the bows of their boats to attract the animals. Most of the squid caught back then were dried and shipped to San Francisco or China. Today, some 5,000 tons are harvested annually right here in Monterey Bay for both domestic and foreign markets, and it continues to be a well-managed, sustainable fishery. Other spawning grounds in California are located off southern California, including the waters around the Channel Islands.

most extensive kelp forests. The nutrient-rich waters of the sanctuary support hundreds of species of fish, 100 or more species of birds, and 26 species of marine mammals. When you start counting the smaller marine animals and plants that thrive here, the numbers soar into the thousands.

The National Oceanic and Atmospheric Administration (NOAA) manages all marine sanctuaries for recreational and commercial use, and both biological and cultural resources fall under NOAA's jurisdiction. (For

A school of northern anchovy

Anchovy *(Engraulis mordax)*

These metallic-blue nine-inch torpedoes seem to be constantly on the move. Anchovies are important food species for both humans and wildlife, though here in Monterey Bay they've always played second fiddle to sardines, at least in terms of fishery catch. Between the 1920s and the 1940s, when the sardine reigned supreme, the average anchovy take in California was only around 1,300 tons. At around that time, though, the sardine fishery began to collapse—and anchovies quickly took up the slack. By 1953 the anchovy fishery had exploded, with a take of some 39,000 tons statewide. Today, anchovies are still very important—and they again play second fiddle to sardines, averaging only some 3,750 tons yearly in Monterey Bay.

Rockfish *(Sebastes* spp.*)*

Dozens of rockfish species live in Monterey Bay, generally in and around the kelp beds and in deeper areas around rocky outcroppings and reefs. When they are harvested, all species are processed simply as "rockfish"; they account for some 1,500 tons annually. Some of the common names of local rockfish include the black, blue, olive, gopher, kelp, cannery, copper, flag, rosy, chilipepper, yelloweye, and vermilion rockfish.

Grenadier *(Coryphaenoides acrolepis)*

Grenadier—also known by the decidedly unappetizing name of Pacific rattail—is a relatively new commercial species, with some 1,000 tons taken every year. In fact, it became a fishery by chance: grenadier, a deep-water fish, kept coming up in the nets of sole and sablefish fishermen. This fish is not exactly nice to look at, but someone was brave enough to fillet one and give it a taste test. It turns out the fish processes well, and it has mild-tasting light meat that is adaptable to a variety of cooking methods. It is also low in oil and so keeps well. Grenadiers will probably prove to be an increasingly popular commercial species, since they appear to be extremely abundant.

MONTEREY BAY AQUARIUM

Yelloweye rockfish, just one of the many species of rockfish found in the bay and throughout the marine sanctuary

example, there are hundreds of shipwrecks within the limits of the Monterey sanctuary.) There are two sanctuary-related websites worth checking out. One is maintained by the sanctuary's office (http://205.155.38.2/Intro/index.html), and the other was produced through a cooperative agreement between NOAA and the Moss Landing Marine Laboratories (http://color.mlml.calstate.edu/www/mbnms/docs92/main.htm). You can also give their office a call (831-647-4201) to find out about educational programs, research projects, and public events.

You might notice that the Monterey Bay Coastal Trail is very straight as it parallels Cannery Row and then skirts the Monterey Bay Aquarium to access the shoreline. That's because this trail was once a train line, operated by the Southern Pacific (SP) Railway. It was popularly called the Del Monte Express, since it stopped at Charles Crocker's opulent Hotel Del Monte, now on the grounds of the Naval Postgraduate School. First opened in 1880, the hotel, a favorite destination for well-off San Franciscans, has had three incarnations. Fire consumed the first structure in 1887, and partially destroyed a sec-

ond in 1924. The current building is a combination of what remained after 1924 and additions made over the next two years. You can go on a self-guided tour of the former hotel, which now serves as the administration building for the navy school (the old lobby is well worth a look, as is the ballroom); just drive onto the school grounds and look for Herrman Hall. In front of the building you'll see what remains of the cacti-dominated "Arizona Garden," designed by noted botanist Rudolf Ulrich in the early 1880s. You can also call the school's public affairs office (831-656-2023) for directions.

From the hotel, the Del Monte Express followed the shore all the way to Monterey's wharf area. Eventually the line was extended past today's Cannery Row (before there were canneries) and along the low coastal bluff to Lovers Point in Pacific Grove. From there it crossed over the peninsula to Lake Majella (now dry) near the Inn at Spanish Bay. The line was intended to continue to Carmel, but when an abundance of high-quality sand was encountered here, SP stopped construction of the rail line to mine it. The Del Monte Express was in operation until the late 1960s.

Monterey Bay Aquarium

The Monterey Bay Aquarium is one of the world's premiere aquariums and centers of marine education. When it opened its doors at the site of the old Hovden Cannery in 1984 it proved that innovative displays, an educational approach, and great architecture can be mixed together quite successfully.

The aquarium focuses on the fertile waters of Monterey Bay with numerous exhibits that walk you through the major habitats of the bay, including the kelp forest most spectacularly, as well as a progression from deep reefs to wharf pilings, the rocky shore, and the slough with special exhibits on bat rays (that you can touch), sea otters, octopus and kin, and the ever-popular touch pool. Be sure to find the wave crash (a real crowd pleaser). The Outer Bay wing, with its million-gallon open ocean exhibit, tanks of jellyfish, and "plankton lab," is stunning. There are also displays on local history and contemporary marine issues.

The Monterey Bay Aquarium

TIDES

The daily rise and fall of the ocean along coastlines worldwide is vitally important to many species, especially those that live on rocky shores. In fact, the vast majority of tidepool species simply couldn't survive without this regular movement of water.

Tides are caused by the gravitational pull of the moon and the sun on the earth's oceans. These forces create antipodal bulges, or long-period waves on opposite sides of the planet: at the point closest to the moon, and at a point on the other side of the globe. As the earth rotates these bulges move across the oceans, creating tides twice a day. The highest tides occur when the moon is full, and the lowest tides happen around the time of the new moon. When the earth, the moon, and the sun are arranged in a straight line, thereby combining their pull, we experience so-called spring tides, which have the greatest range (higher highs, lower lows): beaches and rocky shores are fully covered during high tide and well exposed during low. Neap tides—tides of minimal change—occur when the sun and moon are at right angles to each other and negate each other's pull.

The particular character of tides on a given shoreline depends on the shape of that shoreline and the configuration of the offshore continental shelf. In Monterey Bay, tides range from about three to six feet. To find out the particulars, look for the small books of tide tables, available free or for a nominal cost at boating and fishing stores and recreational equipment companies around the bay.

Thanks to these fluctuations, nearshore rocky outcroppings and vibrant tidepools are regularly exposed for viewing. Be very careful if you venture out into wet areas, though: rocks, especially ones covered with seaweed, can be very slippery. And don't take any souvenirs; the coastal areas of the Monterey Bay National Marine Sanctuary are protected as well.

Some 1.8 million visitors seek out the aquarium annually, and thousands of school kids arrive for special programs. Where else can you walk beneath full-size gray whales and a family of orcas while gazing out across Monterey Bay? For information about visiting hours (and best times to visit), call 831-648-4888 or check out their website, http://www.mbayaq.org.

Monterey Bay Sports Museum

And now for something completely different: a sports museum. Immediately up David Avenue from the aquarium, on Lighthouse Avenue, is the Monterey Bay Sports Museum, the perfect retreat for the shoreline explorer who doubles as a sport aficionado. You enter by pushing your way through an antique turnstile from Pittsburgh's Forbes Field. Mosey your way through exhibits that focus on baseball, football, and boxing. Items worn by Babe Ruth, Rocky Marciano, and Muhammad Ali are on display. And check out that old football equipment: can you believe they once played with thin pieces of leather strapped to their heads? Call ahead (831-655-2363) for hours; admission is free.

Hopkins Marine Station, situated on Point Cabrillo next to the Monterey Bay Aquarium, is the oldest marine facility on the Pacific coast. Founded in 1892—and originally located at today's Lovers Point—the station is operated by Stanford University's Department of Biological Sciences. There are no public facilities or programs at the station.

Chinese Fishermen Start an Industry

Between the Monterey Bay Aquarium and Hopkins Marine Station is a small, inconspicuous beach that was once home to a vibrant and colorful Chinese fishing village. From the mid–19th century until 1906 this village, according to an early government report, was one of the most thriving Chinese settlements on the West Coast.

These fishing pioneers collected abalone, oysters, and mussels from nearshore waters and hauled in rockfish, halibut, flounder, yellowtail, sardines, squid, and shark from farther out in the bay. The meat from these animals was dried, and most was sent to San Francisco. From San Francisco a portion of these goods headed to the Sierra foothills and the gold country; most, however, was destined for China, as were the impressive quantities of bay shrimp caught and dried in San Francisco Bay during the mid to late 1800s.

Today, absolutely nothing remains of the village. A fire of suspicious origin destroyed the settlement in 1906. Some of the Chinese moved to a new village at McAbee Beach, but they were eventually forced to leave as California's 1882 exclusion laws, enacted to put a stop to Chinese immigration and to deny Chinese residents the right to become citizens or own property, slowly but inevitably took their toll. Some Monterey Chinese returned to their ancestral land, others traded in their boats for livelihoods as merchants, yet others drifted away to less hostile areas of California and the western United States.

Hopkins Marine Life Refuge

About one and a half miles of shoreline straddling the Hopkins Marine Station, extending to a depth of 60 feet, was designated as the Hopkins Marine Life Refuge in 1931—the second oldest such refuge in the state. The taking of anything from this area—sand, rocks, plants, or animals—is prohibited. The refuge extends as far as Lovers Point.

Tidepools

Tidepools are bursting with life and decorated with an impressive array of colors: hermit crab blue, urchin purple, sea star orange, anemone green. Along the greater Monterey Bay, some 800 species of invertebrates (animals without backbones) are known to survive where the ocean meets the shore, though the actual number might be closer to 2,000 once all these animals have been discovered. This exuberance of life is well represented by species of clams, barnacles, mussels, abalone, limpets, chitons, sea stars, hermit crabs, worms, snails, and anemones. You can also find an abundance of fish, algae, and sea grasses.

Although species in this habitat are subjected to radical fluctuations on a daily basis—inundation then desiccation, cold water then warm air—they are well adapted to this regime, and each species has developed its own strategy for preventing water loss. Barnacles, for example, simply close their shells at low tide. Limpets create depressions in rocks into which their shells fit exactly, thereby minimizing water loss at low tide. Snails close the opening to their shells at low tide with a device called an operculum to avoid desiccation.

Just like beaches, tidepools can be divided into distinct zones, or habitats. The highest zone is the splash or spray zone. It receives the least amount of water and is home to certain algae and species such as periwinkles.

TIDEPOOL TIPS

As far back as 1939, Edward Ricketts cautioned the tidepool collector to "carefully replace all rocks right side up in their depressions; otherwise many of the delicate bottom animals are exposed to fatal drying, sunlight, and wave action." Of course, we aren't collecting anymore, but Ricketts's advice holds true today for people simply wanting to poke around and see the beautiful animals and plants of the tidepool.

In addition to replacing everything where it belongs (if you don't, the spirit of Ricketts will gently tap you on your shoulder), the following tips should be followed:

1. Be prepared to get wet, and never turn your back on the ocean.

2. Be careful where you walk. Don't step on those tough-looking, rock-hugging species: you will kill them. They can withstand smashing waves, but not human trampling.

3. At low tide, carefully work your way as close to the waterline as possible. You'll see more that way.

4. Tips 2 and 3 do not cancel each other out: It is possible to walk around a tidepool without stepping on beds of barnacles, anemones, and other tidepool life.

5. Don't poke or touch animals or plants. Let your eyes, ears, and nose do all the work. And don't remove a thing. Remove it, and you kill it.

The hermit crab, a common tide-pool discovery

The upper intertidal zone is inundated only during high tides. More species reside here, including crabs and other snails. The middle intertidal zone, which is bathed twice daily by the tides, is characterized by thick beds of mussels and cloning anemones. And the low intertidal zone is unmasked only during low tides. This is where the greatest diversity can be discovered, from abalones to *Zostera marina* (eelgrass, a true flowering plant rather than an alga).

The richness of life in tidepools is due partly to the moderate climate that predominates throughout the marine sanctuary, with little annual variation of air and sea temperatures. There is also plenty of food and shelter in tidepools. Below you'll find a small sampling of tidepool residents. (California mussels—perhaps the most abundant tidepool species; purple and striped shore crabs; owl limpets; sunflower stars; giant green anemones; and kelp species are described elsewhere in this book.)

■ Spray zone: Eroded periwinkle *(Littorina keenae)*

Although this rather nondescript snail blends in well with its rocky surroundings, when you look close it seems to be everywhere. In fact, this periwinkle, along with others of the genus *Littorina* (meaning "shore-dwellers" in Latin), is the most numerous animal of the spray zone. It eats microscopic and drift algae with its sharp radula (filelike tongue). When the tide goes out and it needs to conserve moisture, the periwinkle simply shuts its door, called an operculum.

■ Upper intertidal: Fingered limpet *(Lottia digitalis)*

This common neighbor of the snail-like periwinkle is shaped like a miniature volcano (not to be confused with its cousin, the volcano limpet). Although often dingy in color because of algae growing on them, their shells can be very beautiful when free of algae. Fingered limpets might look sedate, but when the tide moves in they move about, grazing the rocks for algae. As the tide retreats, they gather back together and hunker down until the next influx of water. Groups of limpets are often seen among barnacles and periwinkles.

■ Upper intertidal: Hermit crab *(Pagurus spp.)*

Edward Ricketts described hermit crabs as the "clowns of the tidepools," and rightly so: although these crabs act tough, it's really all a show. Their claws are rarely used for fighting, and they eat mainly seaweed and dead animals.

Hermit crabs wear borrowed shells on their oddly shaped soft body. When they outgrow their shell, they simply find a larger one. Hermit crabs are a great joy to watch in tidepools, but you must be quiet and still, otherwise they'll retreat into their shell until the coast is clear. If you can sneak up close and look carefully, you might be able to see their beautifully colored red antennae, and the blue highlights on their legs.

■ Middle intertidal: Cloning anemone (*Anthopleura elegantissima*)

What looks like a bizarre underwater flower is really an animal. The skinny "petals" are tentacles that sting small animals so the anemone can swallow them. However, anemones' tentacles aren't enough to keep away predators such as nudibranchs, snails, and sea stars. When the tides retreat, the anemone closes up until the water returns. Look closely at their trunks: they're covered with shells and small rocks. This gathered material helps the anemone stay moist when exposed at low tide.

Cloning anemones, seen here underwater at high tide

Cloning anemones are a gray green color with tentacles frosted by pink, lavender, or blue. The large mats of anemones are actually clones from one individual, which reproduces by dividing itself (before this was discovered it was called the aggregating anemone). Neighboring populations of cloning anemones won't mix. In fact, they fight to defend their territory.

■ Middle intertidal: Ochre star *(Pisaster ochraceus)*

Ochre sea stars exposed at low tide

Another popular name for this sea star is the purple sea star (it also comes in ochre). Hundreds of tiny tube feet help this sea star keep stable in the middle intertidal zone, where the water is almost constantly in motion. And stable it is; in fact, it's downright pokey—it's the sloth of the tidepools. Ignorant it's not, though: Every now and again this slow-moving animal (about the size of a large human hand) finds a mussel that

has opened up for air, forcefully pries its shell apart, and inserts its stomach. The sea star then proceeds to digest the hapless mussel in its own living quarters. Although these tough-skinned tidepool denizens don't look very appetizing to us humans, sea otters and seagulls are known to eat sea stars.

■ Middle intertidal: Leaf barnacle *(Pollicipes polymerus)*

Leaf barnacles are extremely common in the middle intertidal zone, where they can be seen growing in large masses cemented to the rocks. You typically see them all closed up, after they've been exposed by the retreating tide. Their bodies are covered with hard white scales of varying size. When the water moves back in they open slightly and send up a feathery-looking foot, which they use to capture plankton and tiny crustaceans.

■ Low intertidal: Red octopus *(Octopus rubescens)*

Red octopus

If you look very carefully, you may be lucky enough to see a juvenile red octopus in the low intertidal zone. Extremely quick in the water and able to change shape and size almost instantly, the red octopus has many tricks up its many sleeves. Although its body is very soft and pliable (they often hide in small crevices), it has a hard mouth that looks like a parrot's beak. It uses that tough mouth to eat fish and other prey, which it snags with its tentacles. Adult octopuses dine on crabs, lobsters, and a variety of mollusks. In turn, the octopus is hunted by bass, rockfish, and other predators. Its defenses include speed, camouflage, and the old ink trick. If it's feeling bothered, it squirts a cloud of ink; it can then either hide, change colors, or dart away.

■ Low intertidal: Tidepool sculpin *(Oligocottus maculosus)*

Many fish frequent tidepools, especially at high tide. One of the most common is the tidepool sculpin. When the tide comes in, the sculpin moves about looking for food. When the waters retreat, it scurries back to its home base. Researchers have discovered that the sculpin has a very good sense of direction. Be patient: although these little fish are common, their ability to change color and their tendency to flit from protected spot to protected spot can make them difficult to see.

■ Low intertidal: Purple sea urchin
(*Strongylocentrotus purpuratus*)

Urchins are among of the more bizarre-looking tidepool inhabitants. They're all spines—or so it seems. Those spines, aided by tidal action, are believed to be the principal tool allowing the urchin to burrow into rocks. Sometimes they grow faster than they excavate, and they get stuck in their own rocky burrows.

Under its mantle of spines the urchin has tube feet, which it uses to move around on the rocks, hold on, and capture pieces of kelp to eat. Urchins are a favorite food item for many different marine animals. And there is a growing market among humans. Although once eaten by California Indians, urchins were considered a pest until recently (divers thought they were destroying kelp beds and they routinely smashed them). Starting in the early 1970s, however, a foreign market was found for the roe, or eggs, from red urchins (which live in slightly deeper water than the purple), and divers are now taking purple urchins as well.

CHARLES SEABORN / MONTEREY BAY AQUARIUM

Purple sea urchins and a giant sea star

Edward Ricketts

Edward F. Ricketts was introduced to the public as John Steinbeck's "Doc" in his 1945 classic, *Cannery Row.* Apparently, Steinbeck's portrayal was pretty darn accurate—though the real person was far more important than the engaging fictional character might lead you to believe.

If you ask any seasoned marine biologist what drew him or her to the field, the answer you get will probably include some mention of the classic book *Between Pacific Tides.* This book, first published in 1939 and now in its fifth edition, is authored by Ricketts and Jack Calvin, but all—including Calvin—acknowledge that the work and thoughts are almost all Ricketts's. Enthusiastic, insightful, and at times very funny, this shoreline bible was the culmination of Ricketts's years of scouring the shore for

Edward ("Doc") Ricketts, here busy at work in his lab, inspired generations of marine biologists.

specimens that he sold through his business, the Pacific Biological Laboratories (the building still stands a few doors down from the Monterey Bay Aquarium).

Ricketts, with his keen eye and sharp intellect, was one of the first true field biologists, in that he thought about species and their environments together. As a result, the book is arranged by habitat, not by species—a novel concept at the time. In it Ricketts presents, in a highly readable text, tips on what to do—and what not to do—while exploring the shoreline.

There is a bust of Ed Ricketts at the corner of Wave and Drake, right on the Coastal Trail. Take a look at the monument, but to do this interesting individual an even greater honor, get out and explore the tidepools he worked in with such zeal, or simply sit and enjoy the rocky shores of the peninsula he loved so dearly.

In 1998 the Monterey City Council approved the designation of the Ed Ricketts Underwater Park, stretching from the Coast Guard Pier to the Pacific Grove city limits just beyond the Monterey Bay Aquarium.

Pacific Grove

As you leave the Monterey Bay Aquarium and move toward Point Pinos on the Coastal Trail, you enter the city limits of Pacific Grove. It's a subtle transition but an important one, for from here until downtown Carmel you won't find any more large commercial strips: it's just you, the Pacific, an impressive number of golf courses and luxury homes once you hit Pebble Beach, and some pretty incredible wildlife. Sound like a lengthy oxymoron? It isn't.

The town of Pacific Grove began as a religious retreat in the 1870s and slowly grew into Monterey's beautiful little-sister city. Early pictures of the seaside resort show thick stands of Monterey pines growing right down to the water's edge, with a few small cabins peeking through. Today, unfortunately, most of the trees are gone, long ago replaced by streets of quaint bungalows and a charming downtown (on Lighthouse Avenue, just up from the shoreline).

Pacific Grove is still slow and quiet compared to Monterey. You can feel a special quality to the air and neighborhoods here, which might start you thinking about otherworldly matters. No wonder people have been gathering here to worship and contemplate life for over 130 years.

Pacific Grove's spectacular shoreline, just beyond Cannery Row

If you really want to blend in while visiting this city, never use Pacific Grove's full name. Just call this quiet home of the monarch "P.G." Like, "Oh yes, we've been coming to P.G. for years. And you?" Got it?

Pacific Grove's Shoreline Park

From the northwestern edge of Hopkins Marine Station all the way to Asilomar Beach the shoreline is open for exploration. A good portion of this section of coast—from Hopkins to Point Pinos—is Pacific Grove's Shoreline Park, which winds along Ocean View Boulevard for some two miles. An eclectic and beautiful mix of houses, including some grand old Victorians refurbished as bed-and-breakfasts, front the boulevard. The Coast Trail threads through the park, first as a paved trail to Lovers Point, then on the roadway. From Lovers Point all the way around Point Pinos and beyond, walkers and runners will find a blufftop footpath. Throughout, beaches large and small can be discovered, though you'll have to venture close to the bluff's edge to spot some of them.

Shoreline Park is actually a series of parks. As you move along Ocean View you'll discover large pullouts along the way, where you can park and explore bit by bit. It is safe to say that for the entire length of the park—and the stretch extending around Point Pinos—the views are without equal.

Immediately past the marine station, between 6th and

Pacific Grove's shoreline is graced with numerous parks.

7th Streets, you'll come across Andy Jacobsen Park. Next comes the one-acre Berwick Park, between 9th Street and Carmel Avenue. This nicely land-scaped piece of greenery has a beautiful lawn, just made for having a rest or enjoying the view. Greenwood Park, between 12th and 13th Streets, is one of the city's oldest parks, dedicated in 1875. The small creek running through this gorgeous spot was once a principal source of water for local residents.

Lovers Point Park and Beach comes next, at the foot of 17th Street, and the smaller Chase Park is here too, attached to the inland side of Lovers Point. This park has something for everyone. In addition to stunning vistas from the tip of a granite head-land, Lovers Point has an enormous lawn area, a pro-tected beach, picnic sites with grills, a small pier, bath-rooms, a children's swimming pool (open in summer), snack bar, a sand volleyball court, and for you art lovers, even a couple of sculptures. It's not uncommon to stroll past here and find a wedding in progress. It's the perfect spot for such an occasion. You can also rent open-deck kayaks here.

Hays Perkins Park extends Shoreline Park from Lovers Point to the foot of Coral Avenue. Its namesake, Hays Perkins, who designed the park and then maintained it, died in the 1960s, but his legacy lives on in this exquisite strip of greenery against the blue of the Pacific. In late spring, look for the abundant pink-flowering iceplant; although a nonnative, it is spectacular when in bloom. Just past Beach Street you'll see Esplanade Park immedi-ately inland. Cross the street and walk around under the truly enormous Monterey cypress trees—this is what most of the immediate coast once looked like. Continu-ing along the shore you'll come across the first of several dirt turnouts equipped with barbecue stands, and before too long the Pacific Grove Municipal Golf Course begins to dominate your inland view.

Throughout Hays Perkins Park you'll find benches along the footpath. Look before you sit: All of the benches have been dedicated to the memory of a loved one. Once comfortably perched, take in the vista of the bay. Directly in front of you large Pacific waves crash on the rocks with foamy explosions. Composed sea otters bob up and down, watching the surfers from a safe distance, seem-ingly unimpressed with the antics of the neoprene-suited

SANCTUARY NOTE
STORM DRAIN STENCILS

You've probably seen storm drains along the coast and in other areas throughout the state that are "tagged" with a message. The wording may vary, and you may see languages other than English, but basically the message states: "No Dumping, Drains to Bay"—or ocean, creek, or river.

Storm drain pollution is a major source of marine contamination.

Unlike sewer systems, which are linked to wastewater facilities, the vast majority of storm drains bypass treatment plants and drain right into the nearest body of water—water that in turn usually finds its way to the ocean. This means nasty stuff like used car oil and radiator fluid doesn't magically disappear when it is dumped in the street or down a storm drain. Instead it pollutes, and in a big way. For free information on what you can do to avoid storm drain pollution, including how to dispose of waste products like used oil, household detergents, and pesticides, contact your local water district or wastewater treatment plant. When it comes to healthy water, we can't be too careful.

---

humans. Cormorants and pelicans fly by in sleek formations. Across the bay, the coastal mountains rise like dark green curtains, shielding Monterey from the hectic life of nearby San Jose. The panorama is almost unreal.

Pacific Grove Museum of Natural History

Back by Lovers Point Park, maneuver your way a few blocks inland on 17th Street until you reach Central Avenue (continue one more block to get to downtown P.G.). Turn left on Central and you will find tiny Jewell Park and the Pacific Grove Museum of Natural History. Just look for the life-size gray whale sculpture in front: you can't miss it!

This low-key museum, great for adults and kids alike, is well worth a nice long visit. For one thing, it's a fine example of a traditional natural history museum, in the sense that most of the exhibits on animals consist of mounted specimens (kept in excellent condition) and there is little reliance on high-tech gizmos to attract your attention. Even the building is beautiful; look for the informational placard next to the front entrance.

The well-maintained permanent exhibits include information on local Indians, geology, botany, insects (there's a great monarch display), and local history, all with nice photographs. Regular temporary exhibits are mounted as well. Behind the building is an informal garden of plants native to Monterey County—many of them rare or endangered species—with some interpretive signs. A no-frills approach means that the garden can look great in spring and nearly dead by late summer and early fall, but that's only natural. Museum admission is free, but call ahead (831-648-3119) for hours and information regarding special exhibits.

Monarch Butterflies

The monarch butterfly (*Danaus plexippus*) is virtually synonymous with the city of Pacific Grove. Every fall thousands of these orange-and-black-winged beauties glide in to this city to overwinter along the mild Pacific coast. Over the years the city has established one butterfly sanctuary, and another public park—George Washington Park—also serves as an overwintering site. Additionally, the city has encouraged "butterfly hospitality zones" in the residential areas around the butterfly sites. During warm winter days, the monarch will actually wake up from its partial dormancy and fly around looking for nectar. Every night they return to their cluster high in the trees.

Clusters of monarch butterflies

After surviving the winter here, the butterflies head north with vigor. These little dynamos might seem to epitomize the notion of "fragile," but with warm weather spurring them on they've been known to fly at rates of up to 30 miles per hour on the northward journey. They soon stop to mate, lay eggs, then die. After metamorphosis (an incredible five-week process), new butterflies emerge and continue north during the summer months. Some venture as far as Canada, and several generations can be born in one season. Most monarchs live only about nine months, which means that the vast majority of monarchs returning to their ancestral groves have never been there before!

There are two principal populations of monarchs in the United States. The eastern population travels up to 3,000 miles to overwinter in central Mexico. The western population overwinters up and down the California coast. The most famous spot is Pacific Grove, but other well-known monarch sites around the bay include Santa Cruz's Natural Bridges State Park and smaller groupings at Lighthouse Field State Beach and Point Lobos Ecological Reserve (Whalers Knoll Trail) south of Carmel. In P.G., go to the Monarch Sanctuary off Lighthouse Avenue, between Grove Acre Avenue and Ridge Road; during the fall and winter monarch season, docents can answer questions and provide additional information.

An interesting natural history note about the monarch has to do with its diet. Because they've evolved to feed solely on milkweed—a poisonous plant—monarchs themselves become inedible to most birds. Meanwhile, the viceroy butterfly, which is very tasty to birds, employs what is called protective mimicry: by looking almost exactly like a monarch, the viceroy ensures that the majority of birds leave it alone as well.

By observing two simple guidelines, you'll enhance your—and the butterflies'—chances:

1. Don't touch or collect overwintering butterflies.

2. Get out your binoculars. Because the butterflies are hard to approach, binoculars can give you a close-up view with zero impact.

To find out more about P.G.'s monarchs, and about celebrations such as the annual Butterfly Parade, in which Pacific Grove schoolchildren dress up as monarchs, contact the Pacific Grove Chamber of Commerce at 831-373-3304.

Point Pinos Light Station

Sebastián Vizcaíno, who named this rocky tip of Monterey Peninsula in 1602, might have appreciated the helpful orientation of a lighthouse, but he was 250 years too early. When construction began on this lighthouse in the early 1850s by order of the federal government, this windswept section of the peninsula was still covered with dunes and quite remote. It was also often shrouded in fog and a real threat to ships entering the harbor. The granite used in the construction of the

Historic Point Pinos Lighthouse

light station was quarried on site, and by 1855 the large beacon was in operation. It has served its purpose well: today the Point Pinos Light Station is the oldest continuously operating lighthouse on the West Coast.

Although the lighthouse was automated in the 1970s, all of the equipment inside is original. In addition, several of the rooms have been preserved with period antiques so visitors can get a feel for what life was like for a lighthouse keeper in the 1850s. For information about the light station and its self-guided tour, call 831-648-3119.

The shoreline that wraps around the lighthouse and golf course—along Ocean View from Asilomar Avenue and to Lighthouse Avenue—is the Lighthouse Reservation. The footpath continues here, and all plants and animals are protected.

Black-crowned Night Heron

In this land of golf courses, gourmet restaurants, and resorts, the black-crowned night heron (*Nycticorax nycticorax*) is appropriately attired. About two feet tall, these short-necked, short-legged birds look like corpulent gentlemen in formal suits. Breeding night herons have prominent black heads and backs, with wispy white head plumes. Not surprisingly, these birds are most active at night, but small flocks can be spotted during the day as they roost in a favorite tree near a pond or other body of water. When disturbed, they emit a single loud "quok."

Black-crowned night herons come out at dusk to forage.

Killdeer

Killdeer

Killdeers (*Charadrius vociferus*) are a nervous lot, or so it seems. When not standing at attention on the lookout for trouble, they are scurrying this way and that, as if dodging phantom hailstones. Killdeers can be found along the shoreline throughout the National Marine Sanctuary—look for the distinctive double band on the upper breast—but they are also one of those shorebirds that has adapted to human environments very well. School play fields and golf courses are favorite hunting grounds, since they eat a lot of grubs and worms.

As its species name—*vociferus*—implies, this bird is quite the talker. If even slightly disturbed, it runs away or takes to the air with a loud and scolding "kill-dee" or "dee dee dee." This bird is also a fantastic actor: to protect her camouflaged but vulnerable nest on the ground, a female killdeer will feign a broken wing or leg and flutter, squawking, away from the nest, thereby luring intruders away.

MONTEREY BAY AQUARIUM

Asilomar State Beach

Asilomar State Beach and conference grounds have a rich history. People have been coming here since the late 19th century for retreats. Today's park and conference facilities (some buildings of which were designed by famed architect Julia Morgan) became state property in 1956, and since then have been named a National Historic Landmark.

Asilomar covers some 100 acres of wooded uplands, dunes, and rocky shore. Many unique native plant and animal species, such as the Menzies's wallflower, live along the coast here. A footpath runs the entire length of the state beach, and there are numerous pullouts for cars and scores of tiny pocket beaches. Bikers can enjoy the roadway bike path, which serves as the Coastal Trail.

Take notice of the Pacific's mood swing here, compared to the waters off Hays Perkins Park. This section of coast is exposed and receives the full brunt of Pacific storms; as a result, the waters tend to be wilder and more unsettled. The offshore terrain is a diver's paradise, but swimming is strongly discouraged owing to unsafe conditions.

Asilomar State Beach

The dunes at Asilomar—on the land side of the Coastal Trail—are the product of years of restoration. Public boardwalks here guide you through now rare coastal strand habitat that once covered much of the area. These dunes were once so badly eroded that only bedrock remained in most areas. Today, some 55 acres of healthy dunes greet springtime visitors with brilliant and pungent shows of flowers—testimony to the fact that we humans are beginning to learn the healing art of restoration almost as efficiently as we have learned to destroy.

Menzies's Wallflower

One of the truly unique species of this shoreline—which, perhaps not surprisingly, is also endangered—is the Menzies's wallflower. Of its several subspecies, one, *Erysimum*

STRIPED SHORE CRAB

The striped, or lined shore crab *(Pachygrapsus crassipes)* is a common resident of rocky shores and tidepools throughout the National Marine Sanctuary. In fact, it can spend long periods of time on dry land, though it must return to water to wet its gills and feed. This alert shoreline denizen is up to two inches wide and has a dark red to greenish carapace (main body shell) covered with transverse stripes. Its eyes are set very widely apart—which gives it great eyesight. When it sees a human lumbering toward it, the striped shore crab scurries immediately into a protected crevice.

Striped shore crabs eat mainly algae, but they are also known to devour dead animals of all sizes, and even a few live ones such as limpets and unlucky hermit crabs. There is no doubting that they help to keep the rocky shoreline nice and clean. Edward Ricketts described them as pugnacious. They

Striped shore crab

might be pugnacious with one another, but these bite-sized crabs are no match for the quick paws of raccoons and foxes, or the powerful bills of gulls and other large shorebirds.

menziesii ssp. *yadonni,* is found only in the dunes near the town of Marina. It was named after Vern Yadon, long-time director of the Pacific Grove Museum of Natural History. Here, south of Point Pinos, another subspecies, *E. menziesii* ssp. *menziesii,* grows in the dunes around Asilomar (it is also found up by Fort Bragg in Mendocino County). This interesting distribution—called disjunct by experts—is puzzling to casual observers and the endless source of conjecture on the part of botanists and ecologists.

The local subspecies of Menzies's wallflower blooms in late winter (or early spring, depending on how you look at it). It produces a cluster of deep yellow flowers less than a foot off the sand, above a rosette of spoon-shaped fleshy leaves. This subspecies and the one in Marina are both cultivated by State Park employees for local revegetation programs. They are considered endangered because much of their habitat was, until recently, severely degraded owing to erosion, human trampling, and competition by nonnative species.

NICOLE NEDEFF

The endangered Menzies's wallflower

The Bay Trail

Just as you are pulling away from the coast, having passed the sands of Asilomar Beach on your right, watch for a small trailhead tucked between some short willows and coyote bushes. This is the Bay Trail (foot traffic only), maintained by the Pebble Beach Company. The beautifully built and maintained wooden walkway skirts the Spanish Bay golf course (keep an eye open for errant golfballs) and works through the dunes behind Asilomar Beach. Paralleling the beach, the trail continues to the Spanish Bay picnic area in Pebble Beach.

The dunes here, pleasing to the eye, are a joy to walk through. You'll be surrounded by native vegetation dominated by sagewort, lupines, and poppies. As at other places along this coast, however, looks can be deceiving. These dunes look nice and pristine only because they've been painstakingly restored. Before this site was developed as a resort and golf course, it was a sand mining operation for decades. As part of the development agreement, the dunes had to be restored. Although the work is not yet complete, the results so far are spectacular.

If you continue up Sunset Drive, another section of the Bay Trail can be found. Across from where Asilomar Avenue dead-ends into Sunset, look closely for a small "Bay Trail" sign next to the restaurant. From this informal trailhead you can follow a sandy path up through some pines, oaks, yellow lupines, and landscaped terrain sandwiched between a commercial strip and the Spanish Bay golf course. It moves along for just under one mile before spilling out near the Pacific Grove Gate on Seventeen Mile Drive.

Jacks Peak County Park

Even though you are only half done exploring the peninsula's shoreline, how about a side trip inland? At Jacks Peak County Park, a 525-acre preserve atop a ridge, you can get away from the coastal crowds, take in some outstanding views, and walk in the region's most pristine Monterey pine forest. The park was named after the Scottish-born David Jacks, a colorful, even infamous Monterey civic figure of the mid-19th century. (Monterey jack cheese may be named after him too, but that's a long—and controversial—story.)

It will take you about half an hour to drive to the park from the far side of the peninsula, but it's worth it (see p. 233 for directions). Motoring up Jacks Peak Drive—a favorite of local bicycle riders—you meander through deep roadcuts and dense stands of Monterey pine. At the entrance gate (there is a modest fee) you can turn either left or right. Left will take you to the East Picnic Area and a trailhead; the Earl Moser, Madrone, and Sage Trails make a nice loop of about two miles, with the accumulation of pine needles and oak leaves making for soft and quiet hiking. If you turn right at the entrance, you will end up at the Jacks Peak Parking Area. This is the option to choose if you don't have a lot of time. Not only does the picnic area have spectacular views down to the Monterey

SEA FOAM

"Hey Mom, what are these suds from?" asks the child. "Oh, that?" replies the mother. "That's whale foam. You know, it comes out of their blowhole when they breathe, then it piles up on the beach." Child: "Yuk!"

Ever heard that conversation, or a version of it? Well, those suds being pushed up and down the beach are every bit as natural as "whale foam" would be, and have an explanation that might sound just as fanciful—but it's the real one. They're called sea foam, and they're created by the churning action of the waves. It is mostly air and water, but its slightly dirty look hints at the fact that this ocean whipped cream is also packed with small pieces of organic matter. Researchers now believe that sea foam provides a form of natural fertilizer and food for plants and animals of the nearshore, beach, and foredune habitats.

Peninsula, but the self-guided nature walk is fun and informative (look for the brochure guides to borrow near the message board). Make sure to find the Jacks Peak Trail and walk up to the peak (1,068 feet), the highest point of land on the Monterey Peninsula. Actually, it's two adjacent peaks—what a deal—and the walk is only about a quarter of a mile and not very steep at all, since you've driven almost to the summit. The Skyline Trail will let you look down on Carmel Bay and the gnarly coast of Point Lobos. Both here and at the East Picnic Area it feels and smells like you've been transported to the Sierra foothills. On all trails, keep an eye open for poison oak: it grows prolifically here.

Monterey Pine

One of the principal reasons for seeking out Jacks Peak County Park is to have a look at Monterey pines (*Pinus radiata*) the way they grow naturally. Too often these trees, popular in landscaping because they're fast growing and hardy, are sculpted into so much green topiary by well-meaning homeowners or simply clipped to resemble a classic A-shaped Christmas tree. Here you can see that

Monterey pines, en route to Jacks Peak

mature Monterey pines are tall (they grow up to 90 feet), mostly trunk, and almost regal looking with their wide-spreading crown of branches and needles. Still, this park isn't pure pine. You'll also see coast live oaks and some other species associated with chaparral. In the trees you might see lace lichen growing, and maybe even some mistletoe.

Naturally occurring Monterey pines are found in only a handful of locations along California's central coast—including Waddell Valley by Año Nuevo State Reserve—with a disjunct population on two islands off the coast of Mexico. On the Monterey Peninsula these pines once spread across thousands of acres. Today the largest segment of pine forest hereabouts is believed to be around 100 acres.

Not only has this species suffered from years of cutting and human encroachment, but it now faces a serious natural threat: pitch canker. Pitch canker is a fungus that is spread by bark beetles of several varieties and quickly kills trees. Symptoms include browning of the needles and copious amounts of resin flowing from the afflicted portions of the trunk or branches.

Like many California plants and trees, the

Monterey pine depends on fire for healthy growth and regeneration. Its cones, for example, open only on extremely hot days or when heated by ground fires. It may be that well-managed control burns will become necessary to maintain the Monterey pine in Monterey.

Monterey pines are among the world's most popular commercial species, particularly in the Southern Hemisphere. Although some experts are concerned about genetic purity, Monterey's pine forests may be saved by importing individuals from such distant lands as New Zealand.

Pygmy Nuthatch

As you marvel at the towering pines surrounding Jacks Peak, you will likely see or at least hear a pygmy nuthatch (Sitta pygmaea). These tiny birds—about the size of a large champagne cork—are typically found high in the canopy poking around for insects, but they can also be spotted hanging upside down from branches and creeping up trunks probing the bark. They have a grayish back, brownish cap, and white chin. If you can't spot one, then stop and listen. Its call has been described as sounding like Morse code: hear that "pipping" overhead? There's your pygmy nuthatch.

Monterey Formation

To get a good look at the Monterey Formation—the light gray to whitish mudstone on top of which much of the central coast resides—stop at one of the roadcuts en route to Jacks Peak. Basically, it looks like a very well defined stratum of chalk. Formed 12 to 13 million years ago on the floor of the ocean, composed of several thousand feet of quartz, clay, and diatoms (single-celled marine organisms that leave behind silica skeletons), it was later compressed and folded. Fossils can often be found between the many strata of the Monterey Formation. Because it works easily and is pretty, it is often used for building and landscaping.

The Monterey Formation near Jacks Peak Park

NICOLE NEDEFF

Monterey-Salinas Transit:
831-899-2555

Monterey State Historic Park:
831-649-7118

Presidio of Monterey:
831-242-5184

Maritime Museum of
Monterey: 831-375-2553

Monterey Peninsula Museum
of Art: 831-372-7591

Monterey Peninsula Visitors
and Convention Bureau:
831-649-1770

Cannery Row Foundation:
831-372-8512

Hotel Del Monte, Naval
Postgraduate School:
831-656-2023

Monterey Bay National
Marine Sanctuary:
831-647-4201
Website: http://
www.mbnms.nos.noaa.

Monterey Bay Aquarium:
831-648-4888
Website: http://
www.mbayaq.org

Monterey Bay Sports
Museum: 831-655-2363

Pacific Grove Museum of
Natural History and Point
Pinos Light Station:
831-648-3119

Pacific Grove Chamber of
Commerce: 831-373-3304

Asilomar State Beach and
Conference Grounds

Rangers Office:
831-372-4076

Conference and Lodging
Information: 831-372-8016

Jacks Peak County Park:
831-755-4895

Consider for a minute the fact that marine fossils can
be found around Jacks Peak, 1,068 feet above sea level.
Couple this with the fact that the shoreline ringing the
bay was once miles offshore, and you begin to realize that
landscapes, over time, are incredibly dynamic.

Monterey Bay Coastal Trail

Shortly after the Pacific Grove Gate the Monterey Bay
Coastal Trail, now on the shoulder of Seventeen Mile
Drive, behaves as it should and leads back down to the
shoreline. Bicyclists are permitted to enter Pebble Beach
for free; simply sign the registration book, and pick up
a free tour brochure if you'd like. Be
aware that bike access is limited to the
Pacific Grove Gate on weekends and
holidays, though once you have your
Pacific Grove gate pass you can ride
all the way to Carmel and then reenter
via the Carmel Gate. (And remember:
pedestrians can walk in via the Bay
Trail for no charge.)

Once you've reconnected with the
shoreline at Point Joe, the trail hugs
the coast for another mile or so before
coming to the intersection of Seventeen Mile Drive and Spyglass Hill
Road. Although you can ride around

One day the Monterey Bay
Coastal Trail will line the
entire shore.

NICOLE NEDEFF

To find Del Monte Beach, exit Highway 1 at the Del Monte Avenue–Pacific Grove exit. At the first stoplight (Casa Verde Way), turn right, cross over the Monterey Bay Coastal Trail (watch for people running, biking, and rollerblading), go uphill, and continue through the residential area toward the bay. Del Monte Beach is at the end. You can't miss it.

For the remainder of the peninsula to Asilomar Beach, you only need to know five streets, all of which blend into one another to lead you around the shoreline: Del Monte Avenue, Lighthouse Avenue (and tunnel), Cannery Row, Ocean View Boulevard, Sunset Drive.

From Del Monte Beach, return to Del Monte Avenue and go toward the peninsula. Monterey State Beach, the Municipal Beach, the wharves, and ample parking will all be on your right; the Historic Park is easily reached from this area. The city of Monterey has large, legible signs along the

way stating your options. To reach most of downtown Monterey, stay to the left just before the road veers into the Lighthouse tunnel. To get to Cannery Row and the aquarium, go through the tunnel. When you see the light of day you'll be on the edge of Fisherman's Shoreline Park and very close to Cannery Row. You'll soon be given the option of staying on Lighthouse (a commercial stretch) or veering to the right, onto Foam Street; from either of these streets you can turn right to reach Cannery Row. The Presidio is on the hill to your left. There are several large parking complexes on Foam Street.

The Monterey Bay Aquarium is at the intersection of Cannery Row and David Avenue. Ocean View Boulevard begins at David; it's the Pacific Grove extension of Wave Street, between Foam Street and Cannery Row. Ocean View will bring you all the way to Point Pinos. On the south side of the point the road becomes Sunset Drive and continues to Asilomar State Beach and Conference Ground.

Jacks Peak County Park might be a little far from the shore, but it is beautiful and affords a fantastic view of the entire coast. From the wharf area, go back (north) along Del Monte Boulevard, past the Naval Postgraduate School, and follow the signs to Highway 1 south. Once on the highway you'll soon see the turnoff for Highway 68 east (directing you to Salinas and the airport). Take that exit and continue for just under 2 miles; turn right at the second stoplight, at Olmsted Road, and continue on Olmsted for 1 mile. Jacks Peak Drive will be on your left. If you're leaving from the Asilomar area, stay on Sunset Drive up the hill, veer right at Forest Avenue, and keep going for several miles along the twisting Holman Highway (also signed as Highway 68, but the western leg). Eventually you'll reach Highway 1; go north on 1 (to access the highway drive over it, then curve sharply to the right) until you reach the Highway 68 exit moving inland. Proceed as described above.

Cypress and Pescadero Points, it's recommended that you continue up Spyglass Hill on the official portion of the trail. The route around Cypress and Pescadero Points and the last portion of Seventeen Mile Drive are extremely narrow, with very little shoulder. As you move up Spyglass Hill the road becomes Stevenson Drive. The Pebble Beach portion of the Monterey Bay Coastal Trail ends (for now) at the intersection of Stevenson and Seventeen Mile Drive, near the Peter Hay Golf Course.

In Carmel the trail picks up near the corner of Dolores Street and Lasuen Drive, next to the Carmel Mission. The trail skirts a sewage treatment plant, then moves across the Carmel River and into state beach lands. It continues around the headland of Carmel Meadows and lines out toward the parking area next to San Jose Creek State Beach.

Seventeen Mile Drive to San Jose State Beach

There is no dodging the fact that this stretch of coast—from Pebble Beach to the luxurious sands of Carmel—is some of the most exquisite (and seemingly most exclusive) shoreline in the United States. And yet for the cost of a movie you, too, can enjoy this windswept stretch of prime real estate as you tour Seventeen Mile Drive, or stop off at Carmel with its magical beach. Not only that, but a footpath runs from Asilomar Beach by Spanish Bay all the way to Spyglass Hill Road, or you can walk in via the Bay Trail—all for free.

Southward, Carmel River State Beach and San Jose Creek State Beach combine for several more beautiful miles of public shoreline. They also serve as the perfect introduction to what awaits if you continue on: the Big Sur coast.

So, here are your directives: don't mind the occasionally dense crowds of summer, and don't be intimidated by the aristocratic neighborhoods and expensive homes. You are here to enjoy the shoreline, and there is plenty of shoreline here to enjoy.

Spanish Bay

The dunes at Spanish Bay are spectacular. Though neither large nor expansive, they are beautifully vegetated with a full complement of native dunes species, most of which were raised in a native plant nursery maintained by the Pebble Beach Company. Spanish Bay has one of the largest parking lots on Seventeen Mile Drive, and it also has the biggest beach, called South Moss Beach. Benches fronting the beach let you park and picnic easily.

This stretch of beach is a good example of what is in store for you from here on south: brilliant white sand, derived from pure granite. Farther north, many of the beaches have a mixed recipe of riverborne sand and material from coastal erosion. Not so here.

Coastal Granite

Granite is what gives the peninsula its special character. The granite we see here was formed millions of years ago, and far to the south. Granite is a plutonic igneous rock—that is, a rock that formed deep within the earth's crust,

POOCH ON THE LEASH

Dogs must be on leashes when visiting the peninsula's shoreline. It is best for both your dog and the local wildlife. At North and South Moss Beaches dogs are allowed off leash only if they are under voice command. The closest leash-free beach is Carmel City Beach, just around the bend.

Beechey ground squirrels (*Spermophilus beecheyi*) are inordinately common in shoreline parks around Monterey Bay, especially in dirt parking lots. Why? Because, these burrowing rodents are masters of disturbed habitats—such as the blufftop park at Asilomar State Beach and the coast-side turnouts along Seventeen Mile Drive. Grasses, for example, tend to be kept unnaturally low in many public parklands, affording ground squirrels a clear view of potential trouble. Also, bits of food from human hands are simply too tempting—though really, we shouldn't be feeding them. And yes, these quasi-domesticated rodents do have a historic maritime connection: they were named for Frederick William Beechey, who explored large sections of the Pacific coast in the 1820s.

These mottled gray squirrels are colonial nesters, and they can often be heard chirping loudly before diving underground when perceived danger approaches. Although shoreline visitors find the curiosity and antics of this squirrel cute and entertaining, in rural parts of Santa

Ground squirrels are common around shoreline visitor sights.

Cruz and Monterey Counties this animal inflicts serious damage on agricultural lands by eating crops and undermining large portions of cultivated fields.

cooled very slowly, then was brought to the surface through a combination of uplift and erosion of upper rock layers. After surfacing, this dense, erosion-resistant rock was moved ever so slowly north along the San Andreas Fault to its present location. (It's still moving north, but at a fraction of an inch yearly.) The long cooling process formed the crystals that sparkle in the sunlight.

Granite may be dense and resistant to erosion, but it has met its match in the power of the ocean. Not only does pulverized granite make for exquisite white beaches, but the jointing in granite is responsible for the in-and-out appearance of much of the shore here and at Point Lobos. Underwater erosion in these joints has created spectacular caves prized by scuba divers for their wondrous marine life and beauty.

Point Joe

Point Joe is a fine example of a towering granitic outcropping—which explains its former name of Pyramid Point. It was apparently renamed in the late 1800s in honor of a longtime resident of these rocks, a Chinese fisherman and jack-of-all-trades who maintained a house within these rocks for years. Point Joe—and most of this shore—is an excellent spot for whale watching on clear winter days.

"Point Joe has teeth and has torn ships; it has fierce and solitary beauty; Walk there all day you shall see nothing that will not make part of a poem."

Robinson Jeffers,
"Point Joe" (1924)

BIRD ROCK AND SEAL ROCK

Almost two miles from the Pacific Grove Gate is Bird Rock, a major stopping point along Seventeen Mile Drive. It is also a major wildlife site. Bird Rock itself is home to a raucous population of California sea lions and cormorants. Three species of cormorant can be seen here: double-crested, pelagic, and Brandt's. Of the three, the pelagic and Brandt's are by far the most numerous, and the Brandt's nests here every spring. The Pebble Beach Company maintains free spotting scopes here, as well as informative interpretive signs.

Several hundred yards south is Seal Rock, a favorite haul-out spot for sea lions. There is a nice picnic area here.

The walking and running path from Spanish Bay continues to Bird Rock and beyond to Spyglass Hill Road. Although it is strongly recommended that you follow the road uphill from there, it is not against any rules to continue walking or running around to Cypress Point and beyond. The road does become very narrow, however, and you might find cars getting uncomfortably close.

European Starling

Viewed through a pair of binoculars in the proper light, the European starling (*Sturnus vulgaris*), with its shimmering plumage, prominent beak, and rapid movements, can be very beautiful. But if you take off those rose-colored magnifiers and look at the starling for what it truly is, another reality emerges. Ever since this species was introduced into New York in 1890, it has slowly spread across the United States. As it has reproduced and traveled, the starling has used up food resources normally destined for native species and stolen nesting cavities from such natives as red-headed woodpeckers, purple martins, and eastern bluebirds. Starlings are aggressive, loud, messy, and they can form gigantic flocks that demolish agricultural crops and even threaten power lines across the country.

Here, along the shoreline, you'll often see flocks of starlings walking among ground squirrels—two prime examples of very successful invaders.

Pebble Beach Company

As early as the 1880s, the Pebble Beach area was the private touring grounds for people staying at Charles Crocker's Hotel Del Monte (on today's Naval Postgraduate School). One of the main activities for hotel visitors was to ride on horseback, or in a horse-drawn carriage, from the hotel through the forests of Pacific Grove across the peninsula toward Carmel, then back to the hotel, a distance of 17 miles, more or less—hence the name Seventeen Mile Drive. The land was held by the Pacific Improvement Company, the holding company for the Southern Pacific Railroad. Over time, the land has maintained its status as a gated community. Today the corporation that owns and runs the properties is called the Pebble Beach Company. For information about any of their facilities or annual events, call their corporate headquarters (1-800-654-9300) and they'll be happy to fill you in.

Pebble Beach Hiking Trails

Not only does the Pebble Beach Company maintain Seventeen Mile Drive, with ample pullouts and scores of interpretive signs, but it also has several hiking loops that are open to the public. They are all well marked with

The westernmost tip of the Monterey Peninsula is occupied by two nice Seventeen Mile Drive pullouts. Fanshell Overlook is a small parking area above dazzling-white Fanshell Beach. And true to its name, this beach makes for some good shell collecting if you hit the tides correctly. This beach may be closed in spring during seal pupping season.

To find the Cypress Point turnout (no beach access) you have to pay attention: it comes up quickly, between two residences, on the narrow winding road. The entrance

Harbor seals hauled out on Fanshell Beach

opens up into a large parking area ringed with interpretive signs. During the harbor seal spring pupping season you can view the young pups through observation holes in a wall ringing the parking lot, though occasionally the site is closed for the seals' safety.

small signs—an icon of a hiker or simple directional arrows. The only thing the company asks is that hikers respect private property and don't bother residents. A guidebook to the trail system, published by Pebble Beach, is available at the Monterey Peninsula Visitors and Conference Bureau (380 Alvarado Street, downtown Monterey). Below are a few particularly worthwhile hikes:

■ Spanish Bay

This is actually a double loop trail, each one a little over a mile. The north loop starts at the dunes boardwalk at the far end of the large Spanish Bay parking lot, proceeds along Asilomar Beach to Sunset Drive, heads up to Seventeen Mile Drive, passes the Inn at Spanish Bay, and finally works its way back down to the beach. The other loop moves south along the shoreline, cuts inland a couple of hundred yards past Spanish Bay Road, then leads back to Seventeen Mile Drive and the Inn. Remember, follow those symbols—and be alert for off-course golfballs!

■ Bird Rock to Indian Village

Just south of the bathrooms at Bird Rock you'll see the first sign for this short but beautiful hike to Indian

Horse fanatics will find some 25 miles of equestrian trails in Pebble Beach, starting at the Equestrian Center, just off Portolá Road near Alva. The center also offers guided horse rides daily, several times a day. The tour takes just over an hour and goes from the center to the beach and back. For information, call the Equestrian Center at 831-624-2756.

Village, a site reportedly used by local Rumsien Indians before the arrival of Europeans. The trail begins by following the coast, but it soon crosses Seventeen Mile Drive and moves through the dunes.

■ S. F. B. Morse Botanical Reserve

This hike, just under two miles long, will take you up and down some hilly terrain through the beautiful S. F. B. Morse Botanical Reserve. The trailhead is on the inland (east) side of Congress Road, between Bird Rock Road and Chaparral Drive (closer to Bird Rock Road). This 86-acre reserve is named for Samuel Finley Brown Morse, former general manager of the Pacific Improvement Company (which became first the Del Monte Properties Company, then the Pebble Beach Company). He was also the great-grandnephew of the inventor of the telegraph—as in Morse code. This reserve is known for its unique association of Monterey pine, Bishop pine, Monterey cypress, and the rare Gowen cypress.

■ The Lodge

This five-mile loop begins by the putting green directly in front of the lobby of the Lodge at Pebble Beach (off Seventeen Mile Drive just past Pescadero Point). After meandering alongside the Peter Hay Golf Course, it continues as far as Indian Village.

Lone Cypress Point

No matter the time of day, there is always a crowd at Lone Cypress Point. The tree for which this site is named

Lone Cypress Point

is truly phenomenal. So phenomenal, in fact, that it is owned as a trademark by the Pebble Beach Company. You can take a picture of this world-famous cypress, but if you try to sell that image or use it in any shape or form, a lawyer will soon be knocking on your door.

When you do make your pilgrimage to Lone Cypress Point, work your way down the short set of stairs to get a better look. This little section of shoreline is spectacular, and even though the image of the cypress on the rock is overused, it really is amazing to see this tree growing straight up out of the granite boulders. Unfortunately, the old tree has seen better days; today support wires and other paraphernalia help keep the poor thing in place.

As you leave the celebrated cypress and continue south along Seventeen Mile Drive, you'll wrap around Pescadero Point. This is the northern edge of Carmel Bay.

Monterey Cypress and Gowen Cypress

The Monterey cypress (*Cupressus macrocarpa*) is the symbol of Pebble Beach, and for most people it also exemplifies the entire peninsula down to Point Lobos. The gnarly yet graceful countenance of this magnificent tree symbolizes perfectly the hardiness and beauty of the rugged Pacific shore. Although there seems to be a cypress in just about every snapshot ever taken of the Monterey area, this tree is actually very unusual. In fact, there are only two native stands of Monterey cypress in the world—at Pebble Beach (Cypress Point and the Crocker Grove area on Seventeen Mile Drive) and Point Lobos—each of which is genetically unique. All the other cypresses you see along the shoreline have been planted by private and public interests.

In addition to the well-known cypress of the shoreline, there is another, lesser-known species of the interior.

The world-famous 18th hole at Pebble Beach, with Big Sur stretching out in the background

The Gowen cypress (*Cupressus goveniana* ssp. *goveniana*), like the Monterey cypress, occurs in only two places in the world: Huckleberry Hill in Pebble Beach and along Gibson Creek just inland from Point Lobos. The Gowen cypress is one of two pygmy cypresses in the state, the other being up in Mendocino County (*Cupressus goveniana* ssp. *pygmaea*). They are pygmy, or stunted, because of a combination of extreme environmental conditions and nutrient-poor soils.

Cypresses as a group have been around a long time—at least 200 million years, judging from fossil evidence. Unfortunately, both the Monterey and Gowen species are considered rare and endangered by the California Native Plant Society owing to their restricted range. Nevertheless, they are survivors; we can only hope that they will continue to grace these lands here for generations to come.

The Lodge at Pebble Beach and Stillwater Cove

Even if you can't afford to stay at the Lodge at Pebble Beach, it's fun just to stop and look around. Not only is there a trailhead here, but variety of stores and shops are open to the public as well.

The original log cabin–style lodge was built in 1909 as a rest stop for guests of the Hotel Del Monte during their horseback rides along Seventeen Mile Drive. Fire destroyed the original structure, by now known as Del Monte Lodge, in 1917, but it was quickly rebuilt and added on to over the years. The name was changed to the Lodge at Pebble Beach in the 1970s.

The beach at Stillwater Cove is public, but parking at the Beach Club is not. However, you can park back up along Cypress Drive (or by the lodge) and walk down to the cove. Also, although diving is permitted in the cove, the club and harbor master restrict the number of divers to avoid overcrowding and environmental damage. If you'd like to find out more about the Beach and Tennis Club or about diving here, call 831-625-8507.

Carmel Beach City Park

Carmel's city beach is nothing less than spectacular. Snow-white sand is piled up into mountainous dunes at the foot of Ocean Avenue, tidepooling at low tide can be had both north and south, and the water is teeth-rattling cold. From bluff to bluff the beach is about one mile long. Dogs, permitted to run free here, always imbue the scene with a festive mood as they rip up and down the beach

---

PEDAL POWER ALONG THE SHORELINE

To get back to Highway 1 and the Pacific Coast Bike Route from Carmel City Beach, just head up Ocean Avenue. Proceeding steeply at first (you might want to walk your bike), the road soon levels off a bit; keep going to Junípero Avenue, 11 blocks up from the beach. Turn right (south) on Junípero and proceed seven long blocks; the road now merges into Rio Road, which will take you past the mission to Highway 1. There you can either turn left, then right onto Carmel Valley Road, or head south and ride for miles down the Big Sur coast. If you'd like a free biking map for Monterey County, contact the Monterey County Department of Transportation at 831-755-4812.

and sprint through the shallow waters. Offshore you'll notice healthy patches of kelp growing throughout Carmel Bay—and that means sea otters. Pull out those binoculars and scan the watery horizon for some furry heads poking up through the kelp.

While you are snoozing on the sand or strolling along the shore, keep your ears tuned to the voices around you. You'll be amazed at the variety of languages you hear. Carmel is truly a world-class tourist destination. If possible, arrive at the beach early. The parking lot at the foot of Ocean Avenue is always packed.

Ocean Avenue: From Beach to Boutiques

On busy summer afternoons, Ocean Avenue and downtown Carmel buzz with activity. In this approximately seven-block-square area you can purchase just about anything imaginable. You can eat fast food or linger over a gourmet meal, cruise the galleries and novelty shops, or just seek out a park and rest up. (Murphy Park—corner of Monte Verde and 6th—and Devendorf Park—about 11 blocks up from the beach, at the corner of Ocean and Junipero Avenue—are perfect places to find some shaded quiet if the crowds are too much. These parks also have public bathrooms.)

Ever since its incorporation in 1916, Carmel-by-the-Sea, as the city is officially called, has been known for its resident writers and artists. It is a community that has always prided itself on being a little different. There are, for example, no street numbers on any of the houses in town. No kidding!

To really see the town of Carmel, it is highly recommended that you abandon the hustle and bustle of the

SANCTUARY NOTE
EXCIROLANA— TOE NIBBLERS

Have you ever sat on a beach down by the waterline and felt your toes being nipped by a mysterious bug? It doesn't happen often, but it does happen—just a minor little nibble. If you try to spot the culprit, you probably won't find a thing. The villain is a carnivorous isopod—a tiny relative of shrimps and lobsters—that lives in the sand, known as excirolana. It normally eats dead sand crabs and other animals, so when it latches on to you it probably thinks it's struck the mother lode. These animals burrow in just below the surface of the sand at low tide, waiting for the waters to come in, at which point they surface and swim about rapidly looking for food. They are a favorite prey item for shorebirds.

Willets in flight

The willet (*Catoptrophorus semipalmatus*), one of the most common shorebirds throughout the marine sanctuary, is often seen at Carmel Beach working the moistened sand for food such as excirolana. At first sight it seems to be the very definition of dull looking, with its uniform gray-brown plumage, gray legs, and dark bill. When it takes flight, though, it flashes a striking black-and-white underwing pattern that is simply spectacular. The willet is also one of the most talkative shorebirds, and its distinctive call of "will-willet" or "pill-will-willet" is a familiar shoreline sound.

> *"I wish I could describe the coast there, the rocks jutting into the sea, teeming with life . . . Birds scream in the air—gulls, pelicans, birds large and birds small, in flocks like clouds. Seals and sea lions bask on the rocky islands close to the shore; their voices can be heard night and day. Buzzards strive for offal on the beach, crows and ravens 'caw' from the trees, while hawks, eagles, owls, vultures, etc., abound. These last are enormous birds . . . They are called condors by the Americans. A whale was stranded on the beach, and tracks of grizzlies were thick about it."*
>
> William H. Brewer,
> Up and Down
> California (1861)

downtown shopping areas and simply walk through the neighborhoods. The houses are all unique.

For a guide to downtown and information about the city's annual events and festivals, call the Carmel Business Association at 831-624-2522. Another great resource is the Monterey County Travel and Tourism Alliance, with offices at 137 Crossroads Boulevard (in the shopping center at the corner of Highway 1 and Rio Road); give them a call at 831-626-1424 to order free information.

Scenic Road and the Beach Bluff Pathway

Its name says it all: Scenic Road is beautiful. If the beach parking lot at the foot of Ocean Avenue is full, drive back up Ocean a short block and turn right on Scenic Road. The first two blocks of Scenic are hemmed in by houses, but then a vista of the bay appears. And oh, what a vista it is. You may find parking at the foot of 8th Avenue or a little farther south, or just turn left and park on one of the numbered streets.

There is a beautiful walkway here—the Beach Bluff Pathway—which extends about half a mile and is bordered by tasteful landscaping and the occasional bench. You can walk down to the beach at several spots along the way as well. This path is great both for gazing out over the beach and the bay and for admiring the oceanfront homes of Carmel. Even on the busiest day at the foot of Ocean Avenue, the Beach Bluff Pathway is pleasantly free of congestion.

Scenic Road is one-way between 8th and 13th Avenues. Remember, this is a neighborhood, so keep it slow and watch for beach-silly kids running around. Scenic continues by wrapping around the headland as a narrow two-lane road, and soon the beautiful sands of Carmel River State Beach line out to the south. At the corner of Scenic and Valley View Avenue there is a small access point to the northern thumb of the state beach. One more tight turn on Scenic and you'll come across the parking lot for the state beach.

Rock and Hawk

One of Carmel's most noted residents—in addition to author Mary Austin, photographers Edward Weston and Ansel Adams, and actor and director Clint Eastwood, to name but a few—was the poet Robinson Jeffers (1887–1962). He and his wife, Una, first saw Carmel in 1914, and both immediately knew they had to live here. For many years they worked on the now-famous stone Tor House on Ocean Avenue near Stewart Way. Hawk Tower followed. Today the property is managed by the Tor House Foundation and guided tours are offered twice a week. Call the foundation (831-624-1813) for information.

Carmel Bay Ecological Reserve

This reserve, which stretches from Pescadero Point in Pebble Beach to Granite Point in Point Lobos State Reserve, takes in some 1,650 salty acres—most of Carmel Bay. It was created by the state in the late 1970s and affords the bay protection over and above the protection accorded by the Monterey Bay National Marine Sanctuary. No taking of animals or plants is permitted within the reserve.

Carmel River State Beach

Carmel River State Beach provides a great introduction to the shoreline and wild offshore waters of the coast south of the Monterey Peninsula. The parking lot off Scenic is a convenient place to start your adventure. Look for the interpretive signs on the far side of the lot.

Start by going through the dunes into the lagoon area; from there you can skirt the lagoon and, in months when the river is plugged by a sandbar, continue all the way to Monastery Beach, either on the sand or on one of two parallel trails on the bluff. (See the Carmel Meadows entry, page 248, for access information for months when the river is flowing to the sea.)

Carmel River State Beach and lagoon

The Carmel River is a classic California coastal river—or at least it was before two dams were built on it, starting in the 1920s. By the 1960s, groundwater pumping and residential development in the floodplain were severely taxing the already low river. Now in most years it has so little flow in summer and fall that a sand berm builds up across its mouth and the river becomes a brackish, wildlife-filled lagoon, a situation that rarely—if ever—occurred before 1920. Winter storms usually breach the berm, but sometimes humans and machines have to do the job. Nevertheless, this body of water has many friends, and today efforts are being made to restore vast stretches of the river and the wildlife species that depend on it—including steelhead trout.

The area behind the beach, whether it contains a flowing river or a dry-season lagoon, is critical habitat for waterfowl, migratory and resident alike. Here, too, you will find one of the largest coastal marshlands along the central coast, extending over many acres. Even in its reduced and compromised condition, then, this river where it meets the sea is a fertile and exciting area.

A visit to the Carmel River at any time of year is filled with the sounds of wildlife, as the salty breeze blowing off the Pacific mixes with the smell of freshwater. No wonder the local coastal Indians—the Rumsien—lived along its shores. And no wonder that European expeditions, from Vizcaíno on, camped here to rest and stock up on game.

The large agricultural field between Highway 1 and the river is going to be restored to its natural vegetation cover, making hikes through this 106-acre park even more enjoyable.

> "The Carmel is a lovely little river. It isn't very long but in its course it has everything a river should have."
>
> John Steinbeck,
> Cannery Row (1945)

Red-winged Blackbird

The red-winged blackbird (*Agelaius phoeniceus*) is one of the most boisterous and flashy residents of the marsh here. The impressive spring display of the male, with his shimmering red epaulets and his rich call, "kong-ka-ree" and "o-ka-lee-onk," is a sure indication that freshwater is nearby. The lagoon's tule reeds and cattails provide perfect nesting habitat for these birds. During the spring nesting season, don't be surprised if a male dive-bombs you as you approach its territory. They may be small, but they don't lack courage.

Cliff Swallow

During the warm months of the year, one of the birds you will see flying low over the sands and lagoon at Carmel River State Beach is the cliff swallow (*Hirundo pyrrhonota*). These colonial nesters—the same species that descends on Mission San Juan Capistrano every year—build their gourd-shaped mud nests in the bluffs just south of the lagoon.

Mission San Carlos Borromeo del Río Carmelo

The Carmel Mission is perhaps the most completely restored, and most beautiful, of all California's missions. The compound here was built beginning in 1771 (after being moved from Monterey's Presidio, where it was called Mission San Carlos Borromeo de Monterey). The second mission complex to be erected in the state, it served as the headquarters for Father Junípero Serra as he expanded the reach of the missions south and north. Between 1769 and 1823, 21 missions were built in California from San Diego to Sonoma.

Father Serra died in 1784 and was buried here in the mission's church. Over the years several other famous mission priests were also interred with him.

The mission maintained its vitality into the early part of the 19th century, but after Mexican independence in 1821 and the secularization of church lands in the early 1830s the mission was abandoned. It soon fell into ruin, and by the 1860s the once famous mission church was a sad shell of its former self. Restoration efforts began in the 1880s and continued through the early part of this century. You can be the judge of their success: visit the mission grounds and the church and you'll feel like you've been transported back 200 years.

Across the street from the mission is Mission Trail Park, with some 35 acres of native plants and several miles of nicely maintained trails (use Rio Road for access). This park is also home to the Lester Rowntree Native Plant Garden. In the true tradition of Carmel's artistic community, the British-born Lester Rowntree did things her own way, roaming the wild corners of California in the early part of this century collecting native plants and seeds. Her writings on her adventures have become classics.

"We visited the old Mission of Carmelo, in the Carmelo Valley . . . It is now a complete ruin, entirely desolate, not a house is now inhabited. The principal buildings were built around a square, enclosing a court. We rode over a broken adobe wall into this court. Hundreds (literally) of squirrels scampered around to their holes in the old walls. We rode through an archway into and through several rooms, then rode into the church. The main entrance was quite fine, the stone doorway finely cut. The doors, of cedar, lay nearby on the ground. . . . Cattle had free access to all parts; the broken font, finely carved in stone, lay in a corner; broken columns were strewn around where the altar was; and a very large owl flew frightened from its nest over the high altar. . . . So have passed away former wealth and power even in this new country."

William H. Brewer, Up and Down California, (1861)

Mission San Carlos Borromeo del Rio Carmelo

Carmel Valley

Carmel Valley is a long and spectacular 40-mile slice through the coastal mountains. If you're up for it, you can hop on your bike at Carmel City Beach, pump up Ocean Avenue, turn right on Highway 1, then left on Carmel Valley Road and ride for hours (and hours), all the way to Greenfield on Highway 101. Or turn off on one of several side roads—Cachagua, Tassajara, or Arroyo Seco—and learn the true meaning of rough country. It may be rough, but it's also incredibly beautiful. Of course, you can also do this in a car.

The mouth of Carmel Valley inland from Highway 1 is home to a couple of large shopping complexes, and resorts and golf courses march their way up the valley. Carmel Valley Village, about 20 minutes from Highway 1 by car, is a good spot to eat or rest, hidden from the summertime crowds. But the crown jewel of this valley is Garland Regional Park—a spectacular nugget of what most of this valley once looked like.

Garland Ranch Regional Park

The 4,462-acre Garland Ranch Regional Park stretches up and over one side of Carmel Valley just below Carmel Valley Village, some nine miles from Highway 1. It is managed by the Monterey Peninsula Regional Park District, an agency that has been instrumental in cooperative land preservation throughout the area.

The visitor center at Garland Ranch, across the river from the parking lot, is a perfect place to begin your visit. From there you can explore the willow-covered riverbanks, or high-step it through enormous stands of cottonwoods and sycamores en route to higher elevations and steep trails shadowed by maples and oaks. In fact, you can ascend to approximately 2,000 feet in the Santa Lucia Range.

Local Rumsien Indians once lived in this area, and even a brief visit makes it easy to see how they prospered. The river would have provided quantities of fish, the forests are filled with wildlife, and seeds and acorns abound.

This is wild country, and it borders even wilder country: the Ventana Wilderness and Los Padres National Forest. Although dogs are allowed off leash in this park, they should be under voice command at all times—both so they don't harm wildlife and for their own protection: this park is home to mountain lions and wild pigs, and a runaway dog could get into some serious trouble. If you'd like to find out more about Garland Park before your visit, give their office a call at 831-659-4488.

Carmel Meadows

BIG SUR LAND TRUST

The Big Sur Land Trust is one of the organizations the Monterey Peninsula Regional Park District has teamed up with over the years. Launched in 1978 to help preserve the natural and cultural resources of the Big Sur Coast and the Monterey Peninsula, the Carmel-based trust has been involved in safeguarding over 15,000 acres in coastal Monterey County through some 70 transactions worth more than $50 million in appraised value.

Although no signs on Highway 1 indicate that there is beach access in this neighborhood, it's there, and it's open to everyone: this is the south side of Carmel River State Beach. But please, respect driveways and private property.

Turn off Highway 1 onto Ribera. As you approach the shore you'll see Calle La Cruz on your right, at the end of which is a public-access trailhead. If you continue on Ribera around to its end, just past Cuesta Way, there is a similar access site. Both will lead you down to the beach, where you can work your way back north to the Carmel River or south toward San Jose Creek State Beach. The second trailhead also gives access up onto the bluff; there you can walk through some nice grassland mixed with coastal sage scrub, then head down to a wide service road at the base of the bluff or onto the beach.

The beach immediately below Carmel Meadows is sometimes called Middle Beach, because it is situated midway between the wider stretches of the state beaches. Good tidepooling opportunities abound, and there are often nice smelly piles of kelp wrack to poke around in.

San Jose Creek State Beach

About a quarter of a mile south of the Ribera turnoff is San Jose Creek State Beach, known locally as Monastery Beach.

To access yet another trailhead for the bluffs, the beach, and the Monterey Coastal Trail (parking for about six cars), turn onto the rough frontage road by the small school in the eucalyptus grove. A hundred yards beyond this tricky turnoff Monastery Beach is right alongside the road. You can park immediately off the road here. There are bathrooms at the southern end of the beach with a telephone that sometimes works.

Carmelite Monastery

It is somehow fitting that a monastery devoted to prayer, nonmaterialism, and improvement of the human spirit stands watch over Monastery Beach and a good portion of Point Lobos and Carmel Bay. The Carmelite Monastery (which has a much longer official title) was started in 1925 in the town of Carmel. Several years later, the community moved to its present home in this donated building.

The Order of Our Lady of Mount Carmel, founded in the 12th century, required absolute poverty of its followers. In the 16th century Saint Teresá of Ávila instituted reforms to the order; she is considered the founder of today's Order of Discalced, or Barefooted, Carmelites. The monastery's doors are open most days from 7:30 in the morning until 4:30 in the afternoon; visitors are welcome to tour the chapel and the lovely grounds. To get there, simply turn inland off the highway into the monastery's driveway and go uphill about a quarter of a mile.

GETTING AROUND

The Pacific Grove Gate for Seventeen Mile Drive is located due south of the intersection of Sunset Drive and Seventeen Mile Drive. On the far side of Pebble Beach, Seventeen Mile Drive will drop you two blocks up from Carmel City Beach. This popular drive is very well marked.

Once in Carmel the main arteries are Ocean Avenue and Scenic Road. Ocean Avenue runs directly from the Carmel City Beach through downtown to Highway 1. Scenic Road hugs the shore all the way to Carmel River State Beach. To get back to Highway 1 from the state beach, continue on Carmelo Street to 15th Avenue. Turn right at 15th, then continue straight, veering slightly right onto Dolores Street, to the Carmel Mission (the road curves around the mission). Turn right onto Rio Road, which will take you out to Highway 1. To reach Carmel Valley, cross Highway 1, take the second left onto Carmel Rancho Boulevard, then turn right at Carmel Valley Road. (If you're on Highway 1 coming down the hill from Carmel, there's a left-hand turn onto Carmel Valley Road.) To reach points south, turn right off of Rio Road onto Highway 1. Ribera Road with its coastal access points is about 1 mile down the road, and Monastery Beach is just beyond.

The Big Sur Coast:
Point Lobos to Point Sur

The Big Sur coast has been variously described as mysterious, treacherous, a state of mind, and too painful to behold. It is all those things, as well as splendid and accessible. Stretching out for some 90 miles—more or less from Point Lobos south to San Simeon, and inland to the crest of the Santa Lucia Range—this bone-rattling shoreline was so intimidating to early explorers that they simply bypassed it.

When Gaspar de Portolá and his men, traveling north from San Diego in the fall of 1769, reached the southern escarpment of the Big Sur coast, they tipped their hats and turned inland. It was easier to cross over the Santa Lucia Range than continue north along the towering bare-knuckled coast.

A road was completed in the late 1930s along the entire length of Big Sur. Fortunately, instead of increasing settlement and development of the region, it simply made what was to

The rugged and spectacular Big Sur coast

become a string of spectacular parklands more accessible to the public. In fact, at the height of the region's logging days, in the late 19th century, the human population of this coast was larger than it is today.

It is fitting to complete your exploration of the greater Monterey Bay shoreline in this portion of the Big Sur coast. In many ways, this area is the ecological southern sister to the lands lining out northward from Santa Cruz to Point Año Nuevo. Both the Año Nuevo and Point Lobos reserves are home to amazing animal and plant life, terrestrial as well as marine. Whereas the northern lands are dominated by smooth marine terraces and coastal bluffs, the region south of Carmel is famous for its dramatic topography and tough granitic looks. To the north the land is well populated, but here people are few and far between, and the earth has much unsettled business to

◄ Point Lobos State Reserve's China Cove

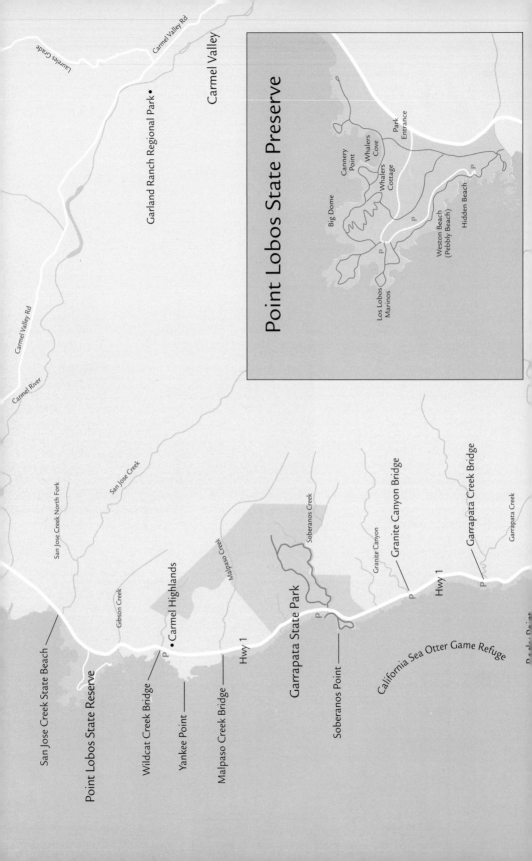

Point Lobos State Preserve

Carmel Valley

Laureles Grade

Carmel Valley Rd

Carmel Valley Rd

Garland Ranch Regional Park •

Carmel River

San Jose Creek North Fork

San Jose Creek

San Jose Creek State Beach

Point Lobos State Reserve

Gibson Creek

Wildcat Creek Bridge

• Carmel Highlands

Yankee Point

Malpaso Creek

Malpaso Creek Bridge

Hwy 1

Soberanos Creek

Garrapata State Park

Soberanos Point

Granite Canyon

Granite Canyon Bridge

Hwy 1

California Sea Otter Game Refuge

Garrapata Creek Bridge

Garrapata Creek

Point Lobos State Preserve (inset)

Park Entrance

Cannery Point

Whalers Cove

Whalers Cottage

Big Dome

Weston Beach (Pebbly Beach)

Hidden Beach

Los Lobos Marinos

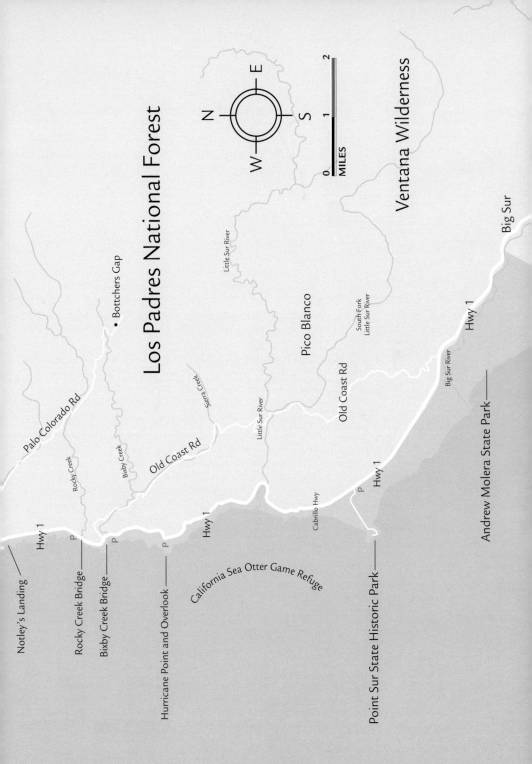

Los Padres National Forest

Ventana Wilderness

Big Sur

Bottchers Gap

Little Sur River

Pico Blanco

South Fork
Little Sur River

Sierra Creek

Old Coast Rd

Little Sur River

Palo Colorado Rd

Rocky Creek

Bixby Creek

Old Coast Rd

Big Sur River

Hwy 1

Hwy 1

Hwy 1

Cabrillo Hwy

Hwy 1

Notley's Landing

Rocky Creek Bridge

Bixby Creek Bridge

Hurricane Point and Overlook

California Sea Otter Game Refuge

Point Sur State Historic Park

Andrew Molera State Park

N

E

S

W

MILES

0   1   2

attend to. In the north the land listens to distant choral music brought to shore by steady winds; here, storm-wrought symphonies slam up against the mountains in D minor, retreat to the rocky shore, then ease back in.

Meandering down Highway 1 along the Big Sur coast is like drawing in a cool, deep breath without needing to exhale. Hiking its wild shores and stony overlooks will give you wondrous pause and make you question if true beauty has any limits.

Point Lobos

Point Lobos State Reserve's
China Cove

What better way to start your Big Sur experience than by visiting Point Lobos State Reserve? There is no better way, but there is a problem: you shouldn't just drop by Point Lobos en route to other sites down the coast. Point Lobos deserves at least half of a day of your time. Even then, return visits will always present new discoveries and wildlife as the seasons come and go across this knobby outcropping of land.

This beautiful reserve was established in 1933 when a few hundred acres were set aside to help preserve the area's Monterey cypress and other species. Today the reserve takes in over 1,300 acres, a majority of which is underwater. The biological richness of this peninsula and shoreline become apparent when you realize that over 250 different animal and bird species and over 350 plant species have been identified here.

But you don't need numbers to figure out that Point Lobos is rich with wildlife and plants. Simply take a walk out by Whalers Cove, for starters. Step up to Cannery Point and look around. Take your time; don't hurry. Look around. Sea lions frolic offshore and snooze on the rocks. Directly below you, sleepy harbor seals gaze up with moist eyes, devoid of fear—as if they know they are in a reserve. Birds are all around: the sky is alive with their calls and disagreements. Surf scoters are diving, western grebes are swimming, and Brandt's cormorants are flying from one feeding area to another.

And then there is the water. This area is famous for its underwater living trea-sures, and scuba divers come here from around the world every day of the year. Even if you're not a diver, you can still see plenty. Just look down through the clear waters, between the waving strands of seaweed. You'll be able to spot fish, sea stars, anemones, and crabs. Offshore, par-tially hidden in the kelp canopy, sea otters rest, play, and pound mollusks on their stomachs, and egrets walk around on top of the water across the slowly undulating carpet of seaweed. The green-brown masses of plant life also have a calming effect on the waves, making this cove look like it's filled with olive oil instead of cold saltwater. Remember to bring binoculars, and you can see even more. You may feel a bit silly gazing into the water with binoculars, but hey, it works.

The reserve rangers and volunteers are friendly and full of information. Most days at the Sea Lion Point parking lot docents staff a fantastic informational booth packed with goodies such as sea lion and otter pelts. If you have a question about anything, they'll probably have the answer. There are also many miles of trails across the reserve. You can access one phenomenal route simply by parking at the entrance station and hiking all the way around the reserve's perimeter, moving from trail to trail. It's about six miles, and it will take you at least two to three hours. (See below for some trail highlights.)

Like Año Nuevo, Point Lobos is wired for communication. Call 831-624-4909 to learn more about the reserve, or go to their website at http://pt-lobos.parks.state.ca.us/index.html (you can e-mail them from there as well). You can also make scuba reservations, which are advisable to secure well in advance, via their website or by calling 831-624-8413. At the entrance station you'll receive an informational brochure with a detailed map of the entire trail network.

Point Lobos is open daily. Also, no matter what time of year, be prepared for changes in weather. It can be warm and sunny one minute, crisp and very windy the next.

"The ocean: A body of water occupying about two-thirds of a world made for man—who has no gills."

Ambrose Bierce,
The Devil's Dictionary
(1906)

Point Lobos Trails

Trails wind throughout Point Lobos.

■ Carmelo Meadow to the Northern Shore

In about two miles, via Carmelo Meadow, Granite Point, and Moss Cove Trails, you can explore the reserve's northern perimeter by Monastery Beach and several fantastic coves. At the western end of Granite Point Trail you'll come across the Whalers Cabin museum, where you'll soon realize that natural history coexists

SUNFLOWER STAR

At low tide you might be able to catch a glimpse of a very large sea star called the sunflower star *(Pycnopodia helianthoides)*. Got binoculars? The sunflower star normally occupies slightly deeper water, but it does climb into the rocky intertidal area for meals. Once seen, it's hard to confuse with other sea stars. These remarkable animals have up to 24 arms and can grow to two feet or more across (the ochre star, by comparison, is only about 10 inches across and normally grows five arms). Their color-

Sunflower star

ing varies from bright pink, orange, and yellow to red and purple. Although Edward Ricketts wrote that sea stars "are scarcely to be classed in general as active animals," sunflower stars can use their estimated 15,000 suckerlike tube feet to move almost two feet a minute. That's downright flying for a sea star.

These large denizens of the rocky shore eat a variety of

mollusks and other tidepool creatures, but they seem to be especially partial to sea urchins. The sunflower star can overtake an urchin and engulf the entire animal with its stomach. After digestion, all that's left is a pile of spines and the empty urchin husk, which the sea star unceremoniously spits out.

POINT LOBOS

Point Lobos is Spanish for "Wolf Point." There might have been wolves here once, but the reference is to the abundance of sea lions here. The Spanish name for sea lions is *lobos marinos*—sea wolves. Lions? Wolves? Humans have a way of confusing matters when it comes to animal names. Anyway, Punta de los Lobos Marinos literally means Sea Wolf Point. It is believed to have been named in the early 19th century.

closely with human history in this reserve. From California Indians to whalers, Chinese fishermen and abalone packers to granite miners, the land and coves of Point Lobos have many stories to tell.

You might notice in Carmelo Meadow and elsewhere that some of the trees look brown, disheveled, and slightly burned. For the most part, this is a good thing. The charred trunks and occasional blackened meadow are the result of prescribed burns managed by park personnel. Many native grass and flower species, as well as pines and cypresses, benefit from properly timed annual burns. Ask any ranger about their burn program to learn more. Some of the damage comes from strong winter storms—par for the course on this exposed headland. There is some bad news, though: the pines are starting to suffer from bark beetles, for which no cure exists (see pp. 230–231). Only time will tell what the future forests of Point Lobos will look like.

■ North Shore Trail to Cypress Grove

In about one and a half miles you can hike between Whalers Cove and the beginning of the Cypress Grove Trail on the North Shore Trail. This spectacular trail is rather hilly and rocky in parts, but well-maintained steps ease the ascent and descent. You stay high and above it all on this trail as you head into the wind past Guillemot Island and Big Dome. During the spring the offshore

GIANT GREEN ANEMONE

T he giant green anemone *(Anthopleura xanthogram-mica),* which grows to almost a foot tall and about nine inches across, won't be found in massive clusters like the cloning anemone. It prefers the single life, though it may also be found in small groups at the bottom of deep pools and downslope from mussel beds—its food of choice. When a mussel is dislodged by predators or loosened by overcrowding, it tumbles downward—perhaps into the waiting maw of an anemone.

Giant green anemone

CHARLES SEABORN / MONTEREY BAY AQUARIUM

rocks are home to nesting western gulls, pigeon guille-mots, and Brandt's and pelagic cormorants; overhead, keep on eye open for great blue herons in their nests. A nice detour along this trail is the Whalers Knoll Trail. It's a bit of a climb, but the views are terrific.

When you reach the Cypress Grove Trail, another 30 minutes of your time will take you out through the Allan Memorial Grove of cypress. This is one of only two naturally occurring stands of Monterey cypress in the world.

■ Sea Lion Point Trail

If your time is limited and you can pay only a short visit to the reserve, this is the trail for you. From the Sea Lion Point parking lot out to the point and back takes about 30 minutes. The ocean views couldn't be better along this trail, and you'll see a nice cross-section of the reserve's wildlife and vegetation.

■ South Shore Trail toward Bird Island

From the Sea Lion Point parking lot you can also explore the ragged southern edge of the reserve by hiking down to Gibson Beach. Start out on South Shore Trail, which turns into Bird Island Trail at the south parking lot. The round trip to Gibson Beach and back is about three and a half miles.

PEDAL POWER ALONG THE SHORELINE

All of Highway 1 is designated as the Pacific Coast Bike Route. This is a very popular bike thoroughfare—for obvious reasons. If you want to trek down the coast using pedal power, why not plan on doing some camping along the way at Bottchers Gap or south of Point Sur? In any event, you had better prepare yourself for sharing some tight, narrow turns with recreational vehicles (those hotels on wheels) and the enormous tour buses that scream down the coast to the town of Big Sur and the Nepenthe restaurant.

Scuba divers

STEVEN WEBSTER

Over half of the Point Lobos Reserve is underwater, and diving is the optimal way to experience it. You can dive with just a snorkel and mask, but you really have to know what you are doing. Novices shouldn't jump into the coastal waters and head out into the kelp forest without proper training and gear. And you *must* have a dive partner here, whether snorkeling or scuba diving.

Scuba equipment and wet suits are the gear of choice in these waters. The term SCUBA is an acronym for Self-Contained Underwater Breathing Apparatus. Scuba gear was developed in the 1940s by Emil Gagnan and Jacques Cousteau, after which marine research and recreation were never the same. Now people can move among towering kelp forests and curious fish with ease. Underwater, swaying back and forth inside the kelp forest, you are truly in another world. When a sea lion darts out of the darkness straight toward your mask then turns away at the very last moment, you'll have the best heart-thumping thrill of your life. You can't help but think sea lions perform these maneuvers just to play—or to keep you on your toes.

Of course, to use scuba equipment, you must learn how: you can't just rent the gear and jump in. If you're interested in lessons, contact your local sports store, or check out the Point Lobos scuba page on the internet; it's packed with advice and resources.

No collecting or fishing is permitted within the reserve. However, if you are interested in fishing while diving elsewhere along the coast, be sure to familiarize yourself with Fish and Game regulations and check with local park officials where necessary.

SHORELINE PUBLIC TRANSPORTATION

During the summer (approximately late May to late August) you can take a bus as far as Pfeiffer Big Sur State Park and the Nepenthe restaurant if you don't want to hassle with all those twists and turns in your car. Just catch a Monterey-Salinas Transit bus (number 22) from downtown Monterey, at the intersection of Munras, Pearl, and Tyler. The one-way trip takes about one and a half hours. For schedules, contact Monterey-Salinas Transit at 831-899-2555 or check out their website at http://www.mst.org.

South Shore Trail leads you across open rocky terrain and past some extraordinary geology. Keep an eye open for the quartz-filled granite and the impressive sedimentary formations that have been uplifted and exposed. Out along Bird Island Trail, two small sandy beaches can be accessed. Swimming is allowed here, but be cautious. Watch the ocean for swells and remember that this water is c-o-l-d. Offshore, Bird Island is just that—a rocky outcropping that serves as a springtime nesting site mostly for Brandt's cormorants.

Highway 1

The completion of what we know today as Highway 1 between Carmel and San Simeon was quite an accomplishment. The project was launched in 1918 with a preliminary survey and was finished in 1937 when the road was opened to the public. Before work was through, 29 bridges were constructed and 90 miles' worth of pavement was laid on the ground. When money was first appropriated by the state for construction, there was

A marine species enjoyed by both humans and sea otters is the abalone. Eight species of these savory shellfish can be found off the Pacific coast, the most prized of which—among humans at least—is the red abalone (*Haliotis rufescens*). Although all abalones are strictly herbivores, dining mainly on drift kelp, that diet allows red abalones—the largest of the bunch—to grow to a foot or more in length.

Abalones have been a human food staple along this coast for thousands of years. In coastal Indian middens (or trash heaps), abalone shells make up a large percentage of the buried material. And until recent history, you could walk out at low tide and pick these overgrown snails right off the rocks. Today, sport divers have to brave rough seas and deep water to find their limit. They can only remove abalone of certain sizes (larger than seven inches for red abalones), either by hand or with a special prying device called an abalone iron, and then only north of San Francisco Bay; and seasonal closures are common. Additionally, they are only allowed to "free dive," that is, with only a mask and snorkel and no air tanks.

The commercial harvest, now closed for all abalone species until 2002, once focused largely on the green abalone (*H. fulgens*), but its population has plummeted. Red abalones are also in trouble, and some experts believe they have been completely eliminated from large swaths of their range in central and southern California. Harvesting restrictions extend to commercial harvesters as well. Divers and commercial interests alike agree that illegal poaching is rampant, but they also point to the sea otter as a problem; if the otters could point and talk, you can guess what they would be saying.

The controversy over taking abalone is not going to go away. Demand will always be high for this delicacy (in recent years abalone meat has sold for $60 a pound on the overseas market), and the supply will remain limited, despite efforts to grow abalone commercially.

Red abalone

There are too many informal pullouts along Highway 1 to mention here. Many of these are not officially maintained by the California Department of Transportation (CalTrans), and some are downright dangerous. Also, many of the steep paths down to the shore from these pullouts are unmaintained; they, too, can be dangerous. Be safe and stick to the signed pullouts, vista points, and trailheads. And always be careful when pulling off or on the highway.

Using Carmel's Rio Road stop light as a starting point, a few of the larger pullouts include (with miles rounded off): Carmel Highlands (3), Garrapata Creek (10), the south end of Rocky Creek Bridge (12.5), the north end of Bixby Creek Bridge (13), and a vista site at Hurricane Point (14).

already a rough road some 35 miles long between Carmel and the Big Sur River. South of the river it was a real trail, passable only by horseback or on foot.

Today this stretch of highway offers one of the best-loved drives in the United States, with incredible views, great hiking, and some genuine Big Sur atmosphere.

Complementary Cormorants

Two birds that tough it out here all year long are the Brandt's cormorant (*Phalacrocorax penicillatus*) and the pelagic cormorant (*P. pelagicus*). Double-crested cormorants can be found around the bay in smaller numbers as well. Cormorants are real fishing birds. They are built to paddle along the surface of the water with their body partially submerged, then dive down in pursuit of fish. By using their webbed feet and pumping their wings, cormorants are not only fast underwater but they also can dive deep—100 feet, and then some. Their nesting rocks offshore can be very noisy sites. You'll be amazed at the variation of grunts and clucks you can hear if the wind is right.

The Brandt's is the most common cormorant along this coast. These large black birds nest in sizable colonies on nearshore rocks, developing a brilliant blue throat patch during breeding season. (The patch is there year round, but it intensifies in the spring.) When you see a long thin line of pointy birds moving low and fast over the water, it is most likely a group of these cormorants shifting from one feeding ground to the next. When they stop, they

Brandt's cormorants feeding

Orca

A recent development in marine sanctuary waters has been the increased appearance of orcas, also known as killer whales *(Orcinus orca)*. These magnificent marine mammals are divided into several distinct populations, each of which has a very different vocalization. The first, and perhaps best studied, group inhabits home ranges throughout the Pacific Northwest. These so-called resident orcas live in extended family groups, or pods, that tend to stay together, and they eat mostly fish. There are no resident pods within the Monterey Bay National Marine Sanctuary.

Another category of orca is called the offshore type, though the term is a bit confusing. Here, as in other parts of the eastern Pacific, these orcas spend most of the year well off the coast living in large groups. During the late fall and winter, however, they may come very close to our shores, in groups that sometimes approach 100 individuals. The offshore orcas eat principally fish and squid.

A third type consists of so-called rogue orcas—orcas with an attitude. These transient packs, which roam the waters from Mexico to Alaska, are known for their fierce attacks on prey. Unlike resident and offshore orcas, which are content with fish, rogue orcas go after whales, seals, and porpoises, chasing the smaller marine mammals down or working as a pack against larger prey such as whales, which they harass until exhaustion sets in.

In Monterey Bay, it is the rogue orcas that have been spotted with increasing frequency. They've been seen killing and eating seals, gray whales, and even, off the Farallon Islands to the north, great white sharks. Just when you thought it was safe to enter the water . . . But don't worry—it still is. There has only been one verified orca attack on a human (right here in Big Sur), and that was decades ago.

form large rafts on the surface of the ocean, often just beyond the kelp beds, where they continuously dive in pursuit of fish.

The smaller pelagic cormorant tends to nest apart from others on very steep rock faces. Watching them land and take off from their nesting sites is to see dexterity in action. They feed alone or in small groups beyond the kelp beds. This species also dresses up for the breeding season, sporting a red patch that extends from its eye down to its pouch and white markings on its flanks below the wings. During spring, the pelagic looks like it has a butch haircut with a dip in the middle.

Pelagic cormorant

Remember, the couple of hours right around sunset are best for viewing bats. Find some open country and perhaps a body of freshwater nearby—pond, creek, river. Later in the evening, bats can sometimes be seen around streetlights or floodlights in pursuit of insects.

- Listen for their clicks and squeaks.

- If you find a roosting site during the day, don't disturb it.

- If you find a bat on the ground, don't pick it up. It might bite you.

Bats

There are over 40 species of bats nationwide, some 24 of which are found in California. You may not associate bats with the shoreline, but they are here. As you sit on a bluff or grassland to watch that perfect sunset, cock an eye overhead every now and again. The period from sunset until two or so hours later is prime bat watching time.

In some parts of the country bat watching is a social event. In Texas—where they do everything big—an estimated 20 million Mexican free-tailed bats emerge from Bracken Cave every evening in pursuit of 125 tons of insects! That won't happen here. Instead, the species you are most likely to see, such as the big brown bat (*Eptesicus fuscus*), hoary bat (*Lasiurus cinereus*), California myotis (*Myotis californicus*), and Yuma myotis (*Myotis yumanensis*), flit about alone or in small groups.

Contrary to popular belief, bats can see well, and they make audible noises. But they rely mainly on their hearing to find their prey, including echolocation, which involves bouncing sound off of flying insects. Researchers even think that bats can tell the type of insect they are pursuing by the shape of the rebounding sound. If you see some bats flying overhead and it's a quiet evening, you'll be able to hear their high-pitched clicks and squeaks.

Over half of the bat species in North America are in trouble or already listed as endangered by federal and state governments. Habitat destruction, pesticides, and disturbance of roost sites are the principal reasons for this situation.

Roosting Yuma myotis and Mexican free-tailed bats

WILLIAM E. RAINEY

Along the central coast of California we humans are privileged to witness migrations on a grand scale. Every fall and winter gray whales swim south to warmer climes. The diminutive monarch butterfly glides overhead to ancestral eucalyptus and pine groves. Salmon and steelhead march up coastal streams after the first big rains, while black-tailed deer come down off the windswept mountains to spend a few months in the lowlands. Ladybird beetles mass together in the cool coastal valleys—gigantic balls of red and black wrapped in green. Other animals and insects wait out the cold weather by crawling under rocks or curling up in burrows.

Less obvious are the impressive changes that take place within Monterey Bay and offshore waters. In the fall, when the northwesterly winds subside, open-ocean species like sunfish and massive leatherback turtles can be seen near shore. During the winter, the Davidson Current typically kicks in from the south, pushing water temperatures from the 50s into the 60s. Upwelling temporarily ceases at this time, making the waters less productive, though we do get a few visitors from southern waters, such as different species of plankton.

Perhaps the most visible seasonal movements are those of birds—birds on the move. Estimates vary, but it is believed that some 80 bird species live along the central California coast year round, and about 175 nest here. Over the years, however, well over 375 bird species have been tallied in these parts. The discrepancy in numbers is due mainly to migration. That is, seasonally there is a lot of movement up and down the West Coast as birds ply their way along the Pacific Flyway.

Birds migrate for several reasons that we know of. Migratory species move from one site to the next as the food resources in those regions become plentiful. Although birds expend enormous amounts of energy migrating, they actually improve their chances for survival and reproduction by making these long journeys to avoid severe weather and to rest.

The Pacific Flyway drains shorebirds and other waterfowl from major portions of Alaska and the Canadian provinces of British Columbia and Alberta into the western United States and Latin America. Many other types of birds, such as hawks and swallows, also migrate down this corridor. Here in California, coastal wetlands and the Central Valley are key habitats along the flyway. The flyway has been described as a highway in the sky or a river of birds. During the height of migration, the description certainly fits.

Even brown pelicans, which many people think live here all year, are a migratory species. They spend the summer and winter here but return south to breed on islands off the coasts of southern California and Mexico. The petite western sandpiper that dodges waves on the beach so expertly—a little gray bird no bigger than the palm of your hand—flies thousands of miles yearly between its breeding grounds in the arctic tundra and its wintering grounds here along Monterey Bay.

Seaweeds to Know and Love

■ Giant kelp *(Macrocystis pyrifera)*

Giant kelp is one of nature's fastest-growing plants, able to grow 14 or more inches a day under optimum conditions. Secured to the ocean floor by a rootlike anchor called a holdfast, an individual kelp plant can live several years and attain lengths of 100-plus feet. Buoyed up by gas-filled floats, the kelp fronds spread out in a swirling

Giant kelp

mass on the water's surface to maximize exposure to the sun. Giant kelp is a favorite of nighttime beach visitors; dried-out floats, when placed in a fire, quickly swell and burst with a loud pop.

Bull kelp

■ Bull kelp *(Nereocystis luetkeana)*

If you see kids down the beach swinging something long and rubbery over their heads, you can bet it's a stranded length of bull kelp. A common ingredient of beach wrack, bull kelp is like giant kelp in that it grows to considerable lengths—30 to 60 feet—in order to reach sunlight. Other species, in contrast, don't mind the half-light of the ocean floor at moderate depths, so long as they get some light to allow photosynthesis. Unlike giant kelp, however, which produces hundreds of small floats and numerous blades, bull kelp slowly develops one large, bulbous float at the top of the plant from which blades grow and droop back into the water. This float keeps the plant growing toward the surface.

Sea palms

■ Sea palm *(Postelsia palmaeformis)*

Sea palm is a nearshore species visible throughout the intertidal zone where rocky shores prevail. Held aloft by a semirigid stem, or stipe, this floppy-headed seaweed looks like a miniature kelp tree. With tough-as-nails holdfasts, groups of sea palms can be spotted rocking back and forth in the surging waves alongside barnacles and mussels. These seaweeds are actually annual plants. They produce spores in the summer and fall, then die off, creating space for new sea palms in the spring.

■ Feather boa kelp *(Egregia menziesii)*

Another nearshore species, and another common ingredient of kelp wrack, is the feather boa kelp. Although it too has a holdfast, you wouldn't know it at first glance. Twisting and writhing in the nearshore waters, this delicate-looking seaweed appears to be freely surging in the waves.

Feather boa kelp

Carmel Highlands and Yankee Point

The secluded homes of Carmel Highlands are immediately south of Point Lobos, where Highway 1 narrows and twists through a dense forest of Monterey cypress. Besides the Wildcat Creek Historic Bridge, a small roadside store, and some lodgings, there are few public facilities here, and no coastal access. This area was first settled

KELP WRACK

During stormy weather it is common for enormous strands of giant kelp to be ripped from their holdfast anchors and wash ashore, where they are stranded in sorry piles—known as wrack—beyond the reach of the highest tides. The wrack then warms and slowly decomposes, attracting a wide variety of insects and other beach life.

Intertwined with the gelatinous wracks of giant kelp are other large species of seaweed dislodged from their aquatic homes, such as bull kelp and feather boa kelp, as well as more diminutive species like sea lettuce and sea grapes. More than 20 species of kelp grow along California's coastline, and within the forests

Marbled godwits and black turnstones feeding on kelp wrack

formed by this kelp myriad animals of all shapes and sizes flourish, along with some 400 types of sea plants.

Kelp wrack is an important food source and habitat for kelp flies and their maggot offspring. Walking past a ripe mound of stranded kelp will often ignite an audible buzz as these flies and other insects momentarily lift off. Because of this insect activity,

it is also common to see a variety of birds—various shorebirds, crows, black phoebes, and warblers—hopping about the wrack, chasing down quick meals. Get down on your hands and knees and take a close look. Pry the pile apart a bit with a brave hand (or a stick, if you must) and look for small crabs and snails. There's a lot going on in there.

in 1916 overlooking the rugged Yankee Point, famed for its towering bluffs. It is where the well-known photographers Edward Weston and Ansel Adams lived.

The Bridges of Monterey County

Many bridges were built along this coast in the early 1930s, and they still stand as marvels of construction. As you continue down the coast, the bridges between here and Point Sur will be pointed out and a bit of their history explained.

■ Wildcat Creek Historic Bridge (1932)

Right in the middle of Carmel Highlands you'll cross over the first of Big Sur's many historic bridges. They are worth the time to stop and look because they are each a little bit different, and they are all very elegant. Unfortunately, this first one—Wildcat Creek Bridge—is situated without any nearby pullouts, so you'll have to bridge-watch on the move.

The Wildcat Creek Bridge is a reinforced-concrete, closed-spandrel bridge with a three-arch span. (A spandrel is the triangular area beneath the roadway, where the structural arch is attached to the right angle of the anchoring abutments and the road.) People who really follow these matters might be interested to know that—are you ready?—this is the only bridge in California to use a pointed-arch main span. Wow! Seriously, though, it is a handsome bridge.

As you leave Carmel Highlands there is a nice blufftop turnout (before Highland Drive) where you can stop and look north to Point Lobos through some cypress trees. To the south you can look out over a cluster of private homes.

■ Malpaso Creek Historic Bridge (1935)

Once you pass Wildcat Creek Bridge and leave the Highlands behind you the landscape begins to open up: the road narrows and coastal sage scrub dominates the land. You may be reminded of Highway 1 between Santa Cruz and Waddell Creek—but in fact it's different. The shore is more rugged here, and you begin to sense that you are heading into a different type of shoreline, a more wild landscape. Soon you'll begin to encounter the small informal turnouts mentioned earlier and the occasional residence.

About four and a half miles south of Rio Road you will cross another beautiful canyon-spanning slab of concrete: Malpaso Creek Historic Bridge. This bridge was constructed with an open-spandrel design (now you can compare a closed spandrel with an open one). It is 210 feet long and was completed for $24,000. How times have changed.

Malpaso Creek was just that—a "bad passage"—before the bridge was built. Apparently, it was very common for wagons to make it down the difficult portage only to get stuck in the sandy wash below.

Coyote

Coyote

Coyotes (*Canis latrans*) are occasionally seen along this stretch of coast. Although they normally hunt at night, you can also spot coyotes during the crepuscular hours—just before sunrise and after sunset. At a distance, these canines look like 50-pound domestic dogs, but the large, bushy tail gives them away. When they run they hold their tails down.

The coyote's scientific name means "barking dog." On still afternoons or quiet nights, you may hear coyotes yip-

Garrapata State Park and the Big Sur coast

ping, barking, and howling down coastal canyons and across shoreline meadows and bluffs. One coyote can make so much racket that it sounds like an entire pack.

Coyotes might have the mystique of being solitary individualists, but they are actually very social animals and often hunt in pairs. At night they can cover 10 miles while hunting, and some have been recorded traveling 100 miles. These opportunistic and smart predators eat mice, rabbits, and just about anything else they come across. Although revered by native cultures, the coyote was ruthlessly hunted for the last 150 years by government hunters to protect livestock. Regardless of such concerted efforts to eradicate them, coyotes have survived and are actually recovering some historic range and opening up new habitats, such as downtown Los Angeles.

Garrapata State Park

Garrapata State Park starts about half of a mile south of Malpaso Creek Bridge (look for the small sign on a coast-side bluff). Encompassing just over 3,000 acres, it is well disguised: there is no entrance station or interpretive center, just a dirt turnout along the highway. It's easy to miss, but don't—it's simply too beautiful to pass up.

The twin turnouts for Garrapata's coastal and inland trails are approximately six and a half miles south of Rio Road, midway through the park. As you pass through three heavily eroded road cuts look for the line of wind-blown cypress trees and the old tin shed on the inland side of the highway. This is the best place to stop. From here you'll see Whale Peak and Soberanes Point on the shore. You can also pull off the highway at a few points to the south, just around the corner, but they aren't as safe.

The hike out to Soberanes Point is a nice one. The trails, which weave across the coastal terrace, make for

NAMES ON THE LAND

GARRAPATA

Garrapata is Spanish for tick. That's right, you are visiting California's Tick State Park. Actually, it is an apt name because these little blood suckers can be found here on a regular basis, as the early Spanish explorers discovered to their dismay.

Where better to discuss ticks than near Garrapata State Park? Where there is European dune grass, native bunch grasses, or chaparral, there are ticks. Okay, so ticks don't occur only in these types of vegetation, but it seems like it at times. Regardless of where you are hiking—but especially in brush or grasslands—make sure to do a tick check when you get back to camp or to your vehicle. If these creepers are still crawling, just pick them off; they move slowly. If they have already burrowed into you, the best thing to do is remove the tick quickly.

You can purchase a commercial tick-removing device and have it on hand, but simple tweezers work just fine. Use the tweezers to grasp the head of the tick (actually its mouth parts) as close to the surface of your skin as possible. Don't squeeze the tick's body. Now gently pull straight back—with little tugs—until the tick releases. Be patient; it might take a while. Clean the bite thoroughly. Lyme disease is not prevalent on the central coast, but if you want to have the tick tested, save it in alcohol. Record where you were and where on your body you got bit, then contact your physician or your county or state health department.

easy walking. It's a bit of a climb up and down Whale Peak, but worth it. After passing through the gate, start out by taking the trail to your left and pass through the cypress grove (there's an outhouse here). Soberanes Point is an ideal spot for whale watching, and people fish out here for rockfish and other species. (As always along the coast, keep an eye on the ocean. Sneaker waves have plucked people off the shore here before.) Glance out over the water and you'll realize the kelp beds here are particularly dense. Keep an ear cocked for the bark of the sea lions and your eyes open for black oystercatchers with their brilliant orange bills.

As you ease your way out to the point, take note of the different heights of the coastal scrub. Back by the parking

Wildflowers of Soberanes: paintbrush and lizard tail

area it's almost five feet tall. The closer you get to the shore the shorter it gets, until out on Soberanes Point is looks like an overgrown putting green. Wind and salt spray sculpt the vegetation here. If you have binoculars, scan the Lobos Rocks offshore for birds. This trail continues all the way around Whale Peak. In the spring the entire area is splashed with color as numerous wildflowers and native shrubs come into bloom.

On the inland side of the highway from the turnout

BLACK OYSTERCATCHER

Black oyster-
catchers on an
outcropping of
the Monterey
Formation

Much of the rocky shoreline of the dramatic Big Sur coast is inaccessible to us. It is simply too steep and too dangerous. However, it's the perfect habitat for the black oystercatcher *(Haematopus bachmani)*. This bird has a loud laugh of a call—like a deep-throated sandpiper—which can be heard over the breaking waves near the rocky shores of Monterey Bay year round. If you don't hear one, scope the rocks with binoculars and be patient.

The black oystercatcher is a dramatic-looking bird, with its deep orange bill, reddish-orange eye ring, black feathers, and pinkish legs. The colors are beautiful, and they also help the bird to blend in with its rocky habitat. Its radiant bill is a very important device as the oystercatcher pursues meals of mussels, limpets, and marine worms—but not oysters. Perhaps it should be called the mussel-catcher because of its great skill in eating those mollusks. It can pry open a mussel, cut the muscles that hold the animal to its shell, and slurp the contents down for a meal, leaving the shell in place! Its bill is flattened laterally to help it push into shells.

you will find two trails—Soberanes Canyon and Rocky Ridge Trails. You should take advantage of these tracks because there are few inland hikes along this section of coast. Walk past the tin shed, then drop down by the refreshing sight of Soberanes Creek with its calla lilies and borders of willows. Even at the driest times of year clear water gurgles through this small creek. Cross the creek and you'll see the trail junction. To go up the canyon, turn right; a left turn will take you to Rocky Ridge Trail, which heads up the ridge. Note the hillside here covered with opuntia cactus planted by early settlers.

These trails form a lovely loop—with an accent. The accent is the half-mile Peak Trail, which ascends very steeply from the canyon to the ridge. The views of the shoreline from the upper reaches of these trails are spectacular. But they'll cost you a few calories. Rocky Ridge Trail is also steep, so consider starting out on the Soberanes Canyon Trail, which works along Soberanes Creek and eventually moves through some nice redwoods. After one and a half miles you'll see the Peak Trail working upslope (it looks like an old road). Assess your condition and if you're ready for a workout, proceed; otherwise, ease back into the redwoods.

White-throated Swift

Every now and again you come across an animal whose way of life is so different from ours that it boggles the mind. Aquatic species fit this category almost by definition simply because their water-based habitat is so unlike our terrestrial home. Birds also fit into this category because they can fly (most of them can, anyway). Of the fliers, the swifts are right up there with some of the best. In fact, these birds spend so much time on the wing, and so little time sitting, that their feet have evolved into tiny little appendages. Which explains their family name: Apodidae, "without feet."

Along the greater Monterey Bay shoreline the white-throated swift (*Aeronautes saxatilis*) regularly entertains the keen-eyed coastal explorer with its dramatic aerial displays and distinctive call. (Its scientific name means "rock-dwelling air sailor.") These birds are usually spotted very high in the sky as they search for insects; their chattering call—an excited, shrill "je-je-je-je-je-je-je-je-je-je-je-je"—will help you pinpoint the group zooming about overhead.

Unlike the relatively slow-moving swallows, with their shorter wings and chubby-looking bodies, swifts have slender bodies and long, tapering wings. Swifts don't flap their wings a lot; instead they spend most of their time gliding, diving, and working the thermals. When they do flap, their wingbeats are shallow and fast. If you see a mixed flock of swifts and swallows it will be easy to tell

WRENTIT

The wrentit *(Chamaea fasciata)* is one of the great little secrets of the coastal chaparral. Although this bird is little, nervous, and secretive, with just a little bit of work you can see wrentits on a regular basis. Look for a bird that is smaller than your fist and grayish-brown all over, possibly with its longish tail held erect. Its call is distinctive: it starts out as a single note, turns into a trill, and descends like a bouncing ball. Sometimes it just performs the bouncing part.

If you don't happen to come across a wrentit but think you hear one or see one hopping around in a bush, try "pishing." Bird-watchers will tell you this works, and it really does. Stand still and make a "psh-psh-psh" sound with your lips. The curious wrentit may well pop out of the bush and take a good long look at the spot where the noise is originating. While it is studying you, study it back, making sure to look at its light yellow or cream-colored eyes.

Wrentits are thought to be monogamous for life and relatively stationary within their home territory. They work through the coastal scrub in pursuit of insects and spiders, although in winter they can be seen eating small fruits as well. Remember, "psh-psh-psh."

which is which: the swifts will be flying circles around the swallows (without flapping), chattering all the while.

These birds are so well adapted to constant flight that they actually couple on the wing. When mating, swifts will clasp one another high in the sky, then spiral downward several hundred feet, spinning like a black and white star. Whereas most other swifts migrate south to warmer climates, the white-throated swift overwinters here. On warm days in the middle of winter they break out of their sleep and fly about in search of a meal. These swifts nest in crevices and cavities along the face of coastal cliffs back from the shoreline.

Lupine

One very striking flower of the shoreline is the lupine. Some lupines here grow very tall, up to four feet, and just as wide. Lupines also flower for a long time, starting in late winter and lasting through early summer. When you find a lupine bush in flower, take the time to walk around it. Look closely at the flowers (and take a whiff), inspect the stems, and survey the ground beneath the plant —you'll see a lot of insect activity. Touch one of the palm-shaped leaves—it's as soft as a mouse's belly (to borrow an image from Steinbeck).

Yellow lupine

Along this stretch of coast you'll find two prominent species of lupine—bush lupine (*Lupinus arboreus*) and silver bush lupine (*L. chamissonis*)—from among the dozens of species in California. This genus got its name, *Lupinus*, or "wolflike," from the popular belief that lupines sucked the nutrients out of the soil. That's not true, but overall, lupines do prefer poor as well as disturbed soils.

The bush lupine, by far the more common of the two, can be found as both yellow- and blue-purple-flowered plants. This plant is native to central and southern coastal California, but the yellow version has been introduced as a sand dune stabilizer in northern California and other parts of the world. Around Eureka, in coastal Humboldt County, this plant is considered an aggressive

Silver bush lupine

pest because it takes over wide areas of dunes, shading out native species, and cross-fertilizes with native lupines of the area. People actively remove the plant up there— but don't do that here.

The silver bush lupine has a distinct grayish cast to its foliage, and its leaves are a little smaller and narrower than the bush lupine's. The silver bush lupine always has purple-blue flowers. This species ranges from central coastal California south to Los Angeles County.

■ Granite Canyon Historic Bridge (1932)

The Granite Canyon Bridge, just over one mile south of Soberanes Point, is another open-spandrel concrete bridge. It crosses above Granite Creek, stretching 288 feet between canyon walls. There are small pullouts on either side of the bridge. Immediately before the bridge you'll see a fenced-in building on the coastal bluff. This is a former military missile tracking station, which has been converted into a state marine pollution lab (no public access).

Black-tailed Deer

In other parts of the state, the mule deer (*Odocoileus hemionus*) prevails, but here on the coast the black-tailed deer (*O. h. columbiana*) is what you will find. A friend of both mountain lions and ticks, it is the largest herbivore on the coast.

Tule elk once frequented areas here, but they were hunted out a long time ago. The bones of elk are frequently found in coastal Indian middens, and the animals were sighted well into the region's Spanish period. Today, elk have been reintroduced in parts of interior Monterey County.

Black-tailed deer

The black-tail deer, however, doesn't need any reintroduction efforts here—and it barely needs an introduction. This common coastal resident is often seen grazing next to the highway, on coastal bluffs, and up canyons among tall stands of redwoods. Along developed portions of the shoreline deer are familiar sites on golf courses and in cemeteries. The typical scene is of a mother and her two young quietly browsing together (deer normally have twins) or a lone male strutting through a field.

This guide has not been mentioning specific places to stop and eat, but on this stretch of desolate coast the Rocky Point Restaurant is about the only show in town. Located midway between Kasler Point and Palo Colorado Road, it is one mile south of Garrapata Creek Bridge. Keep a watch out: it comes up quickly on your right after you've passed by a large hill. You don't have to stop here to eat. You can simply drop in to look around, stretch your legs, use a telephone . . . and *then* get something to eat. They serve lunch and dinner. The views are really impressive, and the view down to Rocky Creek Bridge is unparalleled.

This graceful animal has a reddish-brown coat in the summer and a gray or gray-blue coat in the winter. Deer are usually very quiet, but when alarmed they make a very loud sneezing sound. During the mating season, or rut (from fall through early winter), male deer grunt loudly, defending their females. They also rub their antlers against bushes and tree trunks during this period to polish their rack. You can easily find their scrape marks on tree trunks, typically three or four feet above the ground. Unlike bears, which claw trees a few feet higher and make pronounced vertical grooves, deer shred bark in all directions as they thrash about with their antlers.

If you are hiking on a trail or sitting in a coastal meadow or on a bluff and a deer comes bursting through the bushes and bounces away, stay still and keep your eyes open. You might see a mountain lion hunting. Don't worry: they're interested in the deer. Of course, it might be that a branch fell from a tree and spooked the deer . . . but you never know.

■ Garrapata Creek Historic Bridge (1931)

About one and a half miles south of Granite Creek Bridge, as the terrain opens and flattens slightly, you'll cross another historic structure, Garrapata Creek Bridge. Smaller than the Granite Creek Bridge by only two feet, it is just as elegant. As you approach this bridge you'll see some private homes on the bluff and a beautiful beach. Park before the bridge and follow the informal trail to the beach. This is a nice place to stretch your legs before continuing south or to spend a few hours. About a quarter of a mile past the bridge is a narrow vista point turnout.

Palo Colorado Road, Bottchers Gap, and Notleys Landing

A few hundred yards south of the Rocky Point turnoff (or if you're keeping track, about 11 miles south of Carmel) is Palo Colorado Road. *Palo colorado* is Spanish for redwood tree—an appropriate name, considering the towering redwoods near the entrance of the canyon. Scattered residences line this meandering road, but if you work your way up its length—about eight miles—you'll come to Bottchers Gap Campground in the Los Padres National Forest, at an elevation of about 2,000 feet. As the road moves in and out of the sun the vistas inland toward the Ventana Wilderness are breathtaking.

Like all Forest Service sites, this campground—the only place to camp between Monterey's Veterans Memo-

MOUNTAIN LION

The mountain lion (*Felis concolor*), also known as the cougar, panther, or puma, is tawny colored with black-tipped ears and tail. Young lions are covered with black spots. If you think you've seen an adult mountain lion, ask yourself how long the tail was. If you demonstrate by stretching out your arms as far apart as possible, you probably did . . . their tails are that impressive.

These cats are highly adaptable. They live in deserts and at high elevations, but they also live along coastlines—such as most of the lands ringing Monterey Bay. The mountain lion population in Monterey County is very large, and these big cats are seen all along the Big Sur coast as well as up north in the Waddell Creek area.

Although their culinary tastes center on large mammals, particularly deer (biologists will tell you that if you see deer, you can assume there are mountain lions close by), they also eat mice, birds,

Mountain lions are common, but rarely seen, residents of the coastal mountains.

and even insects. After the black bear (of which there are few in Monterey County), the mountain lion is the region's largest carnivore. Males have impressive home ranges, covering up to 25 miles in a single night.

When hiking in mountain lion territory, use common sense:

- Keep children close to you.
- Avoid hiking alone.
- If you do come face to face with a mountain lion, don't run. Try to look as big as you can.

rial Park and Andrew Molera State Park—is open year round. There is a fee both for camping here and for parking if you want to take a day hike or backpack into the wilderness. This is a no-frills campground—just water (most of the time), pit toilets, fire grills, and tables. But what else do you need? If you add a tent and some food, you're set. Five campsites are located right next to the parking lot, and a scattering of walk-in sites are a short distance away. If you walk past the sites near the parking lot and look inland you'll be treated to a breathtaking view of heavily forested wilderness lands: the hillside drops out below you some 1,000 feet to a

The Ventana Wilderness area takes in some truly wild country, about 165,000 acres' worth, all in the Los Padres National Forest in Monterey County. The national forest, comprising two sections (north and south), takes in approximately two million acres. In addition to Bottchers Gap, Pfeiffer Big Sur State Park provides good access to the wilderness area. For information about the Ventana Wilderness or the Los Padres National Forest, call the district office in King City (831-385-5434).

rugged valley, while in the distance Skinner Ridge rises to a height of over 3,300 feet. The campground is also a trailhead for various routes into the Ventana Wilderness. For information about camping here and in the wilderness area (and to check about water), contact the Los Padres National Forest at 831-385-5434.

Just south of Palo Colorado Road on Highway 1 is the site of old Notleys Landing. Look out across the wide coastal terrace here (now a pasture) and imagine a thriving business based on timber and tanbark. The old Palo Colorado School House (now a private residence) is on the inland side of the highway, behind some trees. The landing was named after its founders, the Notley brothers, who arrived here in the 1890s. All goods were loaded onto ships via a winching device. Taking a good look at the coast; you'll marvel that they made it work. After local supplies of redwood and tanbark were used up, the Notleys moved north to Humboldt County to continue their trade.

■ Rocky Creek Historic Bridge (1932)

To the south of Palo Colorado Road you'll find Rocky Creek Bridge. It is often overshadowed by the more famous Bixby Creek Bridge immediately to the south, but it shouldn't be. Consisting of a single graceful arch, Rocky Creek Bridge is almost 500 feet long and hovers some 150 feet above the creek. There is a turnout on the north side of the bridge from which you can look up the rugged canyon to the east. This canyon was the setting for Robinson Jeffers's epic poem "Cawdor."

You know you are entering some rough terrain when you see the highway sign by this bridge that warns: "Hills and curves next 63 miles." Just past Rocky Creek Bridge, as you proceed uphill, slow down for the turnout. It's nice and big, and the view north is spectacular. Notice how small the Rocky Point Restaurant looks in the surrounding landscape

Crow

Crows (*Corvus brachyrhynchos*) are commonly seen along the shoreline fronting the Monterey Bay National Marine Sanctuary. (Interestingly, ravens are extremely rare between the Pajaro River and Point Sur, and nobody knows why. They mostly stick to points north, in Santa Cruz County, although bird-watchers have recently seen pairs of ravens in Moss Landing, along the Salinas River, and at Point Sur.)

The crow can grow up to 20 inches long and is known for its large build and strong bill (though the raven's bill is much larger). Although the crow is basically black, if the sun is just right and your binoculars are clean you may see shades of glossy violet and dark blue-green on its wings. Crows are opportunistic feeders and will consume just about anything, including roadkills and beached marine mammals.

Crow behavior displays a distinct seasonality, which can be observed by even the most reluctant naturalist. During the mating, nesting, and fledgling times of the year—spring and summer—crows are seen in pairs or very small groups. At these times they are very aggressive toward one another. When that work is over, however, and fall is in the air with winter right around the corner, these gregarious birds form enormous flocks. At night you can watch as the flocks coalesce and form even larger megaflocks, which roost together. It's a very noisy affair, sometimes taking an hour or more to simmer down.

Crows, ravens, and jays are all in the Corvidae family of birds. As a group they tend to be loud, aggressive, and very intelligent. They imitate other birds easily and also produce their own sets of metallic clicks, clucks, whistles, and rattles. Crows exhibit all these traits, along with another family attribute—the ability to have fun. Crows will gang up on any hawk or owl they spot and harass it to no end, even though the likelihood of a hawk or owl harming a crow is slight. Crows can also be seen pulling one another's tail feathers in flight, performing aerobatics while calling, and even flying upside down.

Wild Turkey

One wildlife species you might see on the Old Coast Road, and elsewhere on the eastern escarpment of the Santa Lucia Range, is the wild turkey (*Meleagris gallopavo*). These are amusing-looking birds, not unlike large roadrunners that have put on a bit of weight. Except for their coloration and general shape, they have no resemblance to the pumped-up turkeys placed on dinner tables around the country every November. Wild turkeys are lanky and awkward-looking birds that stay relatively lean by foraging across the countryside in small groups.

There are many subspecies of wild turkey, all native to the eastern and

Wild turkeys are often seen on the Old Coast Road.

midwestern states and parts of Mexico. That's right: not one of them occurs here naturally. In fact, this popular game bird was introduced by the Department of Fish and Game for hunting purposes. Turkeys were first seriously introduced in Monterey County in the 1930s (possibly earlier by ranchers and hunters), and the program has continued up to today, particularly in Los Padres National Forest.

■ Bixby Creek Historic Bridge (1932)

This well-known bridge graces the covers of countless books, posters, and postcards. Bixby Creek Bridge, called the Rainbow Bridge by the engineers who designed it, is over 700 feet long, and it has the longest single arch of any bridge in the West—some 360 feet. Its construction was a challenge because, for starters, it sits 260 feet above the creek. To build this masterpiece the work crew first had to build a 26-story scaffolding, called a falsework, within the canyon walls.

As with many of the bridges along Highway 1, most of the cement for this bridge came from Davenport up north. Amazingly (especially considering the pace of road projects nowadays), Bixby Bridge took only a year to build. There is a nice—and popular—turnout at the north end of the bridge, and the northern entrance to the Old Coast Road spills out on the highway here. About one mile south of the southern anchor is a vista point turnout at Hurricane Point. From here you can study Bixby Creek Bridge a bit more, and also look down on Point Sur to the south. Sensational!

The bridge—and creek—are named for Charles Henry Bixby. An early settler of Big Sur, he came west in the late 19th century to set up a logging operation and mill. He also built Bixby Landing on the coast, immediately north of the creek, for shipping his products north to San Francisco. Eventually a lime operation was started up this canyon and a little community developed. Some of the components of the cable system they used to transport materials to waiting ships can still be seen on the shore at Bixby Landing.

"But you look up into the sky, bend way back, my God you're standing directly under that aerial bridge with its thin white line running from rock to rock and witless cars racing across it like dreams! From rock to rock!"

Jack Kerouac, describing Bixby Bridge, Big Sur *(1962)*

Bixby Creek Historic Bridge

Old Coast Road

At the north end of the Bixby Bridge you'll see the entrance to a dirt road that slams up into the mountains. This is the Old Coast Road, the main thoroughfare before Highway 1 was completed, and it twists and bumps along for a good 10 miles. It's a real adventure in driving. Don't try driving this road during the winter after rains: it will be a long walk out. (The southern entrance to the road can be accessed one and a half miles south of the Point Sur Lighthouse.)

As you move along you might see signs indicating private property, but these pertain only to the land adjacent to portions of the road. This is a public road, open to all who want an adventure. However, do respect private property. The people back in here don't tolerate trespassers. You'll have to negotiate a few one-lane wooden bridges as you pass over Bixby Creek and the Little Sur River deep in the mountains. The northern entrance starts you off with some wild hairpin turns, so brace yourself. An informal survey of wildlife commonly seen back here includes bobcats, wild turkeys, and golden eagles. Not bad. Also, in 10 miles you move through all the major vegetation types of the coast.

Southern Sea Otter

Along with the Lone Cypress, the southern sea otter (*Enhydra lutris nereis*) has come to symbolize the greater Monterey Bay. The sea otter's antics, appeal, and compelling story command the attention of millions of people yearly. Visitors travel the shoreline hoping to spot a furry head sticking up from an undulating raft of kelp.

Of course, people and sea otters have long been acquainted. This member of the weasel family possesses a high-quality and dense fur that is prized by humans. Before extensive hunting took place beginning in the mid-18th century, it is believed that approximately 15,000 sea otters ranged from British Columbia to Baja California. All together, the different subspecies (southern and northern) might have numbered in the hundreds of thousands, reaching from California up through

Sea otters are perhaps the most famous inhabitants of California's central coast.

Alaskan waters and back down around to Japan. Even though it was widely believed that intense hunting had exterminated sea otters along this coast after the turn of the century, protective federal and state legislation was nonetheless passed in 1911 and 1913.

The sea otter could belong in any of the chapters of this book. But it is most fitting right here because it was along this stretch of coast—between Point Sur and Bixby Creek—that the "lost" sea otter was discovered as early as 1915, living in a small group of some 50 individuals. The information did not become widespread until 1937, when completion of Highway 1 made travel along this coast feasible.

Since their rediscovery the population has slowly recovered, and today sea otters can be seen with regularity from Point Año Nuevo south to the Santa Maria River in San Luis Obispo County. It is believed that their population today is just over 2,100 individuals, though recent declines in the population have puzzled researchers. The deaths can't all be attributed to fish-net drownings; instead, it increasingly appears that infectious diseases are taking their toll on the population. The California sea otter has been on the Endangered Species List since 1977, and although there has been talk of removing it because the population has steadily increased in size since the 1930s, the recent losses will ensure its endangered status at least into the near future.

Many fishermen and abalone divers don't like otters because otters have a remarkable appetite. They must consume up to 25 percent of their body weight every day to survive—and that's a lot, considering that some adult male otters weigh 80 pounds and grow to over four feet long. It would be like feeding a teenage human some 30 pounds of food daily! Sea otters eat copious amounts of urchins and abalone, both of which are also collected by people. But they also eat a wide variety of mollusks and snails. Their well-known habit of floating on their back while preparing and eating their meals has provided countless hours of spectator fun for humans.

The entire Big Sur coast, from the Carmel River down to Santa Rosa Creek (Cambria) in San Luis Obispo County, has been designated the California Sea Otter Game Refuge. Keep your eye open for these endearing marine mammals wherever you see kelp beds. For additional information about the California sea otter and its status, contact the Friends of the Sea Otter at 831-373-2747 or visit their website at http://www.seaotters.org. The Monterey Bay Aquarium has an ongoing Sea Otter Research and Conservation Program, which you can learn more about through the aquarium's website, http://www.mbayaq.org (follow the "E-Q Guide").

Point Sur State Historic Park

Point Sur, with its rock-top lighthouse, is a dramatic and fitting place to wrap up your shoreline adventures . . . for now. Don't forget, though, that the entire coastline to the north of the point—just beyond the Little Sur River—deserves repeated visits at all times of the year. From the top of the point, on a clear day, you can see all the way to the Monterey Peninsula (good binoculars help). To the south you'll see another 70 miles of the Big Sur coast lining out in consecutive ridges until they fade in the distance.

As you slow to a stop in front of the gate leading into Point Sur State Historic Park, you will have traveled just under 19 miles from Rio Road in Carmel. If you have time, schedule your visit around a lighthouse tour; it takes about three hours and is a real treat. If that's not possible, just park and look. Note that the land between the highway and Point Sur is private property—part of an extensive cattle ranch—so don't even think of hopping the fence. The cowboys hereabouts can be a rough lot.

Pigeon Point Lighthouse, north of Año Nuevo, was erected in 1872; the Año Nuevo light went up in 1890; and Santa Cruz's light station was built in 1869. Point Pinos was adorned with a light station in 1855. Although the Point Sur Light Station is a bit of a latecomer, having been erected in 1889, it has weathered the years just as

Point Sur Lighthouse

well as the other light stations. And as far as scenic location is concerned, this lighthouse wins hands-down.

The lighthouse, which is now fully automated, is in excellent shape. The rest of the light station—employee housing, barn, and blacksmith shop—is being restored by volunteers and park employees. On the tour, as you ascend the road, you feel like you're stepping back in time. Look out over the Pacific from the railing of the lighthouse, and you almost expect to see the masts of an old tall ship moving along the coast. The boiler room of the lighthouse, where the steam that powered the foghorns was generated, has been converted into a miniature museum with relics of the lighthouse's past. The current safety beacon was placed about 270 feet up the north side of the 380-foot hill to maximize its visibility for ships at sea. The original 4,330-pound lens now resides in Monterey's Maritime Museum.

The tour leads you not only through the lighthouse, but also to a couple of the light station buildings on top of the point, where a flat area was blasted out. The little visitor center up there is packed with historic pictures and information—including well-illustrated details of the 1935 disaster involving the dirigible USS *Macon*, which went down just offshore here—natural history notes, and a small selection of items for sale. All proceeds go to help restore the facilities. The views from the top are beyond belief. During gray whale migration, visitors can look right down on the whales as they hug the coast on their journey south.

Before venturing to Point Sur, be sure to call (831-625-4419); the tours have strict hours and regulations. And be sure to dress in layers for this trip: the wind can blow pretty fiercely up on the rock, at any time of the year.

Krummholz

What the heck is krummholz? That stuff they sprinkle on top of pastries? No. Krummholz—German for "crooked wood"—is a botanical term usually reserved for high mountain areas where intense freezing and winds shape alpine vegetation into a low-growing mat. But sometimes you'll find krummholz at lower elevations. As you go on your tour of the Point Sur Light Station, keep your eyes on the plants. Although it may look like an overzealous gardener has been out there trimming the shrubs to the quick in a frantic effort to create Pacific Coast topiary, in fact the culprit is the area's intense winds and salt sprays, which shape this coastal scrub much as frosts and winds do at 12,000 feet

Point Sur and tombolo, with the light station slightly obscured by fog

in the Sierra Nevada. Basically, krummholz is a form of botanical self-preservation. By bending and staying low, the trees and bushes are able to survive in this demanding environment.

Tombolo

So what's a tombolo? That fortified Italian drink you order with your krummholz? No. A tombolo is the piece of land you crossed to reach the light station—it's a bar, or ridge, that joins an island to the mainland. Point Sur was once offshore. With time, and nearshore drift, material began to accumulate on the lee side of the point— between the shoreline and Point Sur—until finally they became connected and stabilized with vegetation.

USS *Macon*

On the night of February 12, 1935, the lighthouse keeper at Point Sur looked out and saw the dirigible USS *Macon* just offshore. As he watched, the airship was jostled by a strong gust of wind; it then slowly dipped down toward the water and disappeared. Two crew members out of 83 were lost. This enormous helium-filled dirigible built in 1933 was en route to Moffett Field in the San Francisco Bay Area, just finishing up its 54th mission. You can still see the dirigible hangars at Moffett Field, right off the highway.

"Enormous" is right: this airship was 785 feet long, three times longer than a Boeing 747. It was so large that it carried a fleet of small planes, called Sparrowhawks, in a hangar inside its belly. These planes landed by flying under the *Macon* and connecting to the ship by a plane-mounted hook. The Sparrowhawks were then stabilized by a sling and hoisted inside. To take off, the procedure was reversed: the planes simply unhooked and fell free.

Although the *Macon* was known to have sunk off Point Sur, its exact location remained a mystery for decades. It wasn't until 1980, when a fisherman hauled up a strange piece of metal in his nets, that the story got interesting again. The fisherman brought the piece of metal back to Moss Landing and gave it to the owner of a local restaurant, who hung it on the wall of the eatery without knowing what is was. One day the daughter of the *Macon*'s commander came in for a meal. She saw the artifact on the wall and knew right away that it was a piece of girder from the sunken airship, because as a child she used to crawl around in the girders.

Ironically, a researcher from the Monterey Bay Aquarium Research Institute—next door to the restaurant— had been trying to find the *Macon* for years. Using the boat captain's precise records on where the girder piece was recovered, he located the USS *Macon*, with the help of a navy submersible, in the summer of 1990 in 1,450 feet of water. A January 1992 *National Geographic* article on the *Macon* details this amazing adventure of discovery, as well as the fascinating history of dirigibles. You can find out more about the *Macon* at two informative websites: http://www2.lucidcafe.com/lucidcafe/library/macon.html and http://www.noaa.gov/public-affairs/sanctuary/vol2no1/v1mac.html.

Condors

When these lands knew the scream of the saber-toothed tiger and felt the weight of giant ground sloths, the California condor (*Gymnopyps californianus*) patiently watched and waited. This huge bird may have faced intense competition at mastodon carcasses, or been driven off of beached whales by fifty-pound Pleistocene vultures. This, of course, we will probably never know. What we do know is that of all of North America's megafauna (those really large species), only the condor survived to the present.

California condors

It did so, but not without a lot of help from humans. The condor population, both in the wild and in captivity, was down to a mere 20-odd individuals by the early 1980s; in 1987 the last wild birds were captured and placed in a captive breeding program in southern California. Their population now numbers well over 125 birds, and they have begun to be reintroduced into their former range, including portions of Big Sur.

In 1602 Antonio de la Ascención, chaplain of the Sebastián Vizcaíno expedition, made the first-known recorded observation of a condor near here. Two hundred years later and hundreds of miles to the north, the Lewis and Clark expedition observed and collected condors along the Columbia River. In the early 1800s the condor ranged over the Pacific Coast between the Columbia and Baja California, with probable if infrequent forays into Nevada and Arizona. Today, these magnificent birds survive thanks to high-tech breeding and dozens of dedicated wildlife professionals who watch their every move. The cause of their demise is a source of much debate on the part of ornithologists, wildlife biologists, and laypeople. Basically, humans and human-induced habitat loss caused their decline.

What's important is that today they are back flying over the Santa Lucia Range, reminding us what wilderness means and how fragile a species can be, no matter how large or small. For more information about condors in Big Sur, contact the Ventana Wilderness Sanctuary at 831-624-1202. Or access the websites http://rmcclos. idbsu.edu/~iseee/CACondor.htm and http://www.fws. gov/r9endspp/i/b0g.html.

Points South

■ Andrew Molera State Park

This 4,800-acre park just south of Point Sur takes in a large chunk of the Big Sur coast, including a long stretch of the Big Sur River. There is a large camping area here with some 400 sites. For information, call the Big Sur Ranger Station at 831-667-2315.

Big Sur Chamber of Commerce: 831-667-2100

Monterey-Salinas Transit: 831-899-2555

Point Lobos State Reserve and Garrapata State Park: 831-624-4909

Point Lobos Diving Reservations: 831-624-8413

Website: http://pt-lobos. parks.state.ca.us/index.html

Monterey County Department of Transportation: 831-755-4812

Los Padres National Forest, Ventana Wilderness, Bottchers Gap Campground: 831-385-5434

Friends of the Sea Otter: 831-373-2747
Website: http://www.seaotters.org

Point Sur Lighthouse: 831-625-4419

Condor Information, Ventana Wilderness Sanctuary: 831-624-1202

■ Big Sur

The village of Big Sur sits between Andrew Molera State Park and Pfeiffer Big Sur State Park on Highway 1. It is a good place to stock up on goods and get gas. In fact, it's just about the only real settlement along this stretch of coast.

■ Pfeiffer Big Sur State Park

Just down the road from Andrew Molera State Park and Big Sur is Pfeiffer Big Sur State Park, which takes in about 820 acres on either side of Highway 1 and the Big Sur River. In addition to 200 campsites, there is a lodge and cabins for rent. For information about camping, call the Big Sur Ranger Station at 831-667-2315. For lodging information, call 1-800-424-4787. A few miles south of this park is the famous Nepenthe Restaurant and Cafe and Phoenix Gift Shop.

GETTING AROUND

To find Big Sur and all the sites mentioned in this chapter, simply drive south on Highway 1. It is approximately 19 miles from Carmel's Rio Road to the front gate of the Point Sur Light Station.

Selected Bibliography

I used dozens of written sources for this book. Below I list a few of the books that you might enjoy reading if you have specific interests you wish to pursue. In addition to the excellent natural history series produced by the Monterey Bay Aquarium and the University of California Press (some of which are cited below), the numerous guidebooks published by the National Audubon Society are easy to use and informative.

Brewer, William H. *Up and Down California in 1860–1864*. Ed. Francis P. Farquhar. Berkeley: University of California Press, 1975.

California Coastal Commission, State of California. *California Coastal Access Guide*. 5th ed. Berkeley: University of California Press, 1997.

California State Coastal Conservancy. *San Francisco Bay Shoreline Guide*. Berkeley: University of California Press, 1995.

Clark, Donald Thomas. *Santa Cruz County Place Names*. Santa Cruz: Santa Cruz Historical Society, 1986.

——. *Monterey County Place Names*. Carmel: Kestrel Press, 1991.

Connor, Judith. *Seashore Life*. Monterey: Monterey Bay Aquarium, 1993.

Connor, Judith, and Charles Baxter. *Kelp Forests*. Monterey: Monterey Bay Aquarium, 1989.

Costansó, Miguel. *The Discovery of San Francisco Bay: The Portolá Expedition of 1769–1770*. Lafayette, Calif.: Great West Books, 1992.

Dana, Richard Henry. *Two Years Before the Mast*. New York: Buccaneer Books, 1996.

Dawson, E. Yale, and Michael S. Foster. *Seashore Plants of California*. Berkeley: University of California Press, 1982.

de la Pérouse, Jean François. *Life in a California Mission: Monterey in 1786*. Berkeley: Heyday Books, 1989.

Faber, Phyllis M. *Common Wetland Plants of Coastal California*. Mill Valley, Calif.: Pickleweed Press, 1985.

——. *Common Riparian Plants of California*. Mill Valley: Pickleweed Press, 1988.

Ferguson, Ava, and Gregor Cailliet. *Sharks and Rays of the Pacific Coast*. Monterey: Monterey Bay Aquarium, 1990.

Fitch, John E., and Robert J. Lavenberg. *California Marine Food and Game Fishes*. Berkeley: University of California Press, 1971.

———. *Tidepool and Nearshore Fishes of California*. Berkeley: University of California Press, 1975.

Gordon, Burton L. *Monterey Bay Area: Natural History and Cultural Imprints*. 3d ed. Pacific Grove: Boxwood Press, 1996.

Gordon, David George. *Gray Whales*. Monterey: Monterey Bay Aquarium, 1991.

———. *Seals and Sea Lions*. Monterey: Monterey Bay Aquarium, 1994.

Hedgpeth, Joel W. *Introduction to Seashore Life of the San Francisco Bay Region and the Coast of Northern California*. Berkeley: University of California Press, 1962.

Hinton, Sam. *Seashore Life of Southern California*. Rev. ed. Berkeley: University of California Press, 1987.

Hunt, James C. *Octopus and Squid*. Monterey: Monterey Bay Aquarium, 1996.

Lorentzen, Bob, and Richard Nichols. *Hiking the California Coastal Trail—Volume One: Oregon to Monterey*. Mendocino: Bored Feet Publications, 1998.

McConnaughey, Evelyn, and Bayard Harlow McConnaughey. *Pacific Coast*. Audubon Society Nature Guides. New York: Knopf, 1985.

Monterey Bay Aquarium, in cooperation with the National Oceanic and Atmospheric Administration Sanctuaries and Reserves Division. *A Natural History of the Monterey Bay National Marine Sanctuary*. Monterey: Monterey Bay Aquarium, 1997.

McCauley, Jane R. *National Geographic Society. Field Guide to the Birds of North America*. 2d ed. Washington, D.C.: National Geographic Society, 1989.

Nybakken, James W. *Marine Biology: An Ecological Approach*. 4th ed. Menlo Park: Addison-Wesley, 1997.

Ricketts, Edward F., and Jack Calvin. *Between Pacific Tides*. 5th ed. Stanford: Stanford University Press, 1992.

Riedman, Marianne. *Sea Otters*. Monterey: Monterey Bay Aquarium, 1997.

Robinson, Bruce, and Judith Connor. *The Deep Sea*. Monterey: Monterey Bay Aquarium, 1999.

Silberstein, Mark, and Eileen Campbell. *Elkhorn Slough*. Monterey: Monterey Bay Aquarium, 1989.

Creek, 19; Gibson, 257; Greyhound Rock, 38–39; Hooper, 93; Laguna Creek, 50; Lighthouse Field State, 44, 64–66, 225; Lincoln, 88; Live Oak, 88; Lovers Point, 195, 222; McAbee, 206, 208–209, 214; Manresa State, 113, 114–15; Marina State, 168, 169, 173–75, 176, 186, 187, 189; Middle, 248; Monastery. *See* San Jose Creek Beach; Monterey Municipal, 187, 195, 196, 233; Monterey State, *185*, 186, 187–88, 189, 195, 196, 233; Moran Lake, 89–90; Moss Landing State, 113, 119, 128, 130–32, 133, 135, 140; Natural Bridges State, 51, 56, 58–59; New Brighton State, 90, 93, 99, 113; North Moss. *See* Asilomar Beach; Opal Cliff Recreation District Public Access, 91; Pismo, 120, 166; Red, White, Blue, 51, 53; Rio del Mar State, 108, 114, 115; Salinas River State, 137, 153, 156–57, 160, 161, 162; San Carlos, 195, 199, 243; San Jose Creek (Monastery), 119, 234, 248–49, 255; at Santa Cruz, 61; Scott Creek, 40, 41; Seacliff State, 101, 104, 113, 115; Seaside, 187; South Moss, 234; Sunny Cove, 88, 89; Sunset State, *1*, *100*, 115, 116, 117, 121, 133; Three Mile, 53; Twin Lakes State, 86–88; Waddell, 29, 30–31, 32, 37, 39, 41; Wilder, 53; Window on the Bay, 195, 197; Yellowbank, 50; Zmudowski State, 113, 127–28, 133, 135, 140
Beach Bluff Pathway, 242
beachcombing, 187, *208*, 237
beach hoppers (sand fleas), **119–20**, 122
Beach and Tennis Club (Stillwater Cove), 240, 248
bear: black, 36, 275; grizzly, 35, **36**, 143

Beechey, Frederick William, 235
beetles, 178; bark, 256; ladybird, 263
Benicia, 200
Berwick Park, 222
Beston, Henry, 118
Bethany Green Beltway, **64**
Between Pacific Tides (Ricketts and Calvin), 219
bicycles: on buses, 29, 158, 195; mountain, 32, 106, 181
bicycling: maps for, to obtain, 51, 55, 65, 83, 114, 160, 240; routes for, 24, 26, 32–33, 38, 52, 54, **65**, 77, 85, 99, 126–27, 186, 194, 227, 229, 232, 247; *see also* Pacific Coast Bicycle Route; Pajaro River Bike Path
Bierce, Ambrose, 255
Big Basin Redwoods State Park, 12, 31, **32**, 34, 38; to reach, 41
Big Creek Lumber Company, **36–37**, 38
Big Dome, 256
Big Slide Trail, 106
Big Sur, 155, 158, **287**; map of, 252–53; to reach, 287
Big Sur (Kerouac), 278
Big Sur Land Trust, **248**
Bird Island, 257
Bird Island Trail, 257, 258
Bird Rock, **236**, 237
birds, 140, 175; bills of, **121–22**; butcher. *See* shrike, loggerhead; dune-dwelling, 179; flycatchers, 23; migrations of, 263; numbers of, 1, 66, 141; shore, 31, 47, 119, 144, 149, **170–71**, 173, 226, 242, 265; *see also specific kinds*
bird's beak, Seaside, 177
bird-watching, 15, 47, 53, 66, 69, 87–88, 121–22, 125, 128, 141, 144, 148, 149, 163, 180, 182, 186, 187, 188, 236, 276
Bixby, Charles Henry, 278
Bixby Creek, 279
Bixby Creek Historic Bridge, 276, **278–79**; pullout, 260

Bixby Landing, 278
blackberries, 45
blackbird: Brewer's, 71; red-winged, 71, **244–45**
Black Point, 88
BLM. *See* Bureau of Land Management
bluebird, eastern, 236
bluffs, coastal, **14**, 31, 37, 45, 53–54, 91, 96, 188, 195, 243
boardwalk, through dunes, 175, 176, 186, 196, 227
boating, 131, 142, 154, 197
boats, model, 188
bobcat, 82, **183–84**, 279
bodysurfing, 88
Bonita Lagoon, **88**
bonito, 72, 111
Bonny Doon Beach, **47**, 51; to reach, 53
Bonny Doon Ecological Reserve, **48**, 51
Bonny Doon Road, 47
Bonny Doon Winery, **47**, 51
botany, museum exhibits of, 223
botany; *see also* plants
Bottchers Gap, 257, 276; Campground, 274, 287
bowling, 74
boxing, exhibits on, 213
Brachyramphus marmoratus, **34**; *see also* murrelet, marbled
Bracken Cave, Texas, 262
Branciforte Elementary School, 85
Breakwater Cove, 199, 206
Brewer, William H., 173, 242, 245
bridges, 260, **265–66**, 273, 274, 276, 278
Brower, David, 20
brussels sprouts, **52**
buckeye, 26
buckwheat, 177; coast, 181; seacliff, 181
buildings, historic, 204; adobe, 52, 80, 81, 200–201, 203, 204; in Capitola, 96; in Davenport, 44, 46; haunted, 51; in Monterey, 156, 192, 200–205; Monterey Style, 204